THE LIFE AND TIMES OF JOSEPH SMEDLEY

(1784–1863)

PROVINCIAL ACTOR MANAGER

*The only known photographs of
Joseph and Melinda Smedley
(By kind permission of
Roy Sumners)*

THE LIFE AND TIMES OF JOSEPH SMEDLEY

(1784–1863)

PROVINCIAL ACTOR MANAGER

Richard E. Smedley

London | New York

Published by Clink Street Publishing 2018

Copyright © 2018

First edition.

The author asserts the moral right under the Copyright, Designs and Patents Act 1988 to be identified as the author of this work.

All rights reserved. No part of this publication may be reproduced, stored in a retrieval system or transmitted, in any form or by any means without the prior consent of the author, nor be otherwise circulated in any form of binding or cover other than that with which it is published and without a similar condition being imposed on the subsequent purchaser.

ISBN: 978-1-912562-84-8   ebook: 978-1-912562-85-5

*This book is dedicated to the Memory of
my Parents Daphne and Ernest Smedley*

Contents

List of Illustrations		ix
Introduction		1
1	Joseph Smedley – Beginnings	3
2	Beginnings – The Robertsons	14
3	The Smedleys – Early Stages	22
4	Those In Favour: Grimsby, Dr George Oliver & the Freemasons	36
5	Those Against	58
6	The Smedleys – Intermediate Stages	79
7	Family Matters (1)	90
8	The Robertsons – Again	98
9	The Smedleys – Later Stages	113
10	Family Matters (2)	150
11	The Smedleys – Final Stages and Further Family Matters	152
12	In Retirement	240
13	Coda	269
Appendix 1: The Plays		276
Appendix II: The Theatres		301
Bibliography		304
Acknowledgements		309

List of Illustrations

Frontispiece: The only known photographs of Joseph and Melinda Smedley – by kind permission of Roy Sumners.

Chapter 3: Early Stages

Early playbills – Grimsby 1912 – with the permission of North East Lincolnshire Archives.

Chapter 4: Those in Favour

Etching of Dr George Oliver – public domain.

Chapter 5: Those Against

An Answer to the Defence of the Stage

Another Answer to the Defence of the Stage

A Second Defence of the Theatre – by kind permission of Roy Sumners.

Chapter 6: Intermediate Stages

A contemporary sketch of Joseph Smedley in c 1825 From the private collection of Roy Sumners

View of Sleaford Theatre as it is today – picture by author.

Chapter 7: Family Matters

Contemporary engraving of Spilsby School.

Chapter 11: Final Stages

Print of portrait of John Braham as Orlando - one of a series produced by Robert Dighton – in possession of, and by kind permission of, Roy Sumners. (Original in National Portrait Gallery).

Chapter 12: In Retirement

Grave marker and Memorial in St. Denys' Churchyard, Sleaford – picture by author.

Henry Farren's Rules of the Theatre – from private collection of Roy Sumners, copy in Lincolnshire Archive and reproduced here with their permission.

Coda

Picture of the overgrown graves of Joseph and Melinda Smedley in Sleaford Cemetery – picture by Author.

Introduction

I first became interested in Joseph Smedley when I came across a memorial plaque on a building in the Minster town of Southwell in Nottinghamshire close to where I had moved to live. The building purported to have formerly housed a theatre which had been managed by Joseph Smedley. As he was a namesake of mine, and as I was myself a theatre manager for many years with an interest in theatre history, my curiosity was piqued.

By delving into his working and family life, I also had to research the time in which he lived and the difficulties he faced in order to survive as a 'strolling player' in the first half of the nineteenth century, and consequently this is as much a work about social history as a theatrical biography.

Joseph Smedley spent his life as an actor taking theatrical entertainments to small towns and villages around South Yorkshire, North Lincolnshire (or what we know today as Humberside), Nottinghamshire, Derbyshire and Rutland and further afield. At the same time, the Robertsons were running both the Lincoln Circuit and the Nottingham and Derby Circuit; covering the areas in which Joseph Smedley also operated, so it seemed valid to compare their fortunes during this period.

In her book *Strolling Players and Drama in the Provinces 1660–1765* (Cambridge University Press, 1939), Sybil Rosenfeld states how much she notices that everywhere during the decade 1755–65 new and imposing theatres were being built in provincial towns. This certainly continued during the period covered by this book, when even small rural towns were able to boast a building designed for the needs of the actor and the playgoer, some of which were built by Joseph Smedley himself. However the fit-ups, the yards of inns, the barns, the village commons, the market-places were all still being utilised by the touring companies in the first half of the nineteenth century in much the same way as they had since Shakespeare's time, but many of the problems facing them were, if not new, then variations of those experienced by many a touring company since Elizabethan times.

Also, like many small groups of touring actors, the family played an important part, and Joseph Smedley was no different, using his growing family to fill many roles in the repertoire. More than once, during my research for this book, I came across a comparison between his company and that of Mr Vincent Crummles in Charles Dickens' *Nicholas Nickleby*, first serialised in 1838–39 and the first edition in book form in 1839:

> 'Does no other profession occur to you, which a young man of your figure and address could take up easily, and see the world to advantage in?' asked the manager.
> 'No,' said Nicholas, shaking his head.
> 'Why, then, I'll tell you one,' said Mr Crummles, throwing his pipe into the fire, and raising his voice. 'The stage.'
> 'The stage!' cried Nicholas, in a voice almost as loud.
> 'The theatrical profession,' said Mr. Vincent Crummles. 'I am in the theatrical profession myself, my wife is in the theatrical profession, my children are in the theatrical profession. I had a dog that lived and died in it from a puppy; and my chaise-pony goes on in Timour the Tartar. I'll bring you out, and your friend too. Say the word. I want a novelty.'

This, then, is the story of a man's life; his family, his work, and the trials he faced as he 'strutted and fretted his hour upon the stage' over 150 years ago. At this remove, some gaps in knowledge are, I'm afraid, inevitable, but what survives shows a man of honour, of hard work, of someone trying to elevate his profession – which for centuries had been maligned – into a 'school of eloquence, a temple of the arts.'

1
Joseph Smedley – Beginnings

Joseph Smedley was born on 4th January, 1784, at East Brompton, near Patrick Brompton, in the Parish of Bedale, in North Yorkshire, and baptised there on 8th February. His parents were Abraham Smedley and Abraham's second wife Jane, nee Close, who had married at Barton St Cuthbert on 25th August, 1772. They first had a daughter, Elizabeth, who was baptised at Hornby by Bedale on 20th February, 1774, but who died of consumption, aged only eleven.[1] There were also five children by Abraham's first wife Mary, who had died in 1767.

Family history contends that Abraham was a land agent for the Dundas family[2] whose principal family seat was, and is still, at Aske Hall near Richmond, but who had vast lands in Scotland and Northern England; several houses (including a London base); and many business interests around the world. Thomas (iii) Dundas of Kerse, First Baron Dundas of Aske (1741–1820), became MP for Richmond and was very influential in politics. The archive of the Dundas family (later the Earls of Zetland), is huge, but having trawled through the records for the relevant period, I found no mention of Abraham, neither was he listed in the correspondence to the land agents.[3] However, Abraham did describe himself as a farmer in Parish records and in the land-tax records for 1783, the year before Joseph was born, he paid one pound and sixteen shillings per annum as rent for the farm to its owner, Lady Conyers. The following year, the land he farmed must have been much reduced as he paid only 3s-2d for the year. The Conyers family has owned much land in the area since at least

---

[1] Patrick Brompton Parish Records, Northallerton Public Records Office
[2] Dundas Family: Joseph Smedley entry, Oxford DNB, CMP Taylor, accessed 22.09.2014
[3] Dundas Family Archive, Northallerton Public Record Office

the fifteenth century, which includes Hornby Castle and Parkland near Bedale.[4] It is possible that Abraham, in addition to his farm work, was a sub-agent, or bailiff, for the Dundas family too.

Joseph was destined for the bar, or certainly a career in law, as he was sent to study with two of his half-brothers (by his father's first marriage) who were solicitors in London. However, by about 1801 or 1802 he was seduced by the theatre or by an actress, or both, and left his studies for a life on the stage.

Undoubtedly, by 1802 he was appearing at the theatre in Lincoln on the same bill as Miss Melinda Bullen, an actress from Norwich. In October, 1800, she appeared on a Lincoln playbill for a production of *Lovers' Vows* in which she is listed as 'Country Girl' and, in the play *Saint David's Day* on the same bill, she is listed as playing 'Welch Girl' (sic). In November of that year Melinda also appeared at the bottom of a bill for *Obi, or Three Fingered* Jack, among the supporting cast of 'Negros, Negresses, Dancers, Soldiers &C'.

She was born at Norwich and christened there at the Octagon Presbyterian Church on 10th May, 1781.[5] Her parents were Joseph and Susanna Bullen, this being the English version of the name Boleyn, and throughout her life Melinda claimed descent from that family whose involvement with King Henry VIII proved so fateful. Although unproven, she almost certainly worked at Norwich, or on the Norfolk circuit, under John Brunton.

The Bruntons became quite a famous theatrical dynasty. John Brunton started acting at Covent Garden in 1774, became a leading actor at Norwich the following year, and where he became extremely popular. The theatres on the Norfolk circuit varied, and at different times were visited by other companies. However, James Winston gives us the following information on the Norwich Circuit:[6]

---

[4] QDEL Land Tax Assessment, Northallerton Public Record Office

[5] Parish Records, Octagon Presbyterian Church, Family Search

[6] The Theatric Tourist, James Winston, 1805; STR Anniversary Facsimile Version, 2008

The year is made out thus: first, Yarmouth, then Ipswich, a distance fifty-three miles; forty-three more to Norwich (for the Assizes); back to Yarmouth, twenty-two; then to Stirbitch**, eighty-six; to Bury, twenty-eight; Colchester twenty-two; to Ipswich again, eighteen; to Norwich, forty-three; Lynn, forty-four; back again to Norwich, forty-four; and again to Yarmouth, twenty-two; making in the whole a very pretty twelvemonth tour. (**Now Stourbridge. RS)

After five years of this, Brunton tried his luck in London again, unsuccessfully, and spent the rest of the year in Bristol and Bath, where he eventually started to introduce his children to the stage; Elizabeth, John and Harriet all began acting in 1782. Anne seemed the most promising, even having a brief engagement with her father at Covent Garden. However they returned to Norwich, where they found that the previous manager had retired due to ill health in 1780, to be replaced by Giles Linnett Barrett who had taken the lease. But in 1788 it was reported that the lease had been purchased by Brunton, who proved adept and shrewd as a manager, but the upkeep and maintenance of the building proved not to be his forte, and in 1799 the proprietors decided not to grant him the patent, but to award it to William Wilkins, an architect who had drawn up plans for a complete overhaul of the Norwich theatre. Brunton therefore politely withdrew from Norwich in May 1800.[7]

In the meantime, his son, John Jnr, who was also intended for the law, had settled on an acting career and, unbeknownst to his family, aged eighteen, and against his father's wishes, he joined the theatre company at Lincoln, where he had some success before returning to his family in Norwich where his father hired him as an actor and assistant manager. In 1792, he married an actress, Anna Ross, who was the sister of Fanny Robertson, a leading member of the Robertson Company who managed the Lincoln Theatre and its circuit. Both Ann and John Brunton acted under Brunton the elder at Norwich. John the younger helped his father run the Norfolk circuit, and would have acted with Melinda Bullen, both being of similar age, and who no doubt had much in common. It seems likely that John Jnr and Melinda both left Norwich at the same time as Brunton Snr, for in the Autumn of 1800 Miss Bullen's name started to appear on the playbills of the Lincoln Theatre, where, at that time the company also included Anna Ross. It is likely that Melinda was mentored

---

[7] Oxford DNB entry, Moira Field, accessed 8.07.2015

by the Bruntons. That September, Brunton Jnr appeared at Covent Garden as Frederick in *Louisa's Vows*, and at different periods went on to run theatres at Brighton, Birmingham, Lynn and others, with his daughter Elizabeth frequently acting for him as her career became established, and her fame grew.

In 1804, the elder Brunton became manager of Brighton (Duke Street) Theatre, was successful, and secured the patronage of the Prince of Wales (later George IV). Louisa, Brunton's youngest daughter, had followed her sisters onto the stage, and, in 1805 and 1806 she came to Brighton from Covent Garden to play for her father. In both years, the Prince of Wales attended her benefits. Another patron was William, first Earl of Craven,(1770–1825), and on 12th December, 1807, he and Louisa were married, and Louisa left the stage for good.[8]

During this period a number of actresses married into the aristocracy, the first of these being Miss Farren, who married the Earl of Derby, and provoked these lines published in 1840 in the "Remains" of James Smith:[9]

> Farren, Thalia's dear delight,
> Can I forget the fatal night
>   Of grief unstained by fiction
> (Even now the recollection damps),
> When Wroughton led thee to the lamps,
>   In graceful valediction?"

Followed by:

> The Derby prize by Hymen won,
> Again the god made bold to run
>   Beneath Thalia's steerage;
> Sent forth a second Earl to woo,
> And captivating Brunton, too,
>   Exalted to the peerage.

---

[8] Louisa Brunton, entry Oxford DNB, K D Reynolds
[9] Quoted in *Representative Actors from the Sixteenth to the Present Century* by W. Clark Russell

Further stanzas are devoted to Miss Searle, Miss Bolton, Miss O'Neill (who married Sir W. Wrexham Beecher) Bart; Mercandotte (a beautiful Spanish *danseuse* who married a very rich man) and Miss Stephens, who wed the Earl of Essex.

This would be of little interest to the study of Joseph Smedley's life were it not that amongst his papers has survived a press cutting; a quotation, it appears, from Burke's *Romance of the Aristocracy*:

> *Actresses Raised By Marriages – The first person among "the gentry" who chose a wife from the stage was M. Folkes, the antiquary, a man of fortune, who about the year 1683 married Lucretia Bradshaw, the representative of Farquhar's heroines. A contemporary writer styles her "one of the greatest and most promising genii of her time," and assigns her "prudent and exemplary conduct" as the attraction which won the learned antiquary. The next actress whose husband moved in an elevated rank was Anastasia Robinson, the singer. The great Lord Peterborough, the hero of the Spanish War- the friend of Pope and Swift = publicly acknowledged Anastasia as his countess in 1735. In four years after, the Lady Henrietta Herbert, daughter of James, first Earl of Waldegrave, and widow of Lord Edward Herbert, bestowed her hand on James Beard, the performer. Subsequently, about the middle of the eighteenth century, Lavinia Bestwick, the original "Polly Peachum," became Duchess of Bolton. The next on record was Miss Lenley's marriage to Sheridan, one of the most romantic episodes in the theatrical unions; and before the eighteenth century closed, Elizabeth Farren, a perfect gentlewoman, became Countess of the proudest Earl in England, the representative of the illustrious Stanleys. She was Lord Derby's second wife, and mother of the present Countess of Wilton. In 1807 the beautiful Miss Searle was married to Robert Heathcote, Esq., brother to Sir Gilbert Heathcote, Bart, and in the same year, Louisa Brunton to the Earl of Craven; and her niece, Mrs Yate, still exhibits the dramatic genius of the Brunton family. "The Beggar's Opera" again conferred a coronet. Mary Catherine Bolton's "Polly Peachum" captivated Lord Thurloe. She was married to his lordship in 1813. In more recent times the most fascinating of our actresses, Miss O'Neill, wedded Sir W. Wrexham Beecher, Bart.; Miss Foote the Earl of Harrington; Miss Stephens, the Earl of Essex; and Miss Mellon, then Mrs Coutts, the Duke of St. Albans.*

On the other hand he may have saved it because of its final reference to a Miss Mellon – see Chapter 11.

* * *

There is certainly no doubt that the Brunton family was extremely close to the young Melinda Bullen. Neither is there any doubt that she and Joseph Smedley fell deeply in love, and, on 20th May, 1803, were married at St Peter of Mancroft Church in the centre of Norwich,[10] witnessed by George Clarke and a Miss Winner. The marriage was announced in the *Ipswich Journal* of Saturday, May 28th, 1803:

> Married … Sunday Mr Joseph Close Smedley, to Miss Melinda Bullen, daughter of Mr Bullen, in White Lion-lane, Norwich.

Family lore has it that they were runaways,[11] and this is borne out by the fact that both of them lied about their ages; Melinda, reduced her age by a year, giving her birth date as 1782, while Joseph, who was three years younger than Melinda, and only 19 years old at the time, also gave his birth date as 1782, making both of them appear to be 21 years of age, the legal or statutory age of consent for marriage. Thereafter, Melinda always gave her age as that of her husband.

They continued to act at Lincoln theatre but their billing was as Mr and Mrs Smedley, and, although there aren't any supporting playbills, the *Lincolnshire Mercury* announced on 14th October, 1803, that there would be a benefit performance for Mr and Mrs Smedley at the Lincoln Theatre; another at Newark Theatre on 24th November, 1803 (in the comedy *Delays and Blunders* and the farce *The Deserter*), and another at Grantham Theatre on 13th January, 1804. In September, 1804, they appeared at Lincoln in a new comedy called *Soldier's Daughter* with Mr Ferret being played by Mr Smedley, and Mrs Townley being played by Mrs Smedley, with a note stating that both she and Mrs Norris, playing Mrs Fidget, were from the Theatre Royal, Birmingham. Also appearing were, as Captain Woodly, Mr Brunton, who also appeared in the supporting piece, *Love Laughs at Black-smiths*, a musical farce, as Captain Beldare, and in which a Mrs Playford from the Theatre Royal, Norwich also acted as Lydia.

---

[10] Parish Records of St. Peter of Mancroft, Norfolk County Record Office
[11] Family Lore, conversation with Roy Sumners, 02.07.2015

Richard E. Smedley

The timing of Mr Brunton (Jnr)'s appearance may not have been coincidental, as on 10th March, 1804, Joseph and Melinda's first child was born at Boston in Lincolnshire and named Melinda Brunton Smedley.[12] She was baptised at Boston on 31st March, 1804.[13] Her Godfather was 'Captain Brunton'. I have been unable to trace such a person within the Brunton family or amongst Melinda's friends, but considering Mr Brunton played the part of a Captain in both of the plays at Lincoln in which they shared billing, this may account for the soubriquet of her Godfather's name, and her daughter's middle name. (Brunton also played the part of Captain Winlove in *We Fly By Night* at Covent Garden in 1806; so perhaps he was suited to such roles.) Strangely, and for no reason that I have been able to ascertain, Melinda Brunton Smedley was baptised again, the second time being at Newark on 22nd November 1804.[14]

By 1807, the Duke Street Theatre in Brighton had been demolished and a new theatre built with both John Bruntons as joint lessees, and it opened on 6th June that year, with John Jnr playing Laertes to the Hamlet of Charles Kemble.

Brunton Snr remained at Brighton until 1811, and shortly thereafter retired with his wife to Hampstead Marshall, in Berkshire, close to the Craven family seat at Hampstead Park, where he died on 18th December, 1822.

Brunton Jnr went from strength to strength; he became the first lessee of the new theatre at Lynn, built in 1815 at a cost of £6,400, and at which he opened in *Lover's Vows* and *Raising the Wind*.[15] In the same year he is listed as the author, along with Charles Kemble, George Colman, and others of a play called *Town and Country*, a comedy in five acts, and "as performed at the Theatres-Royal, Drury Lane, and Covent Garden."[16] In 1822 he took out a sub-lease on the theatre in Tottenham Street, off Tottenham Court Road, then in the hands of the Beverley family. He

---

[12] Family archive, Lincolnshire Archive;

[13] Parish records; Lincolnshire Archives

[14] St Mary's Church Newark Parish Register, Newark Library.

[15] Rogues and Vagabonds; Elizabeth Grice

[16] OCLC World Cat.

renamed it the West London Theatre and formed his own company, which included his daughter Elizabeth, and managed it for a season until the Beverlys returned to London.[17]

Meanwhile, the Smedleys disappear from view, no longer appearing in the playbills of the Lincoln Circuit. But by 1806, it appears that Joseph had gone into management for himself, seemingly with a partner, as an advertisement in the *Market Rasen Mercury* of 12th June, 1807, proclaims "Messrs. Smedley and Clarke from the theatres Lincoln, Boston and Co inform the inhabitants that they have fitted up a commodious theatre."[18]

Smedley and Clarke also played at Wainfleet in Lincolnshire on 5th September, 1807, where they presented *To Marry or Not to Marry*, and the musical farce *Matrimony*. On the back of the bills, signed by "your humble servants" and the names of the partners, was a notice informing the public that as it was "necessary for the respectability of the stage to *persecute* those scoundrels and impostors who disgrace it" – two of the company were mentioned as being on the black list. One (a native of Norwich) "who received his discharge from us for Drunkenness and Inattention, instead of remaining till the expiration of his notice (two months) left two days afterwards." The other (an Irishman), discharged for the same fault

> … has gone this day and left his name in the Bills of to-morrow night, although there is three weeks of his notice yet unexpired. Jo' May (of Norwich) and I Clare (whose real name is Clark), of Nottingham have likewise left their names in the Bills without giving any notice at all. As the existence of every Company depends on the Managers faith in the performers the necessity of such a communication speaks for itself.[19]

Joseph, it seems, had started as he meant to go on, and was already developing

---

[17] "The History of the Prince of Wales's Theatre London, 1771-1903; Richard L. Lorenzen (STR)

[18] Quoted by CMP Taylor in 'Right Royal: Wakefield Theatres, 1776 – 1994

[19] Extract from Playhouses and Players of East Anglia by T.L.G. Burley, Pub. Jarrold & Sons Ltd., Norwich, 1928

his ideas on ensuring the rectitude and repute of his company as a means of elevating theatre.

On a playbill of 20th April, 1802, found amongst Joseph Smedley's papers and believed to be of Sleaford's theatre, neither of them is mentioned, but a Mr Obbinson does appear, and this may prove significant later.[20]

On 13th March, 1806, at Rotherham, Melinda gave birth to a second baby girl, who they named Jane, and, later in the year, another playbill, again assumed to be for Sleaford, shows the Smedleys and the Clarkes sharing a bill; evidence of Joseph and Melinda still gaining experience:[21]

Tuesday Evening Sept 23rd, 1806
The Battle of Hexham
Or, Days of Old
Written by Mr Colman Jnr, music composed by Dr Arnold
Gondibert............MR SMEDLEY
Lavarenne............Mr May   Fool............Mr Tuthill
Barton............Mr Clarke
First Robber............Mr Matthews   Drummer............Mr Palmer
Prince of Wales............Miss Clarke   Gregory Gubbins............Mr Hall
Queen Margaret............Mrs Tuthill
Adeline............MRS SMEDLEY
THE ORIGIN OF GUNPOWDER,
Mr Tuthill *
A Comic Song, Mr Hall
COLLINS' ODE ON THE PASSIONS
Mr May
LOVERS' QUARRELS**
Or, Like Master Like Man
Carlos............Mr Smedley
Lopez............Mr May   Sancho............Mr Hall
Leonora............Mrs Smedley
Jacintha............Mrs Clark

---

[20] Playbills in possession of family; copies in Lincolnshire Archives
[21] Playbills in possession of family; copies in Lincolnshire Archives

* Mr Tuthill had appeared at Norwich in 1793, on the same bill as Miss Brunton. There had been a company playing at Sleaford and elsewhere for some time under the management of a Mr Simms, with his daughter. Later, they became occasional members of Joseph's company.

After this, Joseph and Melinda Smedley's attentions were more taken by the area around the south of Yorkshire and North Lincolnshire, today known as Humberside, and, in 1806 Joseph commenced a long association with the new theatre in Burgess Street, Grimsby, which, as we shall see, underwent a somewhat curious history of ownership resulting in a very beneficial arrangement for Joseph.[22] There is no sign of the Clarkes, who may have entered into partnership in another enterprise.

In 1809 Joseph became a Freemason. He was initiated into St. Matthew Lodge at Barton-upon-Humber on 25th May. He gave his address as Barton and his occupation as Comedian. He was now 25 years of age.[23]

** *Lovers' Quarrels*

This is a play by John Vanbrugh, a two-act comedy, altered, probably while being performed at Smock-Alley, in Dublin, and hence the subtitle. It is also the English translation of Moliere's second play, *Le Depit amoureux,* and the title of an engraving by Edward Williams Clay in the Library of Congress.

However, the subtitle, 'Like Master, Like Man' is also the title of a book which became very popular. It was written by John Palmer of the Theatre Royal, Haymarket, who was the son of another John Palmer of Theatre Royal, Drury Lane. It had a preface by George Colman, the prolific playwright of the time. It was published in 1811, by subscription, and the list of subscribers is a list of Who's Who in Society and the Theatre of the time. There were 87 subscribers, of which a few were:[24]

HRH The Prince Regent	£5-5s-0d
HRH The Duke of York	£5-5s-0d
Sir George Beamont, Bart	£2-2s-0d
John Brunton	£1-1s-0d

---

[22] History of the Grimsby Theatre by Guy Hemingway, Grimsby Library, Local Studies

[23] Original record, Freemasons Hall, London, Library and Museum of Freemasonry

[24] British Fiction Database, Cardiff University and AHRR

Richard E. Smedley

Earl of Craven	£2-2s-0d
Thomas Dibdin	£1-1s-0d
R W Elliston	£1-1s-0d
Mrs Elliston	£1-1s-0d
Charles Kemble	£1-1s-0d
Charles Matthews	£1-0s-0d

2
Beginnings – The Robertsons

The city of Lincoln started as an Iron Age settlement, was occupied by the Romans, and then ruled by Vikings in the ninth and tenth centuries, during which time it became a trading town. In 1068, William the Conqueror's Norman invasion arrived at Lincoln, and he ordered a castle to be built, and later a cathedral, on the site of the Roman settlement.

Lincoln was therefore divided into two parts: the 'upper' where the Cathedral and Castle were situated; and the 'lower', where the boats moored and to where the shopping area had spread. Daniel Defoe who liked countryside and had a kind word for the 'upper' city, wrote of Lincoln:

"It is an ancient, ragged, decay'd and still decaying city; it is full of the ruins of Monasteries and religious houses…."

However, in the early part of the 18th century, Lincoln was actually emerging from this state of decay into which it had fallen since the 16th century. Although without any industries of its own, as the capital of the county it had good links by road and waterways, and was dependent on the surrounding countryside through its markets, fairs and shops and the growing demand for wool, meat and corn from its nearby counties as well as in London.

The first theatre in Lincoln was built in about 1732 in Drury Lane (within the castle grounds), and managed by a Dr. Herbert, so titled, according to G Hemingway, as he was "bred to the profession of a Surgeon and Apothecary". He managed a travelling theatre company which covered a large swathe of the country, and he is credited with the founding of the Lincoln Circuit. It was his son, Nathaniel, who eventually took over the Lincoln Circuit as we shall see.

Richard E. Smedley

The first theatre in Nottingham was built in St. Mary's Gate near to the Church of the same name which was at the centre of what was then the main residential settlement of the town. It was variously called the St. Mary's Gate Theatre, the Royal Theatre, the Theatre Royal, just plain 'Nottingham Theatre', and, eventually, the Royal Alhambra Music Hall. In its original form it boasted of a pit, galleries and boxes and could hold 758 people. It was built by James Whitely, and therefore the Lincoln and Nottingham theatres share much of their past in common.

The first of four generations to be connected to the theatre, James Shaftoe Robertson is often mistaken for another James Robertson, (1713–95), who was the principal comedian in the York circuit from about 1740 to 1779 when he retired. Both the Oxford DNB and Dame Madge Kendal (formerly Margaret Robertson), in her autobiography, make this erroneous claim.[1]

An account of James Shaftoe Robertson's life is given in an account of the Lincoln Circuit written in 1803 by his eldest son, Thomas Shaftoe Robertson. In that book, he claims that his father came from Ludlow where he was placed at Grammar School, and from which he ran away at the age of 17 to become an actor.[2]

Mr Robertson married early in life, a Miss Ann Fowler of Loughborough, while in a company there. He then got an engagement in the York Theatre under the management of Mr Achurch and afterwards Tate Wilkinson, where he continued until invited by Mr Whitley to take management of the Lincoln Circuit.

He apparently played in Leicester in the company of James Augustus Whitley in 1761 and 1765.[3] A Nottingham playbill of 24th July, 1765, shows him with Mr Whitley's Company of Comedians at the Theatre, St. Mary Gate, Nottingham, in the cast of *The Wonder: A Woman Keeps a Secret*.[4]

---

[1] Dame Madge Kendal by Herself, 1933
[2] GH Lincoln Public Library
[3] GH LNJ 4-4-1761 – 18-4-1761; LNJ 9-3-'765
[4] GH – The Robertson Family, Lincolnshire Archives

According to the Lincoln date book,[5] his son Thomas was born at Alford on 2nd August, 1765. His stay at York is fairly well documented by Tate Wilkinson, saying that he was engaged in 1767, that he had a good education, but did not possess Lord Chesterfield's graces: "quite the reverse, for he walked like a crab."[6] Since the more famous James Robertson already filled the principal comedy roles, his newly engaged namesake appeared in playbills as 'Mr Shaftoe'.

He and his wife appeared regularly until, suddenly 'Master Shaftoe' (presumably Thomas Shaftoe Robertson, then aged four-and-a-half), appears on 17th April and again on 2nd May 1770 as Olinthus in *Timanthes*, his father playing Mathasius.[7]

While at York, another son was born, James, baptised on 19th February, 1770, at St. Michael le Belfry, York,[8] but probably born in December 1769, as he was in his 62nd year when he died on 1st January, 1831.

Another son, George, was baptised there on 13th May, 1771, but buried there two days later.[9] A third surviving son, George, was born later, after his parents had left the York Company. The 'Shaftoes' remained with the York Company, after leaving York, at Leeds until the termination of the season on 3rd October, 1771.

It therefore must have been during the summer of that year when Mr Nathaniel Herbert, who had taken over the Lincoln Circuit, being short of money, invited Mr James Augustus Whitley to become a partner. Mr Whitley, having another circuit on his hands, placed Mr James Shaftoe Robertson there as his deputy.[10]

The language used by Tate Wilkinson when later describing his and Robertson's break suggests that there had been some ill feeling over it.

---

[5] The Lincoln Date Book, Lincolnshire Archives, P.330
[6] The Wandering Patentee by Tate Wilkinson
[7] York Courant; 10-4-1770
[8] Parish Register, St Michael le Belfry, York
[9] Parish Register, St Michael le Belfry, York
[10] Lincoln Public Library

On 11th November, 1771, 'Whitley and Herbert's Company of Comedians' played at the Theatre in the Haymarket, Leicester, and 'Mr Robertson', again under his own name, was in the cast of both *Douglas* and *Lethe*, the two plays produced. In February and March, 1772, he was with the company at Newark[11], and also gave the interlude entertainment between the plays.

There is some uncertainty surrounding the events of the next few years, but Thomas Shaftoe Robertson claims that "after some time" – but probably around 1777 – James Shaftoe Robertson purchased Mr Whitley's shares and the firm became 'Herbert and Robertson'.

After some years, Herbert and Robertson entered into partnership with Mr Joseph Younger and Mr George Mattocks in the management of the Manchester, Sheffield, and the Old Theatre, Birmingham, still retaining the Lincoln Circuit. The Manchester scheme lost money, so they soon withdrew from it and took a third partner in the management of the Lincoln Circuit, a Mr Green, who had been an officer and had risen from the ranks. A year after this event, James Shaftoe Robertson died. The dates of these events are confusing. James Shaftoe Robertson was still alive on 6th September, 1780, when his name appears on a Lincoln playbill, and dead by the summer of 1781 when Tate Wilkinson took over the Sheffield Theatre. Therefore the Manchester episode must have taken place in 1780. An article of 1780[12] states that "after only three seasons, Herbert surrendered his management (of the Sheffield Theatre) to Shaftoe Robertson as he did later also in his interests in the Lincoln Circuit." This article lists the Lincoln Circuit as comprising Lincoln, Boston, Grantham, Spalding, Peterborough, Huntingdon, Wisbech and Newark, but in 1780 Lynn should be added to these, and possibly Peterborough was added later.

James Shaftoe Robertson made a loss at Sheffield which may have contributed to his death. According to Tate Wilkinson, he was buried with great pomp by a large body of freemasons at Sheffield where he had been a brother of their Lodge. However, Thomas Shaftoe Robertson disagreed with Wilkinsons's account, which he found offensive. He says that the Freemasons

---

[11] GYHCreswell's Nottingham and Newark Journal; 1-2-1772

[12] GH Hunter Archaeological Society Transactions

only attended the funeral out of respect. No aid or support was needed. Since local Masonic records show no such payments, his account has validity.

Thomas Shaftoe Robertson, then aged 16, was left in charge of his father's share in the company's affairs – which were encumbered by debt – and managing his mother's. Shortly thereafter the company began to decline in reputation.

Ann Robertson survived a further 22 years after her husband died, latterly living at Peterborough. Her death notice in the Nottingham Journal reads "Died, Monday, 25th (April 1803) at Peterborough, Mrs Robertson, mother of Mr James Robertson, one of the managers of our (Nottingham) theatre". (Nottingham Journal, 30-4-1803).

Thomas Shaftoe Robertson

The eldest son of James Shaftoe Robertson and his wife Ann, Thomas is said to have been born in Alford on 2nd May 1765, and made several appearances on the stage as a child, and then, in 1786, being of age, his mother signed over her share of the company to him., and the name of the company became 'Miller and Robertson'.

Thomas was married on 8th September, 1793[13] at Spalding (on the Lincoln Circuit) to Frances Mary Ross, a daughter, by a former marriage, of Mrs Brown of Covent Garden. Frances, or Fanny, as she was known, was a gifted actress who became a great favourite at Lincoln, where she starred for almost fifty years. It is said that she acted in the style of Siddons.

As we have seen, Fanny's sister, Anna, also an actress, married John Brunton Jnr and they visited Lincoln, and played in Robertson's company several times.

As far as is known, the only child of the marriage that can be traced is John, baptised at Newark on 21st October, 1796.[14] He probably died early as there is no further trace of him.

---

[13] Spalding Parish Register
[14] Newark Parish Church Records

The partnership with Mr Miller continued until 1796 when Thomas bought out his partner and then sold a share in the company to Robert Henry Franklin, who died on 26th June, 1802 at Peterborough, aged only 32.[15] Thomas became the sole owner, and remained so until his death.

In 1803 he wrote an account of the Lincoln Circuit up to then for the use of James Winston in his intended publication *The Theatric Tourist*.

We will continue with Thomas Shaftoe Robertson's career later on so that we can adhere to an approximate time-line with that of Joseph Smedley

James Robertson, was the second son of James Shaftoe and Ann Robertson. Born in York, probably in December 1769, and baptised on 19th February, 1770. He appeared on stage as a child at Lincoln and on the Circuit.[16]

Some time after 1788, James left the Lincoln Company and joined the Nottingham & Derby Company of Comedians, formerly managed by James Whitley who had died in 1781, and been replaced by William Pero who'd married one of Whitley's granddaughters, an actress named Miss Villars, in 1778. On his retirement in 1818,[17] James Robertson thanked the people of Nottingham for "support over 30 years" suggesting 1788 as the year when he joined the company, but on 22nd June 1790, at Stamford, as Squire Acres in *The Rivals*, this was noted as "his first appearance here."

In August, 1791[18], he played the Piper in *The Highland Reel*. Also in the cast was, Miss Robinson, elder daughter of Mrs Taylor (who was also acting). Mr Robinson, Mrs Taylor's first husband, had died around the end of 1785, and around 1789 she married Mr Taylor who, in February, 1791, was also with the company. On his death, his widow, in 1802, became Mrs Wrench. This arrangement evidently caused some amusement, and was recorded as an anecdote by Walter Donaldson:

---

[15] GH Lincoln Public Library
[16] GH Lincoln Theatre Playbills
[17] GH Nottingham Journal; 25-7-1818
[18] GH Nottingham Journal; 30-7-1791

Wrench, the original in several characters at the Adelphi, began his career at Nottingham. So awkward and spiritless was this comedian, that the general remark was, he must have been mad to think of the stage; yet this actor became a popular man at the Adelphi Theatre and at the Lyceum.

At the period of Wrench's probation at Nottingham, a Mrs Taylor, an actress of talent, had a share in the management, and Manly and Wrench paid their addresses to her and Miss Taylor, her daughter. Manly was the adorer of the mother, and Wrench of the young lady. What then was the astonishment of every one to find an exchange of sweethearts take place, Manly marrying the daughter, and Wrench the mother! The latter union was not a blissful one.[19]

In the following October, James Robertson married Miss Robinson at Retford[20] where the company was then playing. Shortly afterwards, perhaps in 1792, was born a daughter, Georgina, who later made many appearances with the company as a child dancer. Other children were:

Henry (c 1795) & {both of whom went on the stage}
William (c 1798) (became manager of the Lincoln Circuit)
Fanny (c 1799)
Caroline (1800)
Maria
Eliza

In April, 1794, Mrs Robertson appears in the cast[21] as Lady Douglas in *Mary Queen of Scots*. In the summer of the same year, James Robertson became part-manager with Mrs Taylor, whose husband had recently died, of the Nottingham & Derby Company and, in August 'Taylor and Robertson, late Pero' opened in Nottingham.[22]

---

[19] Recollections of an Actor, Walter Donaldson, 1865
[20] GH Nottingham Journal; 22-10-1791
[21] GH Nottingham Journal; 19-4-1794
[22] GH, Nottingham Journal; 19-4-1794

James' responsibilities were varied. As well as management and acting, he gave comic songs and other 'interludes' during scene changes. He painted scenery,[23] wrote his own comic songs, and was an artist of some talent.

According to the Nottingham Journal of 19th January, 1799, a tragedy hit the Robertsons when "a few days ago, a child of Mr Robertson, one of the Managers of our (Nottingham) Theatre was burnt to death in Sheffield, in consequence of a spark flying from the stove on its clothes." Neither the name nor sex of the child is given, but the birth may have fallen between those of Georgina and Henry.

As we have seen, in 1802, Mrs Taylor married Mr Wrench, and the management became 'Wrench and Robertson'. In November, 1804,[24] James Robertson made an appearance at Lincoln – where his older brother, Thomas Shaftoe Robertson, was manager – "His first appearance at Lincoln for 16 years," which confirms that he left Lincoln in 1788. There he sang "comic songs, originally written for his theatres at Nottingham, Derby, Stamford, Halifax, Retford, &c."

On 2nd April, 1806,[25] the following announcement appeared in the press: "Died at Derby, aged 29, universally regretted by all who knew her, Mrs Robertson, wife of Mr J Robertson, Manager of the Theatre, Nottingham, Retford, Chesterfield, &c." The age given is clearly incorrect. No cause of death is given, but may have been in childbirth.

In October, 1810,[26] James married again, in Chesterfield, "to Miss Marie Lynam of that place." The second Mrs James Robertson appeared at Retford on 15th December with a song between the acts, and in the cast of *Budget and Blunders*. No further appearances have been noted in surviving Retford playbills, though she did appear at Nottingham.[27]

---

[23] Nottingham Journal; 8-8-1800
[24] GH LSM 16-11-1804
[25] GH Nottingham Journal; 5-4-1806
[26] GH Nottingham Journal; 1-6-1811
[27] GH LSM 13-9-1816

3
The Smedleys – Early Stages

By the autumn of 1809, Joseph had put together a troupe of actors that he knew (the company was twelve strong and included five females), a mixed programme of entertainments and a list of theatres they would tour. Straight theatre, as such, was still the province of those houses with the Royal warrant, and any plays were interspersed with melodrama, farce, dancing, musical interludes and recitations.

Scenery in theatres was usually confined to a series of scene rolls; cloths with scenery painted on them which could be unrolled quickly rather like a set of roller blinds, to form a backdrop. Stage furniture was rare, limited to the minimum necessary to establish where the 'action' was taking place, plus any hand-props they could muster to help delineate their characters. The actors' lines were not directed to each other but toward the audience, and without movement, in a rather stiff and stilted manner. Not until Dion Boucicault presented *London Assurance* in 1841 did a more naturalised style of acting become fashionable, when the characters actually addressed each other. The company of actors had little time to rehearse or to study new roles, particularly when playing in a different programme every evening. They would usually rehearse in the mornings, and such rehearsal would often take the form of a briefing on the plot, the characters and any 'business' they were able to include, and in consequence there was much improvisation and ad-libbing.

It was usual in forming a company of players to ensure that as many characterisations as possible could be covered by them. There would therefore be a member capable of major dramatic roles, a tragedian; someone good in comic roles, someone able to play elderly men, etc. Women were, by now, playing female roles, but it was still common to find them being played by young men or boys. Farce and other entertainments such as comic songs, dancing, monologues helped to form part of the bills, and so the more able, rounded and experienced the performer the better. They termed themselves 'comedians' for actors performed drama which was the province of the Patent Houses in London (the Theatres Royal in Drury Lane and Covent Garden).

There were no copyright laws at the time, and it was quite usual for plays which had a legitimate airing in London being copied or stolen and a version reproduced at theatres in the provinces, sometimes with little bearing on the original, and sometimes quite faithfully, with no redress for the author.

Joseph Smedley, however, wanted to behave in an honest and upright manner in order to gain a reputation as an even-handed and fair-minded man of business. He chose a programme containing tried and tested material, all published, and therefore legitimately in the public domain (although there was no copyright system then, and payments to playwrights rare unless the authors were tied to one of the Patent Houses; nor do we know how faithful they were to the original). With a different programme each evening, he opened at Grimsby on Friday, 29th December 1809, and was due to play there until Friday, 22nd February 1810. He no doubt used this initial Grimsby residency to polish and rehearse his company ready for the road ahead. Note that the plays' titles are referred to as they appear in Joseph Smedley's account books, and are frequently abbreviated. I have tried to properly identify these in the list of plays.

He opened with a mixed programme which included *The Rivals* and *Rosina*; *Laugh When You Can* and *Blind Boy*. Expenses for the week included an item for 'carriage of goods' of £4-10s-0d. The Smedleys paid themselves two guineas for the week, an income which was not to change as far as we can tell. Other salaries were:[1]

---

[1] Joseph Smedley's account books; Lincs. Archives: 38/5/1

Tannets	£2-13s-0d
Goldfinches	£1-16s-0d
Kellys	£1-10s-0d
Hodgson	18s-0d
Spragg	16s-0d

Income from the sale of tickets for these opening days amounted to £2-11s-6d .

The first full week commencing Monday, 1st January, 1810, started with *Foundling of the Forest* and *Midas*, followed by *Jew* and *Christian Gambols* and then *Grievings: A Folly* and *Young Hussar*. This last was "by desire of General Loft." The ticket income for the latter was a healthy £13-12s-0d, bringing the income from ticket sales up to a total of £19-12s-6d, with similar wage expenses as the previous week but with the addition of a payment to 'Smith' of 12s-0d; Billing (7s-6d); and Doorkeeper (4s-0d).

The Grimsby season continued with such plays as *Adelgitha* and *Killings No Murder*; *Honey Moon* and *Weathercock*; *To Marry or not to Marry* and *Tekeli*; *Othello* and *Sultan*; *Speed the Plough*; *Macbeth* and *No Song No Supper*; *Man and Wife* and *Paul and Virginia*; *Castle Spectre* and *Irishman in London* and, on 3rd February, for the Smedleys' benefit performance *Earl of Essex* and *Maid of Orleans*, which took £10-0-0 at the box office. There were further benefits for other members of the company too, and on 22nd February they gave a benefit for the poor: *Stranger* and *Lock and Key*; however the takings for this are unknown. Delayed by the awful winter weather, making travel almost impossible, they remained in Grimsby, finally ending the season on 24th February.

In addition to salaries, other expenses shown was a fee for Dr Bell on 12th February, the Rent for the Theatre (in full) of 12 guineas, and loans to Tannett of £3-0s-0d, and to Spragg of 10s-od. There were sundry expenses of £3-17s-6d paid on 19th February, and 6 shillings for coals, window, loading, and nails. Joseph had already sent expenses to Alford, the next stop on the tour, of £1-10s-0d.

This first Grimsby season must have been considered a success and boded well for the tour that was to follow. The total ticket income was £187-8s-6d and, after wages had been deducted, Joseph had cleared £16-1s-6d. However his accounts are not easy to understand, particularly the benefit system. It appears, for instance, that some tickets were not paid for in advance; the entries for Morton for instance. There is one entry for him for 10s, which is later crossed out suggesting a later payment. Joseph's total appears to have included only box office receipts and tickets already paid for. However, despite salaries being listed as paid on fixed days of the week, these amounts were then deducted from their benefit monies; i.e. they were not paid wages as well as benefits. When the actual takings for the ticket sales were received by Joseph he subtracted the 'advance' and handed over the balance.[2]

Note too that the cast here includes the Tannetts. This was certainly a family of a man, his wife and daughter, hence their joint wages being more than the Smedleys paid themselves. Tannett was an itinerant Irish actor and scenery painter, or scenic artist, whom Joseph had come across in his travels. It appears from correspondence in the Smedley family archive that this was B. Tannett, or Benjamin, who was mentioned in Tate Wilkinson's memoir *The Wandering Patentee*, in which he reports on an exchange of correspondence in 1794, with Tannett at the theatre at Malton in Yorkshire, about the capabilities of a certain young actress.

At Alford, in 1810, Miss Tannett appears to have come of age, as she now receives 16s, deducted from her parents' former wage of £2-13s-0d.

The Tannetts were to have a long association with the Smedleys; and were to have a huge impact on the family.

Having closed at Grimsby on the 24th February, they now had just three days until they opened in the tour in Alford, a village south of Grimsby, inland from Chapel St. Leonards. They opened there on 27th February and presented:

---

[2] A Avison notes

Stranger and *Lock and Key (income £1-19-0d)*
Pizzaro and *Yo. Hussar (£5-7s-0d)*
Grievings A Folly and *Spoiled Child (5s-0d)*
Laugh When You Can and *Cinderella (£10-5s-0d)*
Henry II and *Blind Boy (£2-12s-0d)*
Adrian and Orilla and *Cinderella (£2-16-0d)*
John Bull and *Prize (by Desire of Wind Mill Ordinary) (£18-4s-0d)*
Jew and *Tekeli (£8-18s-0d)*
Jane Shore and *Harlequin (£2-17s-0d)*
Speed the Plough (Desire of the George Inn Ordinary) (£19-19s-0d)
Man and Wife and *Lady of Ro (£6-13s-0d)*
Romeo and Juliet and *Jew(£1-13s-0d)*
Provoked Husband and *Blue Beard (£11-15s-0d)*
Cure for Heartache and *Paul and Virginia (£10-5s-0d)*
Point of Honour and *Brittle(?) (12s-0d)*
Iron Chest and *Maid of Orleans (Smedleys' Benefit) (£5-4s-0d)*
The Foundling and *Iron Chest (Spragg and Smith Benefit) (£4-6s-0d)*
Honeymoon and *Killings No Murder (Kelly's Benefit) (£5-14s-0d)*
Everyone's Fault and *(?) (Goldfinches Benefit) (£8-8s-6d)*
Love in a Village and *Who Wins (Benefit of Miss Tannett and Hodgson)*
Deaf and Dumb and *Ella Rosen (Tannett's Benefit) £7-1s-0d)*

At the end of their Alford season of 24 nights, Passion Week caused a hiatus as no performances were allowed. Joseph, however, made some loans to company members to tide them over:

Mr Tannett	£2-15s-6d
Miss Tannett	13s-0d
Mr Kelly	6s-6d
Mr Spragg	6s-0d
Mr Smith	15s-0d

The tour went on to Holbeach at the expense of a carriage and chaise costing £11-15s-0d. Their route would have followed what is today the A16, but without all of the ring-roads around towns. The original route had 16 miles between each town, but would nevertheless have been a most uncomfortable and slow journey given the state of even well-travelled roads.

Richard E. Smedley

The tour continued, with Joseph continuing to add further attractions such as *The Battle of Hexham* and *George Barnwell*. The dates were as follows, together with the income from ticket sales:

Alford	Feb 27th	£130-1s-6d
Holbeach	April 24th	£106-8s-0d
Upwell	June 9th	£66-3s-0d
Brandon	July 14th	£103-8s-0d
Mildenhall	Aug 31st	£80-16s-0d
Stoke Ferry	Sept 20th	£57-5s-0d
Crowland	Oct 31st	£42-0s-0d
Folkingham	Dec 1st	£56-4s-0d

Joseph prepared to tour again, and, as before, opened in Grimsby on 3rd January, 1812. According to C.M.P. Taylor, Joseph discussed with his friend George Oliver, (see chapter 4),the prospects of a winter in Grimsby, "'dependent on the number of vessels laid up in the docks."

In January 1813: "We have lost all the armed ships and the place is in consequence very dull and dead; but the renewal of trade following the defeat of Napoleon is likely to bring better hopes; the closure of the docks at Hull for repairs in the winter of 1814–15 promised a better season at Grimsby, Oliver says."[3]

It seems that, according to T. Edgar Pemberton, in his book on the Kendals, workers in the early nineteenth century valued their playbills and went to some trouble to preserve them. It is also likely that Smedley, or a member of his company, carried surplus playbills to their lodgings. Hence some years ago a number of playbills of Joseph's 1812 season were found in the chimney of a cottage at Horncastle, in Lincolnshire, some photographs of which are included here.[4]

---

[3] CMP Taylor; Right Royal, Wakefield Theatre, 1776-1994
[4] North East Lincs. Archives, Grimsby

The Life and Times of Joseph Smedley

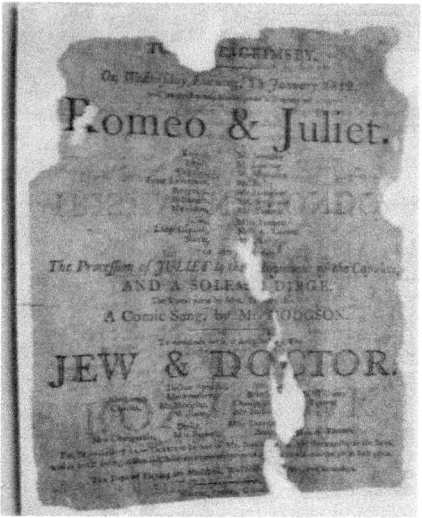
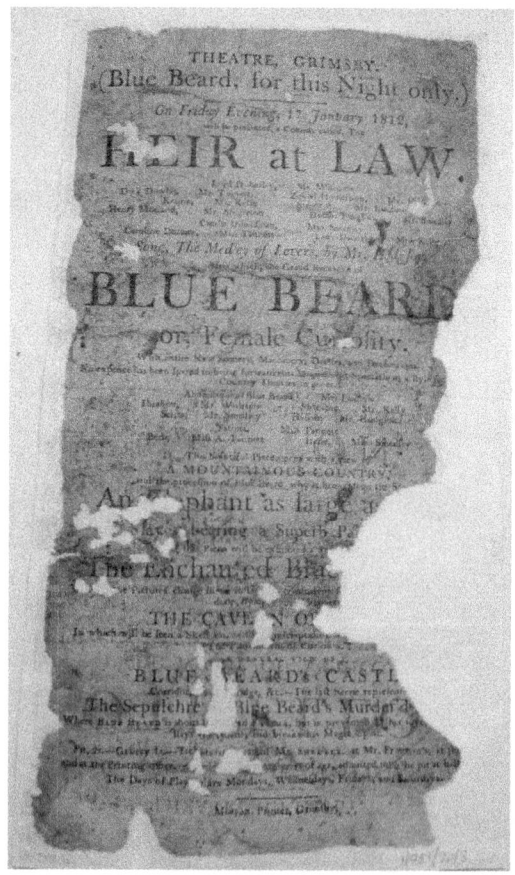

Richard E. Smedley

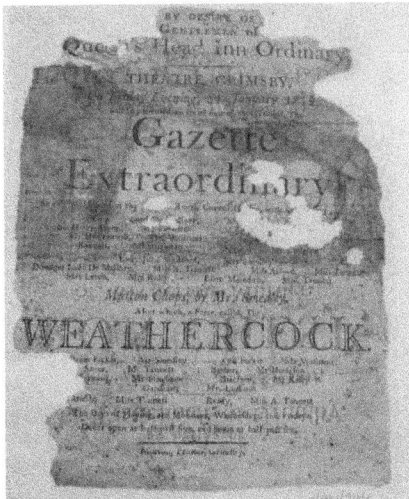

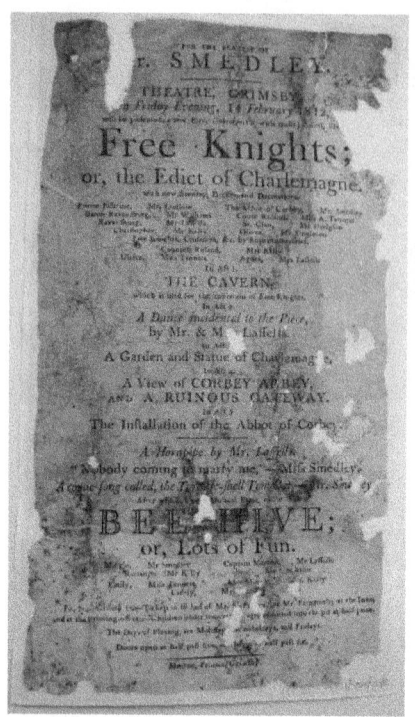 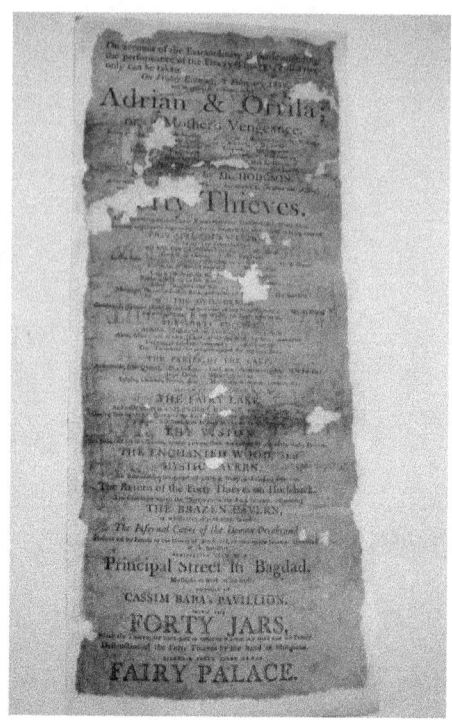

Early playbills – Grimsby 1812
Reproduced here by kind permission of the North East Lincolnshire Archives at Grimsby, and photographed by author.

Joseph's Account books reveal the programme and takings for the Grimsby season:

3rd Jan	*Speed the Plough* and *Lock and Key*	£1-8s-0d
4th Jan	*Alexander* and *Ways and Means*	£3-0s-0d
6th Jan	*Deaf and Dumb* and *Prize*	£1-4s-0d
8th Jan	*Richard III* and *Village Lawyer*	£3-3s-0d
	(By Desire of Spurn and Humber Lodge)	
10th Jan	*Stranger* and *Hit and Miss*	£14-5s-0d
11th Jan	*George Barnwell* and *Trial by Jury*	£4-10s-0d
13th Jan	*Royal Oak* and *Irishman in London*	£3-5s-0d
15th Jan	*Romeo and Juliet* and *Jew and ?*	£3-5s-0d
17th Jan	*Heir at Love* and *Blue Beard*	£8-4s-0d

Richard E. Smedley

18th Jan	*Othello* and *Bon Jon*	£
20th Jan	*Kiss* and *Darkness Visible*	£
	(By Desire of Captain Mott)	
22nd Jan	*Soldiers Daughter* and *Matrimony*	£5-1s-0d
	(By desire of Granby Ordinary)	
24th Jan	*Poor Gent* and *Gay Deceivers*	£10-8s-0d
	(By Desire of the Seamen of the *Prince William**)	

Joseph also performed an evening for this cause in 1810
*The "Prince William" was a man-of-war.[5]

29th Jan	*Wild Oats* and *Turn Gate*	£11-8s-0d
30th Jan	*Iron Chest* and *High Life Below Stairs*	£5-0s-0d
	(By Desire of Queens Ordinary)	
31st Jan	*Gazzette Extraordinary* and *Weathercock*	£8-9s-0d
	(By Desire of Oddfellows) & Tannett's Benefit	
3rd Feb	*Hamlet* and *Paul and Virginius*	£6-18s-0d
	(By Desire of Oliver's School)	
6th Feb	*Wonder* and *Surprise*	£9-10s-0d
7th Feb	*Hypocrite* and *Forty Thieves*	£9-6s=0d
10th Feb	*Gamester* and *Wedding Day*	£1-10s-0d
11th Feb	*Merchant of Venice* and *Forty Thieves*	£4-2s-0d
	Smedley's benefit:	
13th Feb	*Free Knight* and *Bee Hive*	6-11s-0d
17th Feb	*Foundling* and *20 Years Ago* and *Harlequin*	£4-10s-6d
	(By Desire of Freemasons) and Tannett's Benefit	
19th Feb	*Way to Get Married* and *C in Y Wood*	£7-7s-0d
21st Feb	*Pizarro* and *First Frolic*	£7-4s-0d
	(By Desire of Captain of *Game Cock*)	
24th Feb	*John Bull* and *Bee Hive*	£6-19s-6d
	(By Desire of G. Volunteers)	
26th Feb	*Busy Body* and *Bath Prelude* and *Harlequin*	£6-0s-0d
28th Feb	*M.P.* and *Forty Thieves*	£8-2s-0d
	(By Desire of Officers of G. Volunteers)	
2nd March	*Mountaineers* and *Yo Hussars*	£8-1s-0d
3rd March	*Free Knights* and *Killings No Murder*	£6-16s-0d

---

[5] Avison notes

The total income from ticket sales was £178-17s-0d
The total expenses were £167-17s-0d
Giving a clear profit of £11-0s-0d

The expenses included payments to Skinner, who, although soon to be announced bankrupt, was still owner of the theatre at this time and in receipt of rent. Other payments include the purchase of a book of plays, music MS, various loans, making of dresses and mending by sceneshifter.

It is worth mentioning here that the theatres in these days seated few in number compared to theatres of today, and accommodated about 150–200 people on average, and sometimes less. The tour then carried on to the following (with takings):[6]

Caistor	£111-8s-0d	Cleared £13-15s-0d
Southwell	£138-6s-0d	Cleared £6-0s-0d
Belper£	43-4s-6d	Loss of £28-13s-6d
Ripley	£6-19s-0d	Loss of £6-3s-0d
Alfreton	£25-10s-0d	Loss of £23-0s-0d
Wirksworth	£12-0s-6d	Loss of £24-6s-4d
Castle Donington	£35-10s-0d	Loss of £22-13s-6d
Aston (Brassington, Matlock)	£8-18s-0d	Loss of £6-10s-0d
Bingham	£165-2s-0d	Cleared £14-5s-0d
Oakham	£11-15s-6d	Profit and Loss unclear

The players at this time, in addition to Mr and Mrs Smedley, included:

Mr Williams	Mr Ludlow
Mr Tannett	Mr Hodgson
Mr Kelly	Miss Tannett
Mr Singleton	Miss A Tannett
Mrs Kelly	

The tour finished at Oakham at the end of the year.

---

[6] Joseph Smedley Account Books, Lincs. Archive LLHS 38/5/1

Richard E. Smedley

In August of 1812, in his capacity of treasurer of the new Apollo Lodge, Oliver lent Joseph two pounds, commiserating with him on his "losses at Belper and Alfreton."[7] Indeed such a series of reverses must have been devastating to Joseph; the extent of his feelings we can only guess at.

However, undaunted he set out on tour again in 1814, this time starting at:

Sleaford	£58-4s-6d
Folkingham	£46-0s-0d
Bourn	£103-14-6d
Bingham	£103-17-6d
Melton Mowbray	£118-15s-0d
**Southwell	£140-16-3d
Barton	£83-9s-0d
Howden	£142-11s-0d
Driffield	£60-10s-0d
Grimsby	£15-3s-0d

**The plaque outside the restored building which housed the theatre in Southwell claims that "around 1812–16, James Adams, a whitesmith, converted the first floor for use as a theatre. It opened with performances by a travelling company, managed by Joseph Smedley. Playbills show the theatre had boxes, a pit and gallery." It seems to be generally accepted that Joseph took over the management in 1814.[8] However, Richard Shilton[9] states categorically that in 1816 two large rooms in the house of James Adams, Whitesmith, standing in an indent used as a depot for the arms of the Southwell Militia, were converted to a theatre. It further records, "It is neatly fitted up and proves fully competent to the purpose. The public are wisely restricted, in this gratification, to a visit only once in two years for about six weeks each period." The building itself was behind the Cross Keys Inn, and the building shielding it from Queen Street which passes by it has now been demolished as part of a road widening scheme. From contemporary playbills, it is clear that Joseph was including Southwell in his tours before this building was made available, presumably an inn or other facility. Indeed,

---

[7] Oliver, quoted by CMP Taylor (Right Royal: Wakefield Theatre 1776-1994)

[8] Avison notes

[9] History of Southwell by Richard P Shilton, first pub. 1818)

when applying for a licence to perform at the new theatre in 1816, Joseph was informed that his 'uniform regularity and good conduct' had been taken into account by the magistrate[10] in granting it. There are few signs existing today of the sites of boxes, pit or gallery, and windows have been installed at some point.

Presumably, the decision to end the tour at Grimsby was intended to let them finish on a high note. However, as it turned out the ticket receipts appear disappointing, although it should be remembered that the Grimsby theatre was a very small house, even by comparison with other venues of the day. Overall the tour took in excess of £870.

For the record, the Grimsby season commenced on 22nd December: the playlist and takings were as follows:

Play	Takings
Stranger and *Fortunes Frolic*	£0-14s-0d
Hypocrite and *Child in Wood*	£1-7s-0d
Macbeth and *Ro House* (By desire of Freemasons)	£12-19s-0d
Peter the Great and *Love Law*	£
Deserted D? and *Devil to Pay*	£
Wood Demon and *Jukle and Yarico*	£
Jane Shore and *Romp*	£3-2s-0d
Wood Demon and *T. Gate*	£5-0s-0d
Geo. Barnwell and *H.rlle*	£2-10s-0d
Debtor, Creditor and *Purse*	£0-15s-0d
Education and *Weathercock*	£4-0s-0d
Secrets Worth Knowing and *??????*	£3-6s-0d
Rivals and *Prize*	£11-12s-0d
Miller and Men and *??????????*	£3-3s-0d
Wheel of Fortune and *Sleepwalk*	£5-5s-0d
Cure for Heartache, Bleeding Nun and *Die for Love*	£2-5s-0d
Tough at Times and *Peasant Boy*	£6-10s-0d
Alexander and *Intrigue Bombastes*	£4-0s-0d
Riches and *Forty Thieves*	£4-0s-0d
Provoked Husband and *?????????*	£5-4s-0d

---

[10] A letter contained in the Lincolnshire Archive

She Stoops to Conquer and *False Friend*	£9-1s-0d
Venice Preserved and *Darkness Visible*	£5-10s-0d
Farmer's Wife and *Lady of the Rock*	£7-13s-0d
West Indian and *Raising the Wind*	£8-8s-0d

Altogether, after expenses were taken into account, the Grimsby season made a net loss of £4-9s-0d.

These expenses were considerable and included, in addition to salaries, such items as binding thread, binding and gunpowder (3s); sailors' jackets and trousers (18s); writing paper (1s); Craggs Books (11s); Bloom (18s-6d – music); swords (4s); coals (8s-6d); Lumbley, chandler (£5-16-7d); and rent (£9-0s-0d) payable to Goodrick who had now taken over the theatre after Skinner's bankruptcy.

In 1815 the tour again commenced at Grimsby and continued as follows (with ticket receipts):

Grimsby	£100-13s-0d
Alford	£121-11s-0d
Caistor	£73-5s-0d
Barton	£137-3s-6d
Burlington Quay (Now known as Bridlington)	£107-13s-0d
Howden	£105-14s-0d
Grimsby	£22-4s-0d
Hedon	£29-0s-0d

This gives a total of over £766 in receipts. Most of these towns are situated around the coastal area, particularly in what is today Humberside. This may have been in the hope that Joseph's company could cash in on the relief and excitement generated by the news that the war was over and Napoleon and his forces defeated.

4
Those In Favour
Grimsby, Dr George Oliver & the Freemasons

According to Joseph Smedley's entry in the *Oxford Dictionary of National Biography*, written by the late C.M.P. (Coral, known-as-Kate) Taylor, Joseph had a 40-year friendship and correspondence with a clergyman, historian and school headmaster called Dr George Oliver. At the time that she wrote the entry, this correspondence was in the hands of a local historian, Mr Ted Drury; the letters are addressed to Joseph at various theatres in his circuit: Wirksworth (September 1812), Castle Donington (September 1812), Oakham (January 1813), Melton Mowbray (May 1814), Southwell (July 1814, September 1824, August 1826), St Ives Huntingdonshire (November 1816), Holbeach (January 1817, March 1819), Alford (March 1817, June 1821), Barton-on-Humber (June 1817), Sleaford (March 1818), Deeping (September 1818), March (November 1820, November 1828), Thorney Peterborough (March 1823), Sleaford (May 1828, March 1830, July 1830, March 1833), Downham (1830), Spilsby (February 1824).

According to her notes, the correspondence indicated the importance of Masonic connections in ensuring the requisite permissions and licenses were obtained for performances (and for their patronage at his theatres), the threats offered by rival managements, the subletting of Grimsby theatre to supplement Joseph's income, the state of the fishing industry and the number of vessels laid up in the port, Methodist opposition to theatrical entertainment (see Chapter 5), the effect on his business of agricultural depression, and arrangements for Joseph's company to produce, anonymously, plays and other entertainments written by Dr Oliver, apparently in exchange for Joseph canvassing the Freemasons of the towns he visited for orders for subscriptions to some of Dr Oliver's books on Freemasonry.

According to Mr Drury, he was planning to lodge this correspondence with the Lincolnshire Archives, but failed to do so. When he died in 2002, his house in Clee – an area between Grimsby and Cleethorpes – was cleared by a local firm specialising in antiques and house clearances. A local man with whom I spoke recalled seeing piles of papers on the floor of the shop in 2003, however despite a plea in the local paper, and the best offices of the local history librarian, I have been unable to unearth it.

When I spoke to Coral (Kate) Taylor shortly before her death, she said that in fact she hadn't read all of the letters herself, but had been allowed to borrow the letters from which to take notes. Much of this is included in her book *Right Royal, Wakefield Theatre 1776–1994* to which I have referred above and later in Joseph's story. However, I have now managed to secure Kate's original research notes, including those she made of the letters' content which are cited wherever I have used them.

I think that, from these notes, and from existing correspondence in the archive, and that at Freemason's Hall and other sources, it is possible to deduce to a large extent much of what exercised the minds of the two friends.

Grimsby

Popular legend has it that Grimsby's origins lie in the Middle Ages, when it was settled by a Scandinavian, called Grim, who was attempting to flee from justice. He, and later settlers, are said to have valued the haven, a tidal creek off the River Humber, fed by springs of fresh water. Here, Grim built houses from wood, and traded in fish and salt.[1]

The Revd M Davies, in his book *The History of Grimsby*, states that the area was occupied in pre-Roman times by Ancient Britons, or Celts, and quotes *Monumental Antiquities of Grimsby* by Dr Oliver (of whom, more later), describing seven large mounds or hills in the area, largely used for defensive purposes. Dr Oliver's book, published privately in 1825, gives the origin of the name as "Grimsby – Gri-maen-buy – an abode at the sacred mounds."

---

[1] Gillet; A History of Grimsby

Grimsby's trade with the rest of Lincolnshire grew, but was, for a long time, confined to places along the rivers Trent, Humber, and Witham; despite numerous complaints about tolls on these rivers, mainly on the Trent. Grimsby would not have survived but for waterborne trade, and by 1230 there was regular traffic through the port from Scandinavia, from where pine and board were imported, and grain from Grimsby's surrounding countryside was exported to Norway.[2] Fish, however, was the most important trading commodity. There was also necessity for feeding soldiers. (In 1296–97, for instance, 436 quarters of corn were sent to Flanders from Grimsby for the forces of Edward I.)[3]

Over the years, there were many attempts at improving the haven and access to it. However, it was not until 1787 that the first steps were taken to build a dock. Much of these plans were mired in the politics of the period. One of the biggest landowners in the area was Lord Yarborough who had political aspirations. Another landlord, though on a smaller scale, was George Tennyson. A bill was passed in 1796, 'The Grimsby Haven Act' (amended 1799), which enabled the newly formed Haven Company to raise money through public subscription, and authorised it to raise £50,000. George Tennyson personally gave £2,000. It also provided for "the widening, enlarging, altering and improving the existing haven."[4]

The first ships were able to use the new dock in November, 1801. By February of 1802 it seemed that development had gone far enough. Two hundred yards of quays had been built. Although the Borough offered a bounty of one guinea (£1.05) "to the first cobble in any week from Michaelmas to Mayday next with a cargo of fish," few fishermen responded. During the first four years of trading, the port showed a small growth in income. Between 1802 and 1805 the revenue received rose from £480 to £934, an increase of 95%.[5]

Grimsby's glory days of fishing were, in fact, not to come for another fifty years.

---

[2] Great Grimsby' by Crossland and Turner
[3] Crossland and Turner
[4] Edward Gillet, A History of Grimsby, 1970
[5] Crossland and Turner

Nevertheless, with the work taking place on building a new dock, and investment in the fishing industry, Grimsby appeared, on paper at least, to be a thriving and up and coming town . Housing had to be built to accommodate the workers who came to build the port. The population of Grimsby had been in decline in the period to 1790 when it was at its lowest ebb of 982. By 1801 although still no larger than a small village, it had risen to 1524, and in 1811 it was 2747.[6] In 1804, a Special General Meeting of the Grimsby Haven Company was held at the Granby Inn on 10th April, when it was announced that flood gates would be built and the making of staithes or wharves at the head of several lots. During this time there would be employment for 150 diggers and wheelers.[7]

As the town grew, however, the problem of poverty became more acute. In 1783–85 the cost of relieving the poor of Grimsby had been no more than £63 per year. In 1802–03 it was £258. As a means of alleviating poverty without burdening the rates system, the corporation bought, in 1800, a £100 worth of flour to be sold to the inhabitants at cost price. A year later it was decided to form a union with adjacent parishes for the maintenance of the poor and Lord Yarborough was invited to give a piece of land, in exchange for other land, for the site of "a house of industry." Eventually, the land was acquired from George Tennyson in exchange for an area called Coal Hill as well as other pieces of the bank of the old haven. Builders were invited to tender for erecting the house, and Tennyson was appointed Visitor, and a man called John Squire appointed Guardian under the Poor Act. Within a year there were 31 paupers in the house, ten of whom belonged to Grimsby.

Some of the new building in the town was in Burgess Street, where available land was split into lots. Lot 14 was first leased as a separate plot on an indenture dated 6th March, 1802, to a bricklayer named Mark Skinner, upon which he built a public house, the Golden Fleece, with outbuildings; – and a theatre.[8]

---

[6] The History of Grimsby; Rev. M Davies
[7] The Rise of Grimsby; Bob Lincoln
[8] Schedule of title deeds, 1879 Avison

The Life and Times of Joseph Smedley

In 1808, Skinner signed over the theatre's fire policy dated 9th August, 1806, to a Thomas Burringham, whereby "the said messuage or Tenement Hereditaments and Premises stand insured for the sum of £300" as security for borrowing £300 and interest.[9]

Over the next few years, the title to the lease was to change hands several times owing to deaths (including the death of Burringham) and bankruptcies (including that of Mark Skinner). Apparently, by 1814, Skinner had been in business as a victualler, and got into debt with one of his suppliers, Robert Hildyard, a brandy merchant, of Hull. An indenture was made between :

> Charles Tennyson Esq and Joseph Daubney and Marmaduke Dixon, Gentlemen of the one part, and Robert Hildyard and John Garniss, brewer of Grimsby on the other part....stutes concerning bankrupts dated 17th February 1814 have been awarded and issued against Mark Skinner victualler of Grimsby directed to the said Charles Tennyson , J Daubney and M Dixon together with Daniel Sykes Esq and Geo Fletcher gentleman thereby giving the Commissioner full authority to execute the same...

Examination of witnesses showed that Mark Skinner became indebted to R. Hildyard in the sum of £114-15s-0d and in the judgement of the Commissioner he became a bankrupt and was declared accordingly.

The creditors met at the Ship Inn at Grimsby, on March 8th, 1814, in order to choose assignees of his estate. Robert Hildyard and John Garniss were chosen as his assignees and took over Lot 14 and all buildings therein.[10]

However, it seems that Joseph Smedley was allowed to manage the theatre in Burgess Street from its opening in 1806, at which time it appears that he was already managing a theatre at Market Rasen with a man called Clarke. Prior to this it is assumed from contemporary reports and bills that a suitable building in the Granby Inn Yard was used for such entertainments. Joseph himself, on a playbill of 1831, stated that he had been 25 years in occupation of the theatre, although the earliest playbill found is dated 1807.

---

[9] Avison

[10] Avison

Richard E. Smedley

That the theatre was erected in 1804 and completed in 1806 is confirmed by a local historian, Arthur Avison, who photographed the date-stone which still stood in part of a wall in 1950.

This must have been one of the first purpose-built theatres in the country as it was only from the middle of the nineteenth century that permanent theatres began to be built in country towns, often owing to the patronage of leading landowners and businessmen. William Ormsby-Gore Esq built the theatre at Oswestry early in the nineteenth century, before which there had been buildings at Stamford, Grantham (1800), Reading (1788), Bungay, Beccles (1784) and Chichester (1791), and at Tewkesbury in 1823.[11]

Joseph Smedley 'managed' the Grimsby Theatre for many years. In truth, however, as in other towns, the theatre was only opened for high days and holidays, or, in Grimsby's case, principally, Race Meetings.

> The annual races extended over two days in June. The Race ground was on the Cleethorpes Common, beyond the Grimsby boundary. The Corporation gave a £50 plate and the Members for the Borough another £50. On these occasions, the town gave itself up to amusements, and the theatre well patronized. The Theatre was a brick building behind the 'Golden Fleece' facing burgess Street. Smedley's Company performed in it for some years ... Grimsby was also a noted cock-fighting place. The 'Bull and Sun' public house which stood on the site of Spring Church, kept by a notorious character known as Peg-leg Harrison, was the resort of cock-fighters on racing days.[12]

In 1812, for example,

> an ordinary was held at the Granby each day, and there were donkey races, sack races, jingling matches, a greasy pole and hog-tail catching, with cock-fighting at the Crown and Anchor. In 1804 the race [13]course was used for a five-mile running race between a butcher and a cordwainer for £20. The butcher won

---

[11] The English Market Town; Jonathan Brown
[12] "A Gossip about Old Grimsby; Anderson Bates
[13] "A Gossip about Old Grimsby"; Anderson Bates

in just under half an hour after the cordwainer retired, exhausted, in the last half mile.[14]

From correspondence in the Lincolnshire Archives, it is clear that, in time, Joseph had exclusive use of the theatre, the keys to which were held at the Freemasons' Lodge nearby. It is also clear that, for his rent, he expected that no-one be allowed to perform theatrical entertainments in the theatre, without his agreement, although other types of events, such as meetings could be held with the permission of the Lodge.

According to Kate Taylor's notes of the Smedley/Oliver correspondence, one letter from Oliver refers to rival managers, Collyer (sic), formerly in Huggins' company, and Abbotts who was playing in the spring of 1814 at Caistor attempting to secure the lease of the Grimsby theatre and Oliver's own influence in seeking to persuade the magistrates to reject their applications for a licence. In addition, another letter, dated 27th May, 1817 discussed the aftermath of the Hull circuit which broke up in 1816–17, when some members of the Hull company, led by a young man named Elliott, attempted to acquire Grimsby and other theatres in Smedley's circuit, Oliver reports. "Oliver refers to short lets of the Grimsby theatre which brought in modest sums to offset Smedley's rent: Matthews in June 1818 paid £1-12s and some Indian jugglers in August of the same year paid 12s. In 1814 Oliver suggested that Smedley should buy the Grimsby theatre (for £150) from its bankrupt owner and later he negotiated with one of the new owners, William Coney, for Smedley to have a lease of £12 a year; subsequently he treats with Coney's associate, Edmund Goodrick, in regard to Smedley's rent."[15] Joseph's relationship with Mr Goodrick was not always harmonious, and from Oliver's letters it is clear that Oliver kept an eye on Goodrick's activities. It appears too that Joseph did not trust the accuracy of Goodrick's accountancy, as a letter from a fellow freemason, Mr William Smith, would indicate:

---

[14] do

[15] "Right Royal, Wakefield Theatre 1776-1994, CMP;Taylor

Richard E. Smedley

> Dear Sir and Brother,
> I have paid Goodrick £5 as you requested and have now possession of the keys of the theatre....He assures me most solemnly that he only received £1-11s-6d of Matthews and £2 of the jugglers – which I am inclined to think is correct...

Another example Goodrick takes great exception to being accused of losing the keys, although Joseph dismissed his protestations with further stories of Goodrick's maladministration.

The Revd. Dr. George Oliver, D.D.(1782–1867)

George Oliver became a great friend and confidant of Joseph Smedley and as such deserves to be acknowledged here.

He was born at Papplewick, near Nottingham, on 5th November, 1782, and baptised there four days later. His father was Samuel Oliver (1756–1847), a schoolmaster, and, after 1842, rector of Lambley, Nottinghamshire. Samuel married Elizabeth Whitehead (known as 'Betsy'), daughter of George Whitehead of Blyth Spital in Nottinghamshire, on 12th February, 1782. Six years after his marriage, Samuel was appointed headmaster of a school at Lutterworth by the Earl of Denbigh, and, by 1791, was advertising his own school there, The English Academy. George was a pupil at his father's school, and apparently also attended school in Nottingham for a time.[16]

In 1797 Samuel was ordained a deacon and, in the same year, he became a Freemason in a 'Moderns' lodge, being 'made' in St John's Lodge, Leicester which had been founded in 1790. Samuel was a regular attender, walking the 12 miles between the two towns.[17]

Four years later he was ordained priest and accepted a curacy at Gotham back in Nottinghamshire, but very shortly afterward (in 1802) accepted a curacy for an absentee incumbent at Whaplode, a village in Lincolnshire, about 20 miles north of Peterborough, and six miles east of Spalding.

---

[16] "Priest and Freemason"; R.S.E. Sandbach
[17] Sandbach

The church 'living' at Whaplode was then held by an incumbent who was also Master of the Charterhouse, a canon of Salisbury, and rector of a parish in Huntingdon, and who didn't want to bury himself in the depths of the Fens. Under such conditions, the curate was paid by the incumbent in a personal arrangement. During this period, i.e. early nineteenth century, such pluralism was common – the holding by one priest of more than one living – but was soon to be reformed.[18]

In 1802 or 1803, George Oliver was initiated into Freemasonry in St. Peter's Lodge, no. 605, Peterborough.

In 1803, George became usher of the grammar school at Caistor in Lincolnshire, and, in 1805, he married Mary Ann (1785–1856), the daughter of Thomas Beverley. They had two sons and three daughters.[19]

In the early 1800s, some attempts were made to improve the local grammar school. The master, Thomas Wilkinson, was given an increase of salary of £7 per annum, and, in addition to his normal duties, he was to teach reading and writing to ten children of the poorest freemen. He also worked for the corporation as a land surveyor, for which he received additional fees. In 1803, the year of his death, a brick school-room was built for him, 18 by 50 feet, and 10 feet high. Two candidates for the vacancy were referred to the Rev Mr Gray of Waltham. He found both suitable, and Samuel Bucknill of Carlton-le-Moorland was appointed at £40 per year. The appointment was made by election, 82 freemen voting for Bucknill, and 71 for his rival.[20]

The master was given a house, free of tax and window duty, and was allowed 35 days holiday each year in addition to Saturday afternoons and Sundays.

Bucknill's appointment ended in 1808 when he was dismissed for cruelty and gross ill-treatment of the children.

---

[18] Sandbach

[19] Library and Museum of Freemasonry

[20] Lincoln

Richard E. Smedley

Etching of Dr George Oliver

Thus the way was made clear for George Oliver to become the new master of the King Edward Grammar School in Great Grimsby, and probably the most colourful character in its history to hold the post.[21]

He held the title from 1809 to 1826, and, after being ordained deacon in 1812 and priest in 1813, he was curate of Grimsby from 1815 to 1831. In addition, he had the living of Clee, but never lived there.[22]

These promotions meant that he could largely ignore attempts to control his conduct of the Grammar School. He was more comfortably off than any of his predecessors. To make his salary up to £137-10s. per year, the freemen were no longer to have £25 shared among them at the mayoral election, and the mayor gave up his own salary of £50 which he had enjoyed since 1804. The numbers in the school were restricted to 70 children of freemen, and it was expressly stipulated that the master must not take fee-paying pupils. He failed to get an increase in salary in 1812, and three years later was found to be taking fees for teaching 15 children, whom he was required to remove in six weeks. In 1816, he was again formally thanked for his conduct of the school, and, three years later the freemen elected him again, even though the school visitors cleared him of a charge of 'immoderate correction'.

While curate at Grimsby, under George Clayton Tennyson, who was very much an absentee incumbent, Oliver came to know his brother, Charles Tennyson well, and had the good fortune to have the use of his library, and later credited him with being "a friend and supporter of all my labours." George Tennyson was the father of the poet Alfred, Lord Tennyson, later the Poet Laureate. Neither was Dr Oliver backward in using such contacts to his advantage. The following letter survives in the North East Lincolnshire Archives in Grimsby:

---

[21] Lincoln
[22] Oxford DNB accessed 22.09.2014

Richard E. Smedley

Letter from Rev. Geo. Oliver to Charles Tennyson, Grimsby, May 10th 1819

Dear Sir,

Apprehensive that you are pestered with letters from Grimsby on every occasion and shadow of occasion, it is with great diffidence that I presume to trespass on your time and patience, particularly as I am about to solicit the exertion of your friendship in my behalf, if you fortunately possess any acquaintance with the Gentleman to whom I allude. I am informed that the Revd. Mr Gray of Laceby is in a dying state and actually given up by his Physician, who is of opinion that he cannot live three months longer. I am fully impressed with the indelicacy of soliciting for a Gentleman's preferment before his actual decease, but in these days, except an application be made in time there is little prospect of success. Mr Gray is the perpetual Curate of Aylesby, a small Benefice in this neighbourhood in the gift of T. Tyrrwitt Drake, Esq. M.P. for Agmondesham. If you have any acquaintance with Mr Drake, may I beg of you to interest yourself to procure the reversion of this living for me. It will not perhaps be a very great favour to ask of him, as the annual value I am told, is at most, but about 60 or 70£ but it would prove a valuable addition to the certainties of my Income; as the School at Grimsby depends upon the caprice of Individuals who, you very well know, are not wholly to be depended on.

If Mr Drake demand a reference as to my Clerical conduct &c. You may name the Bishop of Lincoln, with whom Mr Drake is acquainted.

Mrs Oliver unites with me in her respects, and

I am Dr Sir

Your obedient servant

Alas, Tennyson's response is not recorded. However, the following letter was sent on June 25th, 1819:

From Rev. Geo. Oliver to Charles Tennyson

My Dear Sir,

I learn on enquiry that Mr Gray is somewhat better, and I think with you that it would be indelicate to make an application for his Benefice under present circumstances. I am very much obliged by your promptness in offering to exert your influence on my behalf, and will take the liberty of troubling further on the subject if Mr G's illness should take an unfavourable turn.

> Mrs Oliver unites with me in best respects, and I am
> My dear Sir
> Very sincerely yours
> Geo. Oliver

In 1814 he attended Trinity College, Cambridge, but never took a degree there, though he was awarded a Lambeth D.D. in 1835. In 1831, having lost the curacy at Grimsby, he became rector of Scopwick in Lincolnshire which he held until his death. From 1834 to 1846 he was perpetual curate of St. Peter's Collegiate Church, Wolverhampton, and from 1846, Rector of South Hykeham in Lincolnshire. He also served as domestic chaplain to Lord Kensington.

He is remembered most for publishing topographical books, such as the aforementioned *The Monumental Antiquities of Great Grimsby*, published by subscription, a commonplace practice at the time. Among the subscribers were Charles Tennyson, the Bishop of Winchester, and Charles Chaplin MP, a considerable landowner in the area of Scopwick, to the incumbency of which Oliver was later to be appointed. Also *History and Antiquities of the Town and Minster of Beverley* (1829), *History of Grimsby* (1825 and 1829), *A History of Wolverhampton* (1836) and *A History of Sleaford and Lincoln* (1837 and 1846). In addition to these, he also published over 30 works on Freemasonry, gave lectures and contributed to the *Freemasons' Quarterly Review* and other publications.

He served as Provincial Grand Steward of Lincolnshire in 1813; Provincial Grand Chaplain in 1816 and Deputy Provincial Grand Master of Lincolnshire from 1833 to 1842, when he was dismissed. In 1815, Oliver had become a member of the Ancient and Accepted Rite in England, and, along with his friend Robert Crucefix, established this body as a Christian organisation. His dismissal reflected the desire of the Duke of Sussex, as Grand Master, to remove religious overtones from Masonic ritual, and Oliver had already given his public support to Crucefix, who had also come into conflict with the Masonic hierarchy over the formation of a new charity, for which he eventually apologised.

It was while George Oliver was at either Caistor or Grimsby, for both offered the opportunity, or at a Masonic Lodge meeting, that he met and began his long association and friendship with Joseph Smedley.

In 1811, Joseph Smedley and George Oliver were co-founders of the Apollo Lodge in Grimsby. [23] This was not the first Lodge in Grimsby. In the early days meetings of Freemasons were held at the Freemason's Arms on Victoria Street in the town, and they also met at Silver Street in the Crown & Anchor, (later the Prince Albert and, later still, the Mason's Arms). In the early 1800s a purpose-built Lodge was constructed behind cottages at 170–172 Lower Burgess Street. After an internal dispute, some members relocated to Silver Street and the lodge was leased to a Baptist Society. The cottages and lodge were demolished in 1939.[24]

Another Lodge was built further along Lower Burgess Street at nos. 240–250 Lower Burgess Street in about 1813, which is the one founded by Dr George Oliver and friends, including Joseph. The theatre that Joseph managed was in Upper Burgess Street, a fair walk away, especially before proper paved paths were introduced.

Joseph gave his address as Great Grimsby, and his occupation as comedian. The building in which it was housed was specially built by a man called Stephen Kitching, (who later became Treasurer under Oliver's stewardship). It had a plain exterior, and was placed east to west so that the west gable abutted the street. The entrance from the street was through an arched doorway, along a pathway of flagstones flanked on each side by a row of poplar trees.[25] These were probably at the insistence of Oliver who had a passion for trees. Originally consisting of a basement (in which Kitching lived), and an upper room, with an anteroom and preparation area. Lodge meetings were held in the upper room which measured 36 feet long, 20 feet wide and 12 feet high.

The Lodge was small, and it elected a candidate whom the members believed would bring in other young men. He proved to be disputatious and the

---

[23] Apollo Lodge founding documents in Library and Museum of Freemasonry.
[24] The History of Freemasonry in Grimsby, 1802-1938, by F J Chapman, 1939
[25] The History of Freemasonry in Grimsby, Anderson Bates, 1892

Apollo Lodge was destroyed by his causing dissension and faction to arise within it. The Apollo Lodge was erased in 1834. Small wonder, then, that in his *A Century of Masonic Aphorisms*, published in 1849, Oliver gave the following advice:

> Be very cautious whom you recommend as a candidate for initiation: one false step on this point may be fatal. If you introduce a disputatious person, confusion will be produced, which may end in the dissolution of the Lodge. If you have a good Lodge keep it select. Great numbers are not always beneficial.[26]

In his account of the formation of the Apollo Lodge, R.S.E. Sandbach states that Oliver had

> arranged for a Brother Kitching to build a Masonic Hall on Burgess Street in 1812 to house the lodge. The inscription on the foundation stone recorded the event… 'This building, erected for a lodge……Bro. George Oliver R.W.M.; Geo. Parker S.W.; T. Travis J.W.; W.Piercy P.M.' This stone, part of the temple of Apollo at Delos, was brought and presented to the Lodge by Bro. Potter.

As a founding member, it is curious that Joseph Smedley's name was omitted from the foundation stone. However there is an account, in Anderson Bates' *History of Freemasonry in Grimsby* (1892), and quoted by C.M.P. Taylor, of a "convivial meeting at Apollo Lodge in 1826 with Dr George Oliver, by then Provincial Grand Master, in the Chair." Bates goes on to say that there was present "Bro. Jos. Smedley, Theatrical Manager (whom the Brethren regularly patronised at his little theatre behind the Golden Fleece." It is also noted that "in the course of time Smedley was awarded Provincial honours, as Past Provincial Grand Steward". He is noted as attending the laying of the foundation stone of the new Masonic Hall in Lincoln on 15th April 1841.

In 1812, Joseph Smedley's company of players performed "*Wonder! A Woman Keeps A Secret* by desire of Mr Oliver and the young gentlemen of the corporation school," and also a comic interlude, written by Oliver himself, called *The Thespian Barber, or, Rhyme without Reason*.

---

[26] Sandbach

Oliver also wrote, anonymously *Jack of Trumps*, which he authorised Joseph to perform and which he described as "a very deep and bloody tragedy."[27]

It is interesting how many of the letters extant in the Smedley family archives in Lincoln are from fellow Freemasons, some of whom are seeking help, but many invoke George Oliver's name and ask that their good wishes be passed on.

In addition to his topographies and his many books on Masonic subjects, George Oliver also published *An Account of the Corpus Pageants, Miracle Plays, Religious Mysteries &C which were Practised at Sleaford* (London, 1838).

It should be remembered that George Oliver was raised in and practised the religion of his father. He was a very orthodox Christian, and believed strongly in the truth of the Bible, (for this was long before Darwin published his book); Christian ideals of clean living and morals. He detected no conflict of interest in his faith and Freemasonry, the ethics of which were entirely compatible. Although he changed over the years, and appreciated the advances of science and technology, he continued to adhere to the fundamental beliefs he learned from his father throughout his life.

In 1854, as his health began to fail, Oliver left his parishes in the hands of curates, and retired to Lincoln, where he died on 3rd March 1867. He was buried with Masonic rites, next to his wife, in the cemetery attached to the church of St Swithin in Lincoln.

In 1910, a meeting was held of Past Masters at Masonic Hall to consider a proposal for a memorial to the late Dr Oliver who had been Deputy Provincial Grand Master. It was decided that a stained glass window would be gifted in his memory to his final church at South Hykeham near Lincoln.

It is truly remarkable how much respect Dr Oliver was afforded. His reputation had spread throughout the world of Freemasonry; indeed he was particularly well-regarded in American Freemasonry, with various Lodges having honoured him.

---

[27] CMP Taylor; Right Royal; Wakefield Theatre 1776=1994

It is also remarkable how much research and writing he managed during his lifetime in addition to his clerical duties, much of which also demanded much travelling to and fro in difficult and demanding conditions compared to our present-day infrastructure. All his works were, of course, written by hand using a quill pen, much written by candlelight, which eventually caused his sight to fail.

Charles Tennyson D'Eynecourt (1784–1861)

The second son and youngest child of George Tennyson of Beacons, Tealby, he was born at Market Rasen and educated at Louth Grammar School, and at St John's College, Cambridge where he received a B.A. in 1805, and an M.A. in 1818. He was admitted to the Inner Temple in 1801 and was called to the bar in November 1806. He married Frances Mary, daughter of the Revd John Hutton at Gainsborough, Lincolnshire, on 1st of January, 1808, and raised five sons and three daughters.

Despite this, the marriage was not a happy one, and from 1816 Charles began an affair with Mary Thornhill, daughter of the Squire of Stanton near Bakewell.

After making a promising start to his career as a barrister, he was elected MP for Great Grimsby in 1818, and became well-known in that town, and, although he served as MP for Bletchingly in Surrey from 1826 until 1831, his association with the town and with the county of Lincolnshire in particular would continue throughout his life. He also became increasingly eccentric. In 1830 to 1832 he served as MP for Stamford and was sworn into the Privy Council on 6th February, 1832. While electioneering in Stamford in 1831, his opponent was Lord Thomas Cecil who mocked his methods, and Tennyson challenged him to a duel. This was fought at Wormwood Scrubs on 18th June 1831. Neither man was injured, both were arrested, and neither was prosecuted.

After the death of his father, and in accordance with his father's will, he assumed, by Royal Licence, the additional name and arms of D'Eynecourt in 1835. He also tried to revive the barony of D'Eynecourt, but Lord

Melbourne, the prime minister, refused. His father left him that major part of his estate which derived from purchase and speculation, with that part relating to and derived from entail and inheritance going to the elder brother, George Tennyson, who by now was a mentally ill alcoholic, who was rector of Somersby and father of the poet Alfred Tennyson. This started a rift between the two sides of the family, as the Somersby branch resented this disposition of the family wealth. Charles moved to the family home, Beacons, and changed its name to Bayons Manor and used his money to recreate the home as a castle, with moat, medieval oratory and secret passages.

According to *Grimsby and the Haven Company* by Gordon Jackson,

> Tennyson enjoyed a far wider circle of friends in the county, but much less respect. He was more or less , nouveau riche, with a homely but inelegant family circle. Above all, he was inordinately proud. They called him 'Dindon' – Turkey Cock – at school in Beverley, and it was rumoured in Lincolnshire that he was regarded with contempt – le plus grand mempris – in London Society. To make matters worse, he stuttered when embarrassed, and it took very little – too little – to make him angry. He had a touch of the Clayton insanity about him; he felt that people were conspiring against him, and he could be vindictive and ruthless to the point of cruelty…

He was elected as a Fellow of the Royal Society in 1829, and also a Fellow of the Society of Antiquities. He served as High Steward of Louth, as a JP and Deputy Lord Lt of Lincolnshire.

He became a joining member of Lodge of Antiquities in London on 28th February, 1827, resigning in 1837. He served as Provincial Grand Master of Lincolnshire from 1827 until his resignation in 1849. From 1813 until 1843 he served as Equerry to the Duke of Sussex who was Grand Master and along with him and Admiral Sir Sydney Smith was architect of an unsuccessful plan to revive the Order of the Knights Templar as a British Order of Chivalry.

This is not quite as eccentric as it sounds, for at about this time there had been a resurgence of interest in the Knights Templar, and there existed a Christian masonic order of Knights Templar in England. The original Order of Knights

Templar, which was suppressed in the Middle Ages, figured in the mythical history of freemasonry current in England at the end of the eighteenth century. George Oliver may well have been a member of the Masonic order, and, when at Scopwick in 1833, he had actively investigated the archaeological site of Temple Bruer, a former preceptor of the Knights Templar, which was not far away from Scopwick. It would have held a double interest for him, firstly as an antiquarian, and, secondly, as an expert and author on Freemasonry.

When first appointed Provincial Grand Master in 1826, he was a busy politician, so much so that he did not attend to be installed in his new office, and therefore unable to act, until 1832, leaving the Province leaderless for six years and fostering hopes in Oliver that he might be appointed Deputy Provincial Grand Master, which finally came about in 1833. In a ceremony at Horncastle, D'Eynecourt said of Oliver: "his profound investigations into the science we profess… have earned him the thanks and gratitude of every Mason who values the true beauties of his science."

There is little doubt that George Oliver and Charles Tennyson D'Eynecourt had a close and longstanding relationship, although it was not always placid.

One of the divisive issues of the time in Freemasonry, the Church and the nation as a whole, was that surrounding Queen Caroline; Caroline of Brunswick.

George IV had fallen out with his wife, and had tried to divorce her for alleged misconduct in a trial before the House of Lords. They had married in 1795 while he was Prince of Wales, and they had a daughter, Princess Charlotte. However he made Caroline live by herself at Shooters Hill and Blackheath. From 1814 she lived chiefly in Italy. When George became King, she was offered an annuity of £50,000 to renounce the title of Queen which she refused. The charges against her by the government for adultery were eventually dropped, largely due to her defence by Lord Brougham, and public support. She was, however, still turned away from Westminster Abbey at the Coronation of George IV just days before she died.

Tennyson D'Eynecourt had supported the Queen's cause in a pamphlet, and had urged the House of Commons to restore her name in the liturgy.

Dr Oliver had actually fallen out with the Grimsby corporation over Caroline's cause, apparently on the other side. Eventually, Oliver was fired as Deputy Provincial Grand Master, by D'Eynecourt, causing a further rift.

* * *

Joseph Smedley's occupation as a comedian afforded him the chance to not only tour to different towns and villages, but to get to know the people of those places by being able to visit other Lodges as a guest, and to sample the hospitality to which he was entitled. He was also aided in finding places for his company to visit by the same network.

One letter in the archive (dated 13th April, 1811) is from a John Stafford, an actor in a company based at Bingham, a small town, no bigger than a village in those days, outside Nottingham:

> Dear Sir, I received yours by W. Hodson. I was glad to hear you and Mrs Smedley were well.
> It appears that your stay at Belper was not of long duration – am afraid not <u>long enough</u> to <u>nail</u> them (underlining in letter) and <u>clinch</u> it. – As Mr Strutt will accommodate you with a theatre in future it is probable it will do – but <u>Strangers</u> cannot always <u>Raise the wind</u>** in their first attempt. A second I hope will be better.

From this it is fairly clear that Joseph had not had a successful visit to Belper, and goes on to suggest that he build a theatre in Bingham at a subscription expense of five or ten shares, and concludes:

> I do not hear anything of Huggins being at Southwell [a small Minster town between Nottingham and Newark]. I intend being there myself in a week or ten days and also at Loughborough – I shall then know if anything is going forward in your way, and if anything worth your notice I will write you.
> I believe Hudson waits of this letter, excuse me saying any more at this time, but that <u>all friends</u> desire their respects to yourself and Mrs Smedley.
> I am yours very respectfully,

This again shows that a fellow freemason is looking out for Joseph's interests.

**The reference in the letter to *Raise the Wind* is a play on words, and intended as a joke. It is the title of a then popular farce of 1803 by James Kenney, which Joseph included in his Company's repertoire for the tour of 1812. (See playlist.)

A letter from Southwell on 6th May, 1816, read:

Sir,

Your application which was communicated to me I only laid before the Justices at the late Easter Session, and obtained their licence for your performing here during a period of forty days to commence on or about the 1st of July next.

The Justices asked me to state, that under the difficulties which oppress this place as almost all others at the present moment, they would have been inclined to refuse the licence, if your uniform regularity and good conduct had not been powerful inducements for them to grant the limited term which I have mentioned, in order that you might not be wholly disappointed.

A letter from William Smith, dated Grimsby, 17th November, 1818:

Dear Sir and Brother,

I have paid Goodrick £5 as you requested and have now possession of the keys of the theatre. He assures me most solemnly that he only received

£1-11-6d of Matthews and £2 of the jugglers, which I am inclined to think is correct. The rent therefore from Michaelmas to Lady Day remains (unclear) paid.

I have left open that door under the stage which communicates with the yard in consequence of a spring of water running through the theatre lest this passage should by any means get stopped and inundate the place I have nailed up the other door which opens on the pit, thereby rendering all access to the theatre impossible.

A letter from Samuel Obbinson from Sleaford, dated 7th May 1826, asked if he could borrow an amusing book that will take his mind off his illness. The whole letter is written in rhyming couplets, but is addressed to 'Friend Smedley'.

This is probably a relation to the R. Obbinson who appeared on earlier Sleaford playbills. Another letter from the same source in 1831, sympathises with Joseph's recent losses: "if you look round you will find many, very many, more unfortunate, or, rather, less fortunate, than yourself."

Another letter from a Robert Bower, on 26th October, 1831 seeks to give the following recommendation:

> Mr Smedley the manager of a Company of Comedians about to act in Beverley is a highly respectable man: this company has prospered in Malton for several seasons, and have ever conducted themselves in a manner highly creditable, and I consider them well-deserving of public patronage.

The letter goes on to mention that Mr & Mrs Oliver were away at Bro. Ashton's at Sixhills, and not expected back until Saturday night.

It is not unreasonable to view Joseph's membership of Freemasonry as the social networking opportunity of its day, providing, as it did, a means of relaxing with like-minded people. It also provided, especially in the form of George Oliver, a friend with whom he could confide and share his worries and concerns. Above all, however, it became a support network for him, his company and its work.

5
Those Against

It is not too hard to see why Joseph Smedley chose the area in which he initially operated. Not far from his childhood home in North Yorkshire, overlapping with the area he knew from his time on the Lincoln Circuit, and bordering on the Norwich Circuit and other East Anglian towns and villages that his wife Melinda would have known.

For some reason, though, Joseph seems to have been drawn to the small towns along the Humber Estuary, to both north and south of the river.

In 1806 this was surprising. Not least because the people of these towns lived in fear; the fear that any morning they might wake up to see Napoleon's warships sailing up the Humber. This would have affected the small fishing concerns in the area, not to mention the fledgling fishing fleet in the growing town of Great Grimsby.

Some of the towns were not far from the theatres which boasted theatrical entertainment like Hull (part of the York Circuit for many years), and Grimsby or Boston on the Lincoln Circuit. However, many were further inland; little more than hamlets or villages in rural and agricultural areas of Yorkshire, Lincolnshire and Nottinghamshire with little tradition of theatre-going but nevertheless welcoming to entertainers who were adding to the fun of holidays, race days, livestock auctions, Statute days and touring fairs.

It is likely that Joseph felt at home amongst such people, not too dissimilar to the farming area of Yorkshire from which he hailed. He may also have had some understanding of (and even empathy for) the changes that were about to sweep through their lives, particularly that part given over to leisure pursuits.

Richard E. Smedley

In the late eighteenth and early nineteenth centuries there was a deliberate attempt to change the traditional cultural practices of rural, largely agricultural folk, not just by the upper and middle classes and institutions, but from below as well – and from within.

During this period such pursuits as bull-running and bull-baiting, cock-fighting, folk dancing, feasting, village races, statute hirings, public hangings, Plough Plays, fairs, drinking, etc., came under attack. These were activities which were not based on literacy, but which were not necessarily for the uneducated either.

The attack was initially launched by the upper and middle classes which attempted to spread ideas and beliefs more acceptable to themselves by the foundation of Sunday Schools, Day Schools, Mechanics Institutes, Temperance Societies, Reading Rooms and other similar organisations. These pursuits embodied a New Culture.

Thomas Hardy, a chronicler of rural life ("change has marked the face of all things"[1]), commented upon the changes of the two cultures when he remarks on the contrast between Tess and her mother in *Tess of the d'Urbevilles*:

> Between her mother, with her fast-perishing lumber of superstitions, folklore, dialect, and orally transmitted ballads, and the daughter with her trained National teachings and Standard Knowledge under an infinitely revised code, there was a gap of two hundred years as ordinarily understood.

Of the 'older culture' certainly bull-running and bull-baiting were still prominent diversions in Staffordshire and Lincolnshire in the early 1800s as were public hangings as in this account from the Stamford Mercury of 1830:

> The execution at Lincoln of the three men… drew an immense concourse at noon on Friday last. The country people had been streaming in from an early hour in the morning: and many foolish parents sent or brought with them crowds of children of both sexes, under the weak and almost hypocritical pretext of 'giving them a warning'.

---

[1] Domicilium, by Thomas Hardy

These traditional elements of the older culture started to come under attack frequently in the pages of rural newspapers, usually on the basis that working people performed them and valued them, ergo, they must be worthless. Rural popular culture was attacked as barbaric, irreligious, indecent and uneducated; it was attacked because it belonged to ordinary people and because it was kept alive by them.

One of the first practices to be attacked was the Village Feast. Notices proclaiming the discontinuance of Village Feasts appeared in the *Stamford Mercury* in 1796. The main objection to these were that they served to encourage drunkenness, the "inlet of Vice and Prophaneness" [sic] and "to check the rapid Growth of Vice and Immorality" said the Overseers of the Poor at Morton whose feast was discontinued in 1797. Similarly, the feast of Sibsey also came under attack in 1796 but was saved, only to be lost in 1824.

Morris Dancers or 'plough-morrisers' also came under attack, particularly in North Lincolnshire, around the Caistor and Barton on Humber areas, largely as an extension of the attacks on Plough Plays. The activities of the Morris Men were eventually restricted as a measure to limit the spread of cattle plague. Plough Plays, which also often included sword dances, denoted the start of the farming year, and almost became obsolete. Almost – because, nearly 200 years later, they have become popular again in rural areas, often supported by local clergymen.

Like so many rural practices passed down from generation to generation, Hiring Fairs (also known as Statute or Mop Fairs), also came into disrepute. These date from the reign of Edward III in the fourteenth century and were a means of arranging for available workers to meet with, and be chosen by, prospective employers, and provided a certain mobility of available labour. Over time these became huge social occasions; an excuse to reunite with ex-workmates which inevitably led to drinking, and, consequently, drunkenness and rowdy behaviour. In a contemporary account, they were described as:

> The annual period when servitude terminates is old May-day, and a series of statute fairs are held in all the large towns and principal villages for renewing the contract. Servants of both sexes assemble early at the statute, and place themselves in groups, the girls decked out in their best bibs and tuckers; and

their personal appearance displayed to the greatest advantage for the purpose of attracting attention; while the "young chaps" sport blue or white slop frocks according to their respective taste, and their avocation is designated by well-known symbols. The shepherd has a lock of wool stuck through his hat-band; the waggoner mounts a thrum of whipcord, and the groom a bunch of horse hair. They are usually engaged for a year at a stipulated rate of wages, and the agreement is sealed by giving and receiving a small sum of money in addition to the wages, which varies from *one* to *five* shillings, and is denominated a "Fessen (fastening) Penny". Should the servant change his mind before he takes possession of his place, he may cancel the bargain by returning the Fessen Penny; and on the other hand, if a master should hear anything prejudicial to the servant's character before the same period, he may get rid of him by announcing that he is at liberty to retain it. A servant can demand the privilege of attending two of these statute fairs, provided he has not been previously hired; but after the actual receipt of his Fessen Penny, without which the hiring is imperfect, the master can legally withhold his consent.

[...]

These fairs are the Saturnalia of servants; and every kind of licence is indulged with impunity. The young men appear, like sailors on shore after a long voyage, to have no idea of order or propriety; and the unpopular master is sure to hear of his faults, real or imaginary, at these places, if he be seen among the crowd. Drinking, dancing, fighting, and every other irregularity prevail; and practical jokes without regard to personal consequences, are played off to an unlimited extent.[2]

However, farmers and farm servants found the Statutes useful and convenient, as well as a pleasant and welcome holiday. This resistance to change saved the Statutes briefly, but by 1856 when they came under a more concerted and bitter attack, the Statutes were wiped out, as much a victim of the Industrial Revolution as anything.

It has to be remembered that such change, especially in rural areas is a gradual process, but these changes in popular culture were assisted by the rise in

---

[2] George Oliver, quoted by R.S.E Sandbach in "Priest and Freemason, the Life of George Oliver

Evangelism at that time, and in particular, the Primitive Methodist movement, also known as the 'Ranters'.

This became an influential force among the labourers themselves, and they in turn gave rise to many of the changes in their own culture witnessed in the early nineteenth century. This is why, although much change was driven by the upper and middle classes, the desire for change came from within the lower classes of agricultural workers. As such they became the instrument for change from the Old Culture, and pioneers of the New.

By the time of the Religious Census of 1851, the Primitives were the third largest denomination in the County of Lincolnshire, after the Church of England and the Wesleyan Methodists, but they were the largest church among labourers; and it was a similar story elsewhere in the country, especially north of the Humber.

The growth of the denomination had started around 1818 or 1819, and had inevitably drawn much hostility. And members were attacked both verbally and physically. In 1821, a long letter appeared in the Stamford Mercury, which said in part:

> As meetings convened by demagogues in the open air, for making political harangues, have been considered by those at the helm of the State to be of evil tendency, it is not a little surprising to find that the same authorities have not taken any notice of those assembled by the Religious Enthusiasts called Ranters. If the former are productive of evil consequences to the State, I can confidently affirm that the latter are in no degree less so to the morals of society.

The consensus of opinion on the history of the Primitives is largely favourable; that they acted as a restraint during a period of disaffection and social tension. After all, the Peterloo Massacre had only taken place in 1819 when a group of dissenters some 70-80,000 strong had protested at their political representation, unemployment and the introduction of Corn Laws. This was a time when only 2% of people had the vote and wages had been cut by two-thirds in the agricultural industry. Public patience was running out, and the desire for change was running high.

In addition, the Ranters were perceived as being against the traditions of the Old Culture and were seen by their social superiors to be firmly in favour of law and order, and recognised as being the leading campaigner for Temperance among the working people. While the Ranters were considered by many to be 'religious radicals', they were not yet radical in a political way. Indeed, it was not until the farm-workers' trade unions were founded and began their fast but short-lived growth in the early months of 1872 that political radicalism emerged from religious radicalism. Nevertheless, the fight of the working class for their own movement helped them to empathise with those Biblical characters who had struggled against oppression and passed through the wilderness on the way to the Land of Milk and Honey, and added emphasis to the words of the prophets.

The Primitives had helped to forge the New Culture and gained the moral high ground. They had endorsed the new Temperance Movement and given it air to breathe. Another part of the New Culture was the formation and rapid growth of the Friendly Societies.

In nineteenth-century Lincolnshire, and mirrored elsewhere around the country, no other secular movement affected so many people.

The Courts of the Ancient Order of Foresters, the Lodges of the Grand United Order of Oddfellows, the Tents of Rechabites, the Lodges of Druids, the Courts of Ancient Shepherds, the meetings of Free Gardeners and the meetings of purely local societies such as Rothwell Interment Society, Louth Friendly Society; these were of great social importance; it was a mass working-class movement.

By 1855 there existed at least one Friendly Society within easy walking distance of every village in the county. For about 80 years from the late 1830s on, these societies made a real impact on town and village life. By the 1860s, every Lincolnshire town boasted four or more Friendly Societies; many more in the larger towns. Their annual feast, often including a procession through the streets with bands, became one of the highlights of the year.

As early as 1841, the *Eastern Counties Herald* reported, on Whitsun week:

> A change has come over the face of the times. This celebrated holiday, one renowned for cock-fights, bull-rings, and footballs, is becoming equally or more remarkable... for processions of industrious artisans in their various orders of Oddfellows, Foresters, Shepherds &c.

Perversely, given that Friendly Societies were a product of the New Culture, the upper and middle classes tended to ridicule and denigrate them. There were attacks on the 'useless' expenditure on regalia. A report from Lincoln in 1840 on the Oddfellows' procession in regalia said critically

> ... a very imposing sight, to the grandeur of which the insignia of the order and the badges of office contributed though some persons consider these displays to be puerile vanities, discreditable to the really rational and admirable principals of the societies.

Similar reports and attacks appeared in 1844 and 1848. However, as described by a report from Louth in 1850, "it is now generally admitted that well-conducted benefit societies are valuable institutions, not only for soothing the bed of sickness, but as having a tendency to form habits of forethought, economy, and self-denial."

The attitudes of the middle classes towards these societies gradually changed; more and more reports stressed that "these and other societies have done much in Grimsby to preserve many from becoming chargeable to the parish, and are consequently worthy of attention and support." It became a matter of self-interest to support them as surely it was better to have a few voluntary donations than heavy poor rates. Some years earlier, the *Stamford Mercury* had stated that Friendly Societies

> ... are in fact one of the rational necessities of the times, forced into existence by some of the Poor Law details and that they will in a great measure ultimately supersede the necessity for parish relief, is no Utopian anticipation.

All of this offered an alternative to the traditional, or 'Old Culture'. The Ranters offered alternatives too. For their followers, chapel became the centre of their New Culture. Maldwyn Edwards wrote: "When people became Methodists they entered on a way of life which occupied all their leisure hours and left them neither time nor inclination for their former pastimes."

For those who did have time, there were now Temperance Meetings or Friendly Society meetings to attend which displaced their former pursuits and led to a higher and worthier, more moral leisure time, (and in time led to the religious revival of the 1830s).[3]

Meanwhile, to these same towns and villages, groups of performers, actors, musicians, tumblers, show people would periodically visit. These were a part of the Old Culture but their appeal lingered, perhaps because of the beneficial effect of drama, which were often historical in subject, religious in content, or jingoistic, or maybe the subject matter generated interest. It was, however, under the New Culture sponsored by a new religious uprising, harder to shake off the reputations of strolling players as worthless vagabonds and thieves with low morals, and the latter particularly as applied to actresses.

As Claire Tomalin points out in her biography of Nelly Ternan[4] this was an age when prevailing sexual rules could be, and were, flouted. Nelly's mother's generation included

> Fanny Kelly, who bore and brought up a daughter unassisted and never married. In the same generation Fanny Kemble left her husband when she found him tyrannous, and later divorced him. Mrs Siddons arranged her life so that she and her husband were never together. Lucia Elizabetta Vestris abandoned her first husband, and Mrs Abington paid hers an annual sum to keep away. Helen Faucit, a byword for respectability in the Victorian theatre, was the child of an actress who left her husband, and Helen's early career was actually managed by her mother's lover, the actor William Farren.

---

[3] This section was extracted from Cock Fighting to Chapel Building by Rex C Russell, by kind permission of the Heritage Trust of Lincolnshire
[4] The Invisible Woman, 1991

The acting profession was very hierarchic, with the more famous actors from Drury Lane or Covent Garden (i.e. the two houses patented to produce drama), having learned their trade by traipsing around the provinces to learn their profession and the stock roles, adding to their coffers by undertaking tours. Many of the greatest actors had graduated from the smaller circuits, most famously that of Tate Wilkinson at York, and many returned to them to prove that the public's faith in them had been proven, to repay that faith; and to collect a large pay day.

It was therefore inevitable that once again the representative of the Old Culture should conflict with the new, highly moral, evangelical membership of the New Culture. This manifested itself in the publication of tracts denouncing the theatre and similar entertainments as devilish, long letters of protest to the newspapers, public lectures , the opposition to the granting of justices' licenses to perform, and by means of moralising sermons from the pulpits of churches up and down the land.

Oddly, a system by which licenses to perform in theatres without patents, and were not allowed to perform drama without other entertainment such as dancing or music, under the Theatres Act of 1737, was the direct result of the Puritans' action during the Interregnum, and their influence which caused plays to have to pass the censor. Now, another upsurge in religious fervour was having an effect on theatres, or theatrical performances, in the provincial hinterlands.

Indeed Puritanism was starting to dominate the respectable classes; the theatre and dancing were branded as immoral. Those able to afford the theatre, the trade and professional people, were staying away and causing a decline in audiences. The *Colchester Gazette,* for example, reported (1st August, 1835), that in Chelmsford "few respectable people are ever found within the walls of country theatres… men are not such fools as to expend their time and money in seeing men and women make fools of themselves."

By 1838, Chesterfield theatre surrendered its tenancy because attendances were so poor that it went into arrears for the rent. Ormsby-Gore's theatre at Oswestry was little used by 1850, and dozens of others had closed.

Richmond's had been converted to wine cellars, and an auction room in 1848. Only two of Lincolnshire's towns, Lincoln and Stamford, still had their theatres in 1850, and Stamford's only lasted until 1871 when it became a billiard hall.[5]

By 1818, Evangelism entered every facet of life, and even prompted Dr Bowdler to publish his sanitised version of Shakespeare.

This was the landscape into which Joseph Smedley threw himself, and his family, in the early years of the nineteenth century. By no means the only one, but in taking it upon himself to provide the entertainment under his own management, he put himself firmly in the firing line. He became one of the targets for the objections, the disparaging letters; the malignant influence of sermonising clergy. As his reputation spread, so did the opposition.

Much of the opposition, however, wasn't personal; it was aimed at 'the Stage' generally, and practitioners of drama by association. One of the first regular accusers was the Revd Thomas Best, whose sermons in St James's Church, Sheffield pulled no punches in demonising the Stage and its followers,[6] and initiated a long debate in the pages of the *Sheffield Mercury*, the *Leeds Intelligester* and other newspapers, with few of the correspondents signing their real names, such as 'VIATOR', who published a response in the *Bristol Gazette* to Revd W. Law's 'Unlawfulness of Stage Entertainments'.

Of those who took exception to the reverend's attacks and so entered into printed argument with him and other clergy, were Robert Mansel, who at the time was manager of the Sheffield Theatre, and F W Calvert, then manager of Hull theatre. In a letter dated 12th November, 1822, to the Sheffield Mercury, and published as a tract, the latter wrote:[7]

---

[5] The English Market Town, by Jonathan Brown, by kind permission of The Crowood Press
[6] The Lincolnshire Archives; LLHS 38/5/5
[7] The Lincolnshire Archives; LLHS 38/5/5

A Defence of the Acted Drama
In a letter
Addressed to
The Rev Thomas Best of Sheffield
By F B Calvert
Formerly of St. Edmund's College and now
Of the Theatres Royal York and Hull

Sir,

An abridged statement of your annual denunciation of the Stage, has been, this morning, conveyed to me, through the medium of the Sheffield Mercury.

Believe me, Sir, it is with no vain presumption that any thing that I can advance upon this long-contested subject, will operate conviction on a mind constituted as yours is, that I hazard a reply; but I feel that some little justice is due to the profession of which I am a member, to the public at large, whose judgment it has been your study to prejudice, and finally to the great cause of truth, which in your periodical attacks on the Drama, I blush to say, you have uniformly disregarded.

Indeed, indeed, Sir, you have done enough; great things no doubt are due to your perseverance in so hopeless a cause, but really it is time to pause from your labours, and withdraw from the contest year after year has found you pursuing the same irksome, the same unprofitable task; and though I make no doubt, you originally fixed your grasp upon the pillars of our Temple with the reckless confidence of a Sampson, that it would soon yield destruction on the needs of its devoted in-mates, – the Classic fabric of the Drama, reared by the hands of genius and cemented by the veneration of ages, trust me, is fixed upon a basis beyond your power to move.

Robert Mansel released a booklet containing some of the sermons and "Letters to Thomas Best through the pages of Sheffield Mercury" dated 2nd November, 1818, with an introduction by himself. It was entitled:

Richard E. Smedley

A Short Struggle
For
STAGE OR NO STAGE
Originating in
A SERMON
Preached by
THE REVEREND THOMAS BEST
In St James's Church, Sheffield.[8]

This provoked further disfavour; in a letter of support to Revd Best, the following appeared on 7th November, 1818:

> A censure having been passed upon you through the medium of the Sheffield Mercury by Mr Mansel, the present "Director of the Theatre" in this Town, in consequence of a Sermon which you delivered in your own Church, on the subject of Theatrical Amusements; we, the undersigned, having ourselves now heard the Sermon, which you kindly preached on Sunday evening last at our particular request, beg leave, through the same medium, to return you our most sincere thanks for so judicial and reasonable an admonition; and we trust that all who were present on the occasion, will be induced to give the subject that serious and dispassionate consideration which it appears to us most justly to demand.
> We remain
> Revered and Dear Sir
> Your affectionate Brethren
> Thos Sutton, Vicar of Sheffield
> M Preston } Assistant Ministers
> E Goodwin } of the Parish Church
> W H Vale } of Sheffield
> Thos Cotterill, Perpetual Curate of St. Paul's Church, Sheffield

However, there were also letters of support for Robert Mansel, such as this letter from Doncaster dated 7th November, 1818, and signed by PHILO DRAMA, which begins:

---

[8] The Lincolnshire Archives; LLHS 38/5/5

Sir,

I have not the honour of being personally known to you, yet I cannot help expressing my warmest thanks to you for the very manly pertinent letter you have addressed to the public, through the medium of the Doncaster Gazette.

The interference of fanaticism, in the cause of any religion, does infinite prejudice to society; because pride, ignorance, or self-interest generally direct the infuriate, uncharitable, and vindictive efforts of this species of phrensy.

and another to the Sheffield Mercury signed AH:

I am one among your numerous readers, who feel a considerable degree of interest in the subject recently introduced to the notice of the public, by the spirited as well as moderate remonstrance of the Manager of your Theatre, Mr Mansel, against a most unwarrantable, indecent, and uncharitable attack upon the exhibitions presented under his direction to the people of Sheffield, as well as upon theatrical representations in general, by the Rev. T Best".

This was the same "AH" who also published:

FACTS AND COMMENTS
Being
OBSERVATIONS
On
THE MORAL TENDENCY OF
THE STAGE
In a letter to a "A Layman"
In answer to
A LETTER TO ROBERT MANSEL, ESQ
On his
REMONSTRANCE
Against the "uncalled for, indecorous, and illiberal Attack" upon the
SHEFFIELD THEATRE
And Theatrical Representations in General
By the Rev. T Best, of St James's Church
SHEFFIELD
"I have heard
That guilty creatures sitting at a play,
Have, by the very cunning of the scene,

Been struck so to the soul, that presently
They have proclaim'd their malefactions"
WORKSOP
Printed and sold by J. Whitlam; sold also by P Sissons, Worksop; and by W. Todd, Sheffield
1819
Price One Shilling

The following is part of the foreword, addressed thus:

To
The Members
Of
THE SHAKESPEARE CLUB
SHEFFIELD

Gentlemen,

The veneration I entertain for the memory of our immortal Bard, as one of the greatest moral philosophers that ever lived, and the consequent respect I must feel for those persons associated in friendship under the powerful influence of his transcendent name, induce me to solicit your patronage and protection of the following pages, in their attempt to rescue the Stage and its legitimate performances, from the illiteral and invidious imputations of Bigotry and Fanaticism.

I am urged to this attempt, in consequence of some supercilious critiques upon a letter of mine which appeared in Mr Mansel's pamphlet, by an anonymous author, styling himself "A LAYMAN", in a letter to that gentleman, and dedicated to you.

The main body of this work contains a quotation from a critique, upon an attack on the Stage, in the *Annual Review*:

Let the comic poet be called to a severe responsibility, when he trifles with the holiest bonds which hold society together; let the matron rise and quit the playhouse with her daughter, if her sacred presence is profaned by coarse ribaldry or systematic licentiousness. Genius can be so taught, that unless he is the slave of virtue, he must become the outcast of fame; that no works of art endure but those which advocate the enduring interests of mankind; and that the true road to permanent praise on earth, is to merit the favour of a retributive Deity.

By the meritorious conspiracy of exemplary characters, by the apt exertion of the social frown, any exceptionable comedies can be cried down, and banished from the Stage: They are not numerous and may be disused unmissed.

Also in favour of Theatre, was a tract entitled *A Vindication of Rational Amusements, in answer to a Pamphlet entitled 'A Review of Certain Publications, &C'*. Printed in Hull, this gave a view based on Biblical quotation in order to oppose those who attack the Stage from a Biblical standpoint. For instance, "He that hideth hatred with lying lips, and he that uttereth a Slander is a fool."

Joseph Smedley considered himself to be a Gentleman. He tried to deal fairly with everyone. He was highly moral, and influenced his family to lead blameless and honest lives. He was a proud man; he attempted to elevate his art to a higher standard and to take it to as many people as possible. This was his work; but above all it was his family's bread and butter. Operating where he did, he must have felt under attack, and probably wanted to respond, or at least give his support to the other managers. That he was concerned about these matters is again reflected in his correspondence with Dr Oliver, as discussed by C.M.P. Taylor:

> Oliver is delighted that a Methodist preacher in Grimsby was silenced on the matter after he had uttered "bitter invective against rational amusement" and "vile and broad abuse against the clergy of the Church of England". He questions whether Smedley's "ill success" in March 1823 is not "more to be attributed to the increasing prevalence of Methodism than to the depression in Agriculture".

This is borne out to some extent by the inclusion in his papers of a handwritten letter, which I am reproducing in full, despite its tortuous syntax and grammar:[9]

At the top of the letter is a note written in a different hand: "This was written + sent by an unknown friend signed Amicus."

---

[9] Smedley papers, Lincolnshire Archives; LLHS 38/5/9/9

Richard E. Smedley

A reply to the observations of Anti-dramaticus

The attempt of the writer stiling himself Anti-dramaticus to sink the stage & its advocates into the depths of iniquity will on an attentive and impartial a perusal be found to voise them still higher in the scale of morality and virtues. His first assertion concerning those celebrated moralists & Divines who have written in defence of the Stage, instead of <u>going to prove</u> that they were fallible & imperfect men does actually prove that their minds being freed from the trammels of bigotry & Puritanism & glorying in the light of reason & exalted feeling, felt that a just delineation of the beauties of virtue, and of the deformities of vice presented to the eye in all of their native colouring, is not merely consistent with, but greatly favourable to the best ideas of true Religion. His extract from the sermon of Archbishop Tillotson refers only to <u>lewdly immodest plays</u>; but as one who had the slightest acquaintance with Shakespeare – Otway, Addison, Rowe, & all our other celebrated dramatic writers will affirm that the tendency of their productions is to cause in the mind sentiments of lewdness and immodesty. Anti-dramaticus exhibits a very confined knowledge of the Drama when he says that in the exhibition of <u>sin,- especially as presented on the stage,</u> will increasingly abate the horrors of it upon the mind" He, who had either read a play or seen one represented knows that the wicked character in the end reaps the fatal effects of his wickedness whilst the virtuous is rewarded for his goodness. If to see the use, progress, & final termination of the impious in the whose not in the mind feelings of horror, and if to see goodness & virtue finally crowned with laurels stir not up our finest feelings to follow the same course. I must confess I know not what will.

Anti-dramaticus continues, "comedians are in general wicked characters, & are as wicked men are of their father (the devil) they will ever be doing his work, and on this account Play-acting proves itself to be the work of the Devil. This is certainly a piece of the strangest reasoning ever produced. The <u>Christian charity</u> of the writer assumes a large body of men to be wicked, and then without discriminating – between the Actor & the Author of a Drama, concludes that if the <u>Actor</u> be wicked the character he performs must necessarily be the same. He might with equal justice contend that if a Parson be ungodly, the Bible, & the doctrine he preaches, must also be false. But I assert (& a strict scrutiny into their characters will bear me out in the assertion) that as a body of men, the virtues of Actors in general will be found to equal those of any other of the same magnitude. Nay, there are many amongst them whose noble & exalted qualities would put to the blush even Puritanism itself. But supposing for the sake of argument that actors were as wicked as Anti-dramaticus would uncharitably have us believe; what have their private virtues or vices to do with the general question, whether the exhibition of the Drama be serviceable or prejudicial to the cause of virtues. We go not to the Theatre to see a private individual, but to see the delineation by that individual of a character for the most part, if not always directly opposite to his own. If the question were to be decided by the weight of authorities I could produce Judge against Judge & Divine but I will place the matter on a broader foundation on the basis of reason & common sense, & I appeal to the understandings of the impartial & unprejudiced & ask, whether to learn to shun the vices & follies of the world without the dear-bought experience of suffering – to infuse into the mind principles of honour, integrity and virtue in the most agreeable & impressive manner, & to check the growth of vice & immorality & cause the heart to turn with disgust & abhorrence from wickedness & crime by witnessing the fatal end of its victims be prejudicial or not to the cause of virtue? If it is not detrimental, and who will affirm that it is; then it only remains to be proved that the sentiments conveyed by the Drama tend to produce these effects. That there are some few plays whose tendency is bad I will not deny; for as long as man continues in his present state the best of human institutions will bear some marks of imperfection. But shall we reject the whole because a part is bad? Shall we destroy the whole body because one member is unsound? That by far the greatest proportion of English dramatic productions have a tendency to produce the good effects for which I have above contended, I leave to the decision of those who have in a spirit of impartiality perused the works of our most admired dramatic writers. The other observations of Anti-dramaticus which I have refrained from noticing are too puerile & too absurd to need a refutation. The Drama was the admiration of the Wisest and Virtuous for centuries before Puritanism had birth & will continue to flourish & be admired by future & enlightened ages when our modern Puritans and their doctrines shall have sunk into merited oblivion.

Dramaticus

There is no evidence that this was used, or that Joseph himself got involved in the mud-slinging. However, there is a surviving bill by 'Dramaticus', which *was* used, entitled *A Second Defence of the Theatre*, and does specifically defend Mr Smedley who was about to embark on a season at Beverley (see illustration).[10] Because of the opposition to him obtaining a licence to perform, he did often get friends or fellow Freemasons to give him a reference, and, on his playbills would occasionally stress the wholesomeness of the production and himself, giving a small lecture or homily, such as this from a playbill from Market Rasen of 28th April, 1836:[11]

> It is desirable that the exhibition of Dramatic Performances should not be neglected. The common business of life, too intensely pursued, makes men unmindful of the precepts and maxims of virtue which they are more apt to forget in the eager pursuits of their avocations; than to abandon through want of principle. The Drama awakens them to virtue, exercises all the kinder emotions and its influence over the mind and feelings, prevents that moral stagnation, which so often tends to degrade and brutify.

Certainly, there is no record of him ever being refused a licence to perform. Throughout the country, managers and actors were having to defend their living. To quote but one further example, Frederic Coleman Nantz, the actor and playwright, had been a member of Manly's Nottingham Company from 1832 to 1835 when he moved to the Norwich circuit. While there, in 1837, he published a ringing defence of the theatre *An Actor's Vindication of his Profession*, dedicated to James Sheridan Knowles with whom Nantz appeared on the Norwich circuit, and written in response to an attack on the stage by the Revd John McCrea, from the pulpit of St. Margaret's Church in King's Lynn.[12] This contained a paragraph which Joseph Smedley was to quote at the top of several of his playbills, although, as was common at the time, without accreditation:

> The common business of life is too intensely pursued – makes men unmindful of precepts and maxims of virtue, which they are more apt to forget in the eager pursuits of their avocations, than to abandon through want of principle. The Stage awakens them to virtue, exercises all the kinder emotions, and by its influence over the mind and feelings, prevents that moral stagnation which so much tends to degrade and to beautify; and while it amuses it instructs – its sole principle being the inculcation of virtue and the punishment of vice.

---

[10] Smedley papers; Lincolnshire Archives; LLHS 38/5/9/9
[11] Smedley papers; Lincolnshire Archives LLHS 38/5/4
[12] F.C. Nantz's entry in Oxford DNB, Paul Schlicke, accessed 11/01/2017

An Answer to the Defence of the STAGE.

If some few of our celebrated moralists and divines, have written in defence of the Stage, it only goes to prove that these were fallible and imperfect men, pulling down with one hand what they were endeavouring to build up with the other. The names of ABRAHAM, DAVID, SOLOMON, & PETER, might be produced in defence of very bad actions, when those eminent men acted unlike themselves in some unhappy circumstances of their lives. But *Dramaticus* has not done Justice to the writers whose names he mentions. Archbishop TILLOTSON in the Sermon referred to says "*I do not see how any person pretending to sobriety and virtue, and especially to the pure and holy Religion of our blessed Saviour, can, without great guilt and open contradiction to his holy profession, be present at lewd and immodest plays, as too many are, who would take it very ill to be shut out of the community of Christians, as they would most certainly have been in the first and purest ages of Christianity.*" He also calls the Play House "*The Devil's Chapel, and the School, and the Nursery of Lewdness and Vice,*" and speaking of parents who take their Children there, he calls them "*Monsters! I had almost said Devils!*" JOHNSON, is mentioned—But take the following instance of his conversation with BOSWELL, "Players Sir!" said he "*I look on them as no better than creatures set upon tables and joint-stools, to make faces and produce laughter, like dancing dogs.*"—"But Sir, you will allow that some players are better than others?"—JOHNSON. *Yes, Sir, as some dogs dance better than others.* Now, Sir, to talk of respect for a player!" (smiling disdainfully)—BOSWELL. "There Sir, you are always heretical; you never allow merit to a player!"—JOHNSON. "*Merit Sir, what merit? Do you respect a rope-dancer, or a ballad-singer.*" (Boswell's Life of Johnson, vol. 2, page 415.) Judge BULSTRODE, in a charge to the Grand Jury of MIDDLESEX, uses these striking words :—"*One Play-house ruins more Souls, than fifty Churches can save.*"

DRAMATICUS vindicates the Stage as "*highly serviceable to the cause of virtue;*" But I contend that Theatrical Exhibitions are destructive of Virtue, and highly serviceable in the promotion of Vice. If we are friends to our Country, to virtue and to religion, we wish well to the rising generation; We wish that their principles and morals, may be conformed to the standard of the Holy Scriptures.—We wish them to be taught to love God with all their heart, and their Neighbour as themselves—But in order to teach them this, who would think of sending them to the Theatre where vice is exhibited; where the modest must be put to the blush by indecency, and the pious ear wounded by profaneness?—The chief argument in defence of Theatrical Exhibitions is *that the young must have recreation, and a good play affords rational and innocent amusement.* But can that play be good which in any part offends the modest or the pious? O how few (if any) are free from this charge? Do not Plays exhibit characters most grateful to human depravity, and most pleasing to corrupt nature?—Pride is exhibited under Greatness of mind; Ambition, and Revenge, under the names of Valour and Heroism; but chiefly Love, the strongest and most dangerous passion of the human heart, is always encouraged upon the stage ; *there,* the young and unguarded heart often receives the most fatal impression. As the most terrible objects would become familiar, and viewed with less emotion, if constantly presented to us, so the frequent exhibition of *Sin,* and especially as presented on the Stage, will increasingly abate the horrors of it upon the mind. Why should the young be induced to see a number of bad characters without necessity ;—to behold them with patience and too often with pleasure? Is there no danger, that a heart softened by delight should be liable to infection ; No danger that the commission of Sin may follow the sense of pleasure? Are Theatrical Exhibitions calculated to imbue the mind with that holy indignation against Sin, which every Christian ought to feel?— If to attend the Theatre be so rational, innocent, and virtuous, as Dramaticus would have us believe, why then are not Comedians the most virtuous and holy persons upon earth? Why does not what they teach to others make themselves virtuous? Why are they not sent for to attend the sick and dying, and why do not we hear vast numbers rejoicing on their dying beds, that they have regularly attended the Play-house, having there learned to love and fear God, and hate Sin? The reason is obvious, Comedians are in general wicked characters, and as wicked men are of their father (the Devil) they will ever be doing his work, and on this account, Play-acting proves itself to be the work of the Devil. If Play-acting at all served the interest of Religion and promoted the glory of God, good and holy men might, and would be common Stage Players. We read in Scripture of holy Plowmen, Shepherds, Fishermen, Tentmakers, Prophets, Apostles, and Evangelists, but never read that any of these Saints were Comedians—hence, we may infer, that Play-acting is altogether Sinful. And who does not believe it? What respectable family (even though they attend the Play-house) will take into their houses a company of Comedians, and make them the companions of themselves, their Sons, and daughters? Let conscience speak, you who attend the Play-house, do you pray for a blessing before you go—have you sweet communion with God while there, have you this testimony that you have pleased God when you return? For God's then sake fly from the tents of these men, least you be partakers of their Plagues.

ANTI-DRAMATICUS.

G. Barnby, Printer, &c. Wheelgate, Malton.

An Answer to the Defence of the Stage

Richard E. Smedley

Another
ANSWER TO THE DEFENCE OF THE STAGE.

In my reply to your Defence of the Stage, I did not appeal to St. PAUL, but not for the reason which you assign viz: "*Because the Book of Sacred Writ, makes my position untenable,*" but because I did not conceive any person (with the exception of Dramaticus) would ever believe that the Apostle in any part of his writings, had defended Theatrical Amusements. If ST. PAUL has cited the *words of a Dramatic Author*, he has quoted the sayings of many Heathen Authors, and very frequently alluded to Olympic Games, i. e. the Heathen Sports as frequently practised both in Greece and Rome, what then! Does this prove that he approved of Theatrical Exhibitions? Of Heathenism? Or of the Exercises to which he refers?

Dr. JOHNSON, whom you so grosly abuse, in your late production, as to call him *an ill-natured Cynic, and Hypocrite,* wrote the tragedy of Irene, but it was the only play he ever wrote, and it was one of his early productions.

I will not deny that you have quoted so much of TILLOTSON, as suited your own purpose, being prudent enough to omit all the rest, " *It is very possible they may be so framed, and governed by such rules, as not only to be innocently diverting, but instructive and useful.* "But this goes as far as to say that they were not "*so framed*" and "*governed by such rules*" in his day, and Dramaticus has not attempted to prove, that they are "*so framed and governed by such rules*" in this day; and at this place; and if he thought they were, surely he would not have omitted to inform us when, and by whom, they were reformed ; or at least he would have referred us to some few for a proof of this.

I did not say that some men of wealth, and influence have not countenanced the Theatre and associated occasionally with Stage Players. Or that some *Comedians* have not, in other respects, been moral characters : but I still contend, that respectable families (generally) will not associate with common Stage Players, or make them the companions of their Sons and Daughters.

If the Scriptures do not directly condemn Theatrical Exhibitions as exhibited in this day, they do it indirectly throughout the whole of the Sacred Pages. They enjoin that "*Whether therefore ye eat or drink, or whatsoever ye do, do all to the glory of God.*" I believe very few if any Actors on the Stage, or its admirers, will affirm, that they obey this precept. The Scriptures say "*Thou shalt not take the name of the Lord thy God in vain.*" But I ask, is not the name of God profaned in almost every Play? *Let no corrupt communication proceed out of your mouth.*" "*All liars shall have their part in the lake which burneth with fire and brimstone.*" If corrupt communication does not proceed out of the mouth and lies are not "*fearlessly*" told on the Stage, then there is no possibility of violating these Scripture Precepts. Are not the Exhibitions, gestures, and language used in most Comedies *indecent, obscene and profane?* And in most of the Tragedies now acted upon the Stage, is there not much of Blasphemy?

I know it is very easy to call all this "*Bigotry and Cant,*" and to brand all who lift up their voice, or take up their pen in defence of purity, and virtue,—in opposition to sin, impurity, and profaneness, with the names of "MODERN PURITANS" Hypocrites, and the like; but it is easy to see that all this "*scurrility*" is adopted not merely in the "*absence,*" but instead of fair argument.

I contend "*fearlessly,*" that Theatrical Exhibitions are altogether Sinful. *It is a sinful waste of Money.* It is not unreasonable to suppose that the money expended this way would be sufficient *to feed and clothe* all the indigent poor in the kingdom, and if it were thus applied, it would turn to a better account. Or suppose it were applied in sending Missionaries to preach the Gospel to the Heathen. Or suppose it were appropriated in translating, printing, and circulating the Holy Scriptures; and if this practice were continued, soon, very soon would heathenism, ignorance, poverty, and sin, be in a great measure banished from the world. But I contend that *it is a sinful waste of time.* *Time*, as well as *money*, is a talent which we are commanded "*to redeem*" and I am persuaded very few, if any, will pretend that the *two or three hours* spent in the Theatre, *three or four evenings in the week,* could not have been better employed. If we profess the Christian Religion, and take the Bible for our Rule of *Doctrine, experience,* and *practice,* then it follows that we are Candidates for Eternity—Upon a state of probation and trial—must give an account of the deeds done in the body, yea for every idle word—That every day we spend on Earth will have some influence on our eternal state. But I contend that the *time spent in a Play-house* is worse *than a Blank!* Are not Duties neglected at home? When is the worship of God performed in such families, before they go to the Play, or after they return? The *mind* is polluted and hardened with the representations brought before them, & it is to be feared *Souls*, yea multitudes of immortal souls are ruined eternally.

Dramaticus did not tell us in his reply why Comedians *are not sent for to attend the sick and dying,* and why vast numbers are not *rejoicing on their dying beds, that they regularly attended the Play-house, having there learnt to love and fear God, and hate Sin?* I ask further, was it ever known that a careless sinner was awakened to a sense of his guilt and danger, as a sinner before God—in the *Play-house?* Did ever a *penitent broken-hearted & contrite sinner,* obtain a sense of divine mercy, by believing on the Lord Jesus Christ—in a *Play-house?* When the great Judge of all shall summon the nations to his dread tribunal, at that awful day of righteous retribution, and final decision, will he pronounce this final sentence upon the admirer of Theatrical Exhibitions "Well done good and faithful Servant" &c.

ANTI DRAMATICUS.

G. Barnby, Printer, &c. Wheelgate, Malton.

Another Answer to the Defence of the Stage

A SECOND DEFENCE OF THE THEATRE

But that silence might be construed into an acknowledgement of the truth of the libellous productions which have been issued by wholesale from the Fanatic Tract and Trash Press for the last twenty years in every town where a Theatre is to be found—I should think it beneath me to reply to the gross scurrility that has been thus ADOPTED instead of rebutting my former defence by fair argument.

Is it to be inferred that he is no CHRISTIAN who attends the Theatre? Then George the Third, whose moral character was never called in question, was lost past all hope, for he was an enthusiastic admirer and advocate of it. Addison, Young, and Johnson were WRITERS of Plays, and they are, by the same rule, hurled to perdition—but by whom?—not in the opinion of the great, the good, the wise—but by these SELF-ELECTED, OVER RIGHTEOUS, ULTRA-PURITANS, who have not christian charity enough to allow any one to be saved who is not within the pale of their own Church. Let them not deceive themselves, the time is at hand, when these denunciations will fall upon their own heads. "Thou hypocrite, first cast out the beam out of thine own eye, and then shalt thou see clearly to cast out the mote out of thy brother's eye." The issuer of the TRACT has sheltered himself by promulgating that which he would not DARE to write himself. What! the Stage "the SINK OF INFAMY," and its professors, "ALL LEWD AND IMMODEST?" What a libel on The Magistrate, Clergyman, and Inhabitants of the Town of Barton who signed the following recommendation—

"Understanding that MR. SMEDLEY is about to open the Theatre at Beverley for a Season;

"We, the undersigned, being the Gentry and principal Inhabitants of the Town of Barton-upon-Humber, do hereby testify, that we have, for upwards of twenty years past, known MR. SMEDLEY as Manager of the Theatre at Barton, and other places, in the County of Lincoln, and that he is a man of most respectable character, and has attended Barton with his Company every other year in succession, for many years past, and that he not only is regular in regard to his own conduct and that of his own family, but that he has always had the whole of his Company under such regular arrangements, that not so much as a single complaint was ever known to be made against any individual of them; and that from MR. SMEDLEY's customary endeavours to please, we have not the slightest doubt but that the Lovers of the Drama at Beverley will experience the same good opinion of him and his company as we have now taken the liberty of expressing."

Did not the late Mr. Kemble number in the list of his private friends, the Dukes of Bedford, Devonshire, and Northumberland, the Marquis of Hertford, the Earl of Aberdeen, Lord Holland, Mr. Canning, Sir James Mackintosh, and a long list of others whose talents and virtues will, like his, be handed down to posterity? Nor would I have you think this is a solitary instance of respect paid to an Actor; there is not a company in existence, but some part of its members can make a similar boast, though necessarily more confined, according to their limited sphere of action. Did you ever hear that the breath of calumny had tainted the moral character of the present Countesses of Derby and Craven, Lady Thurlow, Lady Becher, Mrs. Bradshaw, &c. &c. and yet all these have been what you would call "profane stage players."

As no credit can be gained by parrying the thrust, or even by gaining a victory over bigotry and cant, I shall take my FINAL leave—in the language of an eloquent living defender of the Theatre and its rights; in the firm conviction, "that the Stage is the School of Eloquence, the Temple of the Arts, the Shrine of the Muses, the Chastener of our Morals, and the mild but persuasive Monitress of our Duties." DRAMATICUS.

A Second Defence of the Theatre

6
The Smedleys – Intermediate Stages

Joseph and his Company and family continued to tour, and to grow in stature. He was steadily building a head of steam, making new contacts, playing different towns, but at all times building a reputation for probity and fair-dealing.

Unfortunately, there is little information about the next few years as far as his career is concerned, for Joseph left no memoirs as some others did; there are seemingly few playbills extant, but we pick up murmurs here and there:

For instance, another son, Joseph (Jnr) was born at Sleaford on 4th March, 1816, and christened there on 15th March.

In 1818, another addition to the family, Abraham, was born (17th April) also in Sleaford.

On 4th December, 1821, another son, George, was born at Ely, Cambridgeshire.

The *Lincolnshire Mercury* reported a Benefit performance on 22nd March, 1822 for Mr Smedley, and the following advertisement on 4th October, 1822:

> Theatre, Market Deeping
> On Tuesday Evening, the 8th October,1822, by
> Desire of the Inhabitants of Glinton,
> THE SCHOOL FOR SCANDAL,
> And A CHIP OF THE OLD BLOCK
> On Thursday,
> JOHN BUZZBY,
> And THE LADY AND THE DEVIL
> On Friday,

> THE LAW OF JAVA
> And SHARP AND FLAT,
> And on Saturday,
> THE WONDER: A WOMAN KEEPS A
> SECRET! And
> THE TWO PAGES OF FREDERICK THE GREAT,
> For the BENEFIT of Mrs and Miss SMEDLEY,
> And the last night of performing.

Coincidentally, just above this item was an advertisement for the Lincoln Theatre, allowing a direct comparison of entertainment being offered:

> Theatre, Lincoln,
> Mr Robertson most respectfully acquaints the
> Public, that he has engaged, for Three Nights,
> MESDAMES FERZI
> The celebrated Tight and Black Rope Dancers
> who have been the last two years at the Gardens of
> Tivoli and Beaujou, Paris, and will make their re-
> appearance in England at this Theatre
> This present FRIDAY, October 4th
> Their Second Appearance will be on Monday, the 7th
> Their Third and Last, on Wednesday, the 9th
> On Friday, October 11th
> For the BENEFIT of MR ROBERTSON,
> Will be performed the New Play of
> DAMON AND PYTHIAS
> OR, THE FORCE OF FRIENDSHIP
> (Taken from the celebrated Syracusian story, and performed at the
> Theatre Royal, Covent Garden, with most distinguished applause)
> DAMON............Mr J GANN
> PYTHIAS Mr F ROBERTSON
> CALANTHE............Mrs T.ROBERTSON
> To conclude with the Dramatic Romance of
> VALENTINE AND ORSON,
> Or, THE WILD MAN of the WOODS
> Days of Playing, Mondays, Wednesdays and Fridays

So, it seems, Joseph was continuing to tour to towns and theatres that he knew, and where he was known, and Robertson and Manly continued their policy of importing named players from the London playhouses.

In 1823, for example, Mr Manly announced the appearance at Stamford of Mr W. Farren, and in 1825 Mr Robertson announced that, with the permission of Mr Elliston, he had engaged Miss Clara Fisher from the Theatre Royal Drury Lane to appear at Newark, and then in Grantham, with a programme which included *The Spoiled Child*, *Modern Antiques*, and *The Actress of all Work*.

In 1823, Joseph and his Company played at Malton:

>
> THEATRE, MALTON
> On Wednesday Evening, Nov 26th, 1823
> Mrs Inchbald's favourite comedy,
> EVERYONE HAS HIS FAULT
> Or, The Old Bachelor's Wedding

Mr Ditcher	Mr Major
Mr Smedley	Mr Crawford
Mr Coppin	Mr Richards
Mr Neville	Miss A Smedley
Mrs Neville	Miss Smedley
Miss Simms	Mrs Coppin

> Mr Smedley will sing
> "Wife, Children, and Friends"
> And
> The Echo Song, by Miss Smedley
> RENDEZVOUS
> or, Which is the Lady

On 15th March, 1824, they played at Sleaford, with *Tom and Jerry, or, Life in London*, with a farce *Midnight Hour*.
On Boxing Day, 1825, Joseph was back at Grimsby with:**

> Jane Shore
> Lord Hastings   Mr Ditcher
> Duke of Gloucester   Mr Major Dumont   Mr Neville
> Belmour Mr Fuller   {Their first appearance here
> Ratclif   Mr Reeve {

Catesby   Mr Coppin   Porter   Mr Richards
Jane Shore   Mrs Coppin   Alicia   Mrs Neville
Songs – 'Pudding in a Lantern' Mr Major. And a
Favourite Song, by Mr Fuller
To conclude with a Laughable Farce called The
SPECTRE BRIDEGROOM;
Or, A Ghost in spite of Himself
Mr Nicodemus   Mr Neville   Captain Vauntington   Mr Fuller
Squire Aldwinkle   Mr Major   Dickery   Mr Coppin
Paul   Mr Ditcher
Miss Georgiana Aldwinkle, Miss A. Smedley Lavinia, Mrs Coppin
For this Night, Pit 1s – Gallery 6d

* * *

A contemporary sketch of Joseph Smedley in c 1825

Richard E. Smedley

Still at Grimsby, and by Desire of the Tradesmen thereof, on
MONDAY Evening, January 9th, 1826
Will be presented, A Romantic Play (never acted here) called
IVANHOE
Or, The Jew of York
Founded on the celebrated novel of that name
THE NEW SCENERY PAINTED BY MR REEVE

Ivanhoe	Mr Neville
Sir Reginald Front de Boeuf	Mr Ditcher
Sir Brian de Bois Guilbert	Mr Fuller
Cedric of Rotherwood	Mr Coppin
Sir Maurice de Bracey	Mr Richards
Wamba	Mr Reeve
Robin Hood	Mr Coppin
Friar Tuck	Mr Major
Isaac, (the Jew)	Mr Smedley
Rowena	Miss A. Smedley
Uirica	Mrs Neville
Elgitha	Mrs Coppin
Rebecca	Miss Smedley

SONGS, DUETS, &c

SONG –"The Lullaby," Miss A. Smedley. – DUET – "F al lal la" Mr Reeve & Mrs Coppin SONG – "The Barefooted Friar." Mr Major

MR MAJOR WILL SING
THE ROYAL RADICAL RESTORATIVE
AND COMIC SINGING BY MR REEVE

* * *

To conclude with the petite comedy
SIMPSON & CO.

Mr Simpson	Mr Ditcher	Foster	Mr Reeve
Mr Bromley	Mr Neville	John	Mr Richards
Mrs Simpson	Mrs Neville	Mrs Bromley	Miss Smedley
Madame La Trappe	Mrs Coppin	Mrs Fitzallen	Miss A. Smedley

PIT, 2s Second-price, 1sGALL. 1s Second Price, 6d

** Playbills owned and used by kind permission of Mrs D R Whittingham of Grimsby.

Note that at this point, Mr Reeve is credited with the painting of the scenery for Ivanhoe, but seems to have left the company after this, and doesn't appear on the playbills for Smedley's company again until 1833. In a letter to Joseph, from Newport dated 27th November, 1826, he complains of problems within his company: "When I joined it had been made up but a fortnight, and many of them very bad actors and great dissension and strife…"

The year 1826 brought a sea-change in this policy. He built two theatres, *at his own expense*; the first at Sleaford and the other at March in Cambridgeshire. The former cost £478 to build, and the latter £611.[1]

The site of the Sleaford Theatre was originally owned by Lord Bristol who sold it off, with much of the northern side of Westgate, in 1823 to Revd Friskney Gunniss, who sold the Playhouse and the land on either side and behind it to Joseph Smedley in 1825.

The opening of the Sleaford Theatre was announced thus:[2]

NEW THEATRE, SLEAFORD
Mr Smedley respectfully announces to his
friends and the public that he purposes opening
the New Theatre, on Monday, March 27th, 1826
With the Comedy of
SPEED THE PLOUGH
And the Musical Entertainment of
MY SPOUSE AND I
Days of Playing, Mondays, Wednesdays, and Fridays

A clearly proud owner-manager, Joseph made the following address at the opening[3]: (note that even here he mounts a stout defence of the morals of the stage).

---

[1] Linconshire Arheives LLHS 38/5/3/14
[2] Stamford Mercury, Friday, 24th March 1826 (British Newspaper Archives)
3 Smedley Family papers – Lincolnshire Archives

Richard E. Smedley

As a fond Parent who with anxious heart,
Views a dear Child first take an active part,
On the wide world's vast Stage. So I
With heart as anxious, and a wishful eye
View this my new, but humble Structure. Which,
If you approve, I then am doubly rich.
Here by you cheer'd shall tragedy bewail,
Her many sorrows, then anon she'll rail,
Or vaunt with lofty air some val'rous feat,
How in the midst of Battle's fiercest heat,
Her Hero conquer'd, and the Triumph of Fame
Proclaim'd aloud through Kingdoms his great name,
While Victory hasten'd from her lofty Throne,
To crown with Laurel wreaths her fav'rite Son
Kings, Princes, Heroes, slain in bloodless strife,
Wak'd by your smiles, will rise again to life.
And that gay laughing Muse so blithe and free,
Yelept by Bards of old, fair Comedy,
Hither will come, and with instructive page,
Portray the 'living manners of the age.
"Sweet Shakespeare too, our Country's joy and pride
Shall roam at large with Nature for his guide,
No Horses, Dogs, or Monkeys, brought to view,
But his scenes alone, which are always sure.
Enough for future Years now let us cast
A parting glance at those which long have past,
They have buried with them in Oblivious times
Things that were once of Earth the greater pride,
But in that Tide, while memory holds her sway,
Ne'er shall the favours of those Years 'decay';
No, in any grateful heart they're kept enshrin'd,
Like a spring garland round the firm oak twin'd,
And still shall bloom, fresh, lovely, as when first
From the young bud the opening flowers burst,
Those favours still bestow –
Continue those favours, 'twill be my pride,
And to ensure them, this shall be my guide,

My study, which I will through life pursue,
To keep the Moral of the Stage in view:
Thus to fulfil the Purport of our Art,
While we please the Eye, to amend the Heart
And, as my efforts aid fair Virtue's cause,
Twere heresy to doubt of your applause.

The theatre built by Joseph still stands in Sleaford, and is now a theatre again, after several changes of ownership and uses.

View of Sleaford Theatre as it is today

Joseph firmly advocated incorporating a billiard room in his theatres, and it is believed that this was the case at Sleaford, and that it was situated in the space beneath the stage. Today, there is simply no way of confirming this, as no cellars have been discovered. At the time the theatre was being restored in the 1990s, a report was prepared for the Theatres Trust, which did state that it was most unlikely that a theatre of this period was ever constructed without a cellar for dressing room accommodation.[4] It appears from raising parts of the floor that the pit has been filled with rubble, and so it seems likely that any cellar may also have been in-filled at some point.

Joseph was probably ahead of his time in his inclusion of billiard rooms. They would not only be suitable for the times when players were off-stage, or awaiting cues or for rehearsals to commence, but also supplied a daytime usage for the building which could offset some of the building's overheads. According to playbills of the time, the theatre had a pit, gallery and boxes.

However, Joseph's response to a letter from R. Galpine of Selby in January, 1830, in which it is suggested that Joseph build a theatre there, is indicative of his business sense; not least the theatre's source of income even when 'dark', and Joseph states that he has been

> *Drawing a plan of a theatre similar to the one at Howden and would have 5 in the Selby, or 10 rather than it should stop for want of them.*
>
> *I have two theatres, my own property erected within the last 3 years at Sleaford and March on the very same plan and scale now sent. I let the Deeping rooms, and Money Taker's room with the one opposite as tenements for £9 per annum-and have the use of them to dress in while the theatre is open beside.*
>
> *At Howden 'tis proposed to make a Billiard Room under the stage…*
>
> *I have no doubt that Mr Paver's recommendation of the thing to the Hon Mrs Peters notice (whose liberality is proverbial) will procure the ground at a mere nominal value-and if so-it will be built for £500.*
>
> *I have no objections to take it when erected on a lease and will allow the subscribers two and a half per cent per annum for my occupation of it, say two months once in two years – or five weeks yearly as may be most desirable to the inhabitants, or convenience to myself and if it does not produce two and a half per cent more during my absence as tenements, Billiard Rooms, and other amusements (not theatrical ones) I will make up the deficiency.*

The idea of raising money by public subscription in order to build theatres, and other buildings, was not uncommon in those days. It was an early form of 'crowdfunding', but Joseph seems here to have taken it further in paying

---

[4] Correspondence held by Mr George Shields

for his shares, thus assuring his lease, and then renting out space in his absence, the income thus taken to be set against his rent.

The exterior of the building is constructed from small blocks of Ancaster stone. At the top of the facade beneath the guttering is a small oeil de boeuf, which would have been the only means of admitting light as there was no other fenestration, and which is one of the few features which can be attributed to the original building with some certainty. The present main entrance door is on the right hand side of the front as one faces it, and has a decorated lintel. The width is 3 feet 11 inches wide and access is gained by climbing two steps of stone, also apparently original. Just inside the door to the right, where at present there is a switch room, there would have been a narrow flight of stairs leading to a corridor along the side of the building leading to the pit.

The total internal length is 60 feet, 6 inches. It is assumed that the theatre would have compared well with other surviving Georgian theatres; Richmond in particular, and probably held up to 350 people.

The theatre in March opened in October of the same year. An item in the *Cambridgeshire Chronicle and Journal* of Friday, 27th October, 1826 reported: (v)[5]

> The new theatre at March, which was opened at the fair a few days since, renders that place and its neighbourhood unusually gay. Mr Smedley, the worthy and indefatigable manager, erected it entirely at his own expense, and the very spirited manner in which it is completed does him infinite credit. Its external appearance is neat and respectable, and the interior is commodiously and elegantly fitted up. The decorations and embellishments are of the first description, having been executed by a London artist, who has also been employed in painting the scenery; thus forming altogether one of the most complete and handsome little theatres in the country, and one which is in all respects worthy the encouragement of the inhabitants of that truly respectable and ever improving town in which it is built. ?In addition to those well known performers, whose

---

[5] Cambridgeshire Chronicle and Journal, Friday 27th October 1826 (British Newspaper Archives)

general good conduct, excellent acting, and great punctuality, have created them the regard and admiration of every one who has the pleasure of knowing them, the manager has produced others from the London & Edinburgh's boards and by this means united whatever can possibly tend to engage the attention & rationally amuse the admirers of the stage.

An advertisement in the same paper announced:

> NEW THEATRE, MARCH
> By desire of the officers and Members of the
> Doddington Loyal Cavalry
> ON MONDAY EVENING, October 30, 1826,
> will be presented an admired Comedy, called
> MAN AND WIFE
> Or, More Secrets than One,
> After which, a Musical Entertainment, called
> THE YOUNG HUSSAR;
> Or, Love and Mercy.
> Boxes 3s.............Pit 2s............Gallery 1s

Joseph now owned his own theatres in addition to those he managed. He enlarged his company which gave him more flexibility in his choice of product. He was becoming well-known and admired, and the reputation of his company was enhanced.

7
Family Matters (1)

As we have seen, Joseph and Melinda Smedley's first child, Melinda Brunton, was born at Boston in 1806.

Their second child, whom they named Jane, was born at Rotherham on 13th March, 1806, and another, named Helen Winner Cooke was born at Holbeach on 5th November, 1807.

It was clearly becoming an accepted occurrence by the Smedleys and also experienced by the Robertson dynasty, that their children were born and baptised in whatever town the company happened to be playing in at the time.

Unfortunately, however, a contemporary newspaper report (of 15th April, 1808) said

> A few days ago a child about 3 years old, Daughter of MR AND MRS SMEDLEY at GRIMSBY was left in the care of a neighbour, WHILST THEY WENT TO PERFORM AT THE THEATRE,…the neighbour left the child alone in the house for a few minutes and on her return found it burnt to death.

However, on April 22nd, the same paper wrote: "We are informed that there is no truth in the statement of one of MR SMEDLEY'S CHILDREN being burned to death at GRIMSBY. The child died of a fever." (Capital letters as used in both reports.)

No explanation is given or known about how a newspaper could have got the facts so egregiously wrong. In any case, one must recognise what such a loss must have meant to the parents, for this was undoubtedly a report about the death of Jane, which occurred on 4th March 1808 in Grimsby.

On 26th December, 1809, Melinda gave birth to another girl while at Hedon, a small town east of Hull, and christened Annette there on 17th January, 1810.

Henry Summersett Smedley was also introduced to the world at Hedon on 4th December, 1811; and then another daughter, again called Jane, was born at Bingham in Nottinghamshire on 28th March, 1814.

Two years later, on 4th March, 1816, at Sleaford, Melinda gave birth to another boy, Joseph; and, also at Sleaford, but on the 17th April, 1818, yet another son named Abraham.

On 4th December, 1821, while at Ely in Cambridgeshire, Melinda gave birth to George, who later styled his middle name as Boleyne.

Joseph and Melinda's final offspring was born at Alford on 25th May, 1823, and christened there on 17th June of that year; she was named Georgiana Pennington Smedley.

It is more than likely that either or both George and Georgiana were named after Joseph's friend George Oliver.

Even ignoring the deaths owing to poor diet, sanitation and low wages, or those during the cholera epidemics later in the century, the incidence of infant and child mortality was still very high in the early nineteenth century, especially in more rural areas, although the onrush of the industrial revolution was to bring similar effects to the major towns and cities. This was one reason for the widespread practice of having large families. The Smedley household was not excluded.

Following the early death of Jane in 1808, Henry Summersett died at Malton on 1st December, 1823, when just shy of his twelfth birthday. The year 1821 was something of an *annus horribilis* for the family. Jane passed away on 22nd July, 1821, at Market Rasen, aged just seven years, and a month later, on August 5th, at Caistor, little Abraham died aged just over three years and three months; both at a time when Melinda was pregnant with George.

The infant mortality rate notwithstanding, such statistics, while known and largely accepted by the populace, do not mitigate the pain or the grief of losing a child. The Smedley family was a close-knit unit. It cannot have been easy to tour rural towns and villages, with a young, ever-growing family; fitting-up, rehearsing, learning lines, making or sourcing costumes and props and distributing advertising material, playbills, and overseeing ticket sales, and corresponding with other venues on the tour, and yet mourn the loss of ones' children at the same time.

As the surviving children grew older, however, they started to attend schools; the girls being educated at Market Deeping, and the boys at Spilsby Grammar School, but they all had experience of touring and had experience of performing; each doing so to his or her strengths, with Helen and Annette becoming mainstays of the company.

The Spilsby Free Grammar School had a long history, having been founded in 1550 by order of King Edward VI, with an endowment from local landowners, the Willoughby d'Eresby family. The School was to be funded and administered by Foundation Governors. There was to be a school building, a master's house and three-and-a-half acres of land from the Royal Estates in Spilsby. It seems the Parsonage became home to both the house and the schoolroom. Another house and a schoolroom were donated in 1611, but there seems to have always been a shortage of money and investment in the school and, by 1716, an appeal had to be made for funds. At about this time it was decided to set up a new school with 126 people subscribing. A new school building was planned in 1732; a building 40 foot by 18 foot. Facing onto Church Street, this three-storey building (reduced to two storeys in 1864) formed the basis of the school buildings as they currently exist.[1]

In 1786, a plot of land to the west of the school was leased for 60 years for the building of a 'substantial 2 storey house' to the west of the schoolroom. In 1818 the Revd Isaac Russell was appointed master, and the school was doing well. Revd Russell was allowed to build a house abutting the schoolroom, and this, together with the school gave accommodation for 100 boys.

---

[1] On-line History of Spilsby School

Richard E. Smedley

An advert in the *Stamford Mercury* of 30th December, 1826 announces:[2]

> SPILSBY SCHOOL, conducted by the Rev. I.
> Russell, will be re-opened after the present
> Recess on TUESDAY, JANUARY 24th, 1826.
> At this establishment young Gentlemen are genteelly
> boarded, and carefully conducted through a regular course
> of English, Mathematical, and Classical Literature.
> *Board per annum:*
> Those under the age of 12 years............20 Guineas
> Those of 12 and upwards............22 Guineas
> Cards may be had, and further particulars known, on
> application to the school. *Spilsby*, Dec. 28th, 1825

From correspondence in the Smedley papers[3], it is plain that Joseph got on very well with Revd Russell, who in turn clearly held Joseph in the highest esteem.

A letter dated August 1st 1828, for example, states:

> Mr Russell has great pleasure in assuring Mr and Mrs Smedley that their son Joseph, since their departure from Spilsby has conducted himself in a manner highly creditable to himself and satisfactory to Mr R and the other members of the family.
> Master Smedley enjoys an uninterrupted state of good health, and is making a gradual improvement in the various branches of his education.[4]

Another letter, dated Spilsby, 18th December 1828, concerns arrangements for Joseph Jnr to travel to March to meet his father:

> Dear Sir
> According to your request your son Joseph is just equipd for his journey to March. He and one of his companions start from Spilsby at 11.00 o'clock

---

[2] Stamford Mercury, Dec. 30th 1825; British Newspaper Archive (RS)

[3] Lincolnshire Archives; LLHS 38/5/3/1

[4] Letters in Lincolnshire Archives; LLHS 38/5/3/1/1

tomorrow morning by Sargeant in a very comfortable covered ?. Both the youngsters prefer this mode of conveyance to the uncertainty of the coach, which has been heavily laden every day during the past week, and they will arrive at Boston nearly as soon as the mail. Sargeant promises to take Master Joseph safe to Mrs Oldfield's house.

Mrs Russell has packed up what clothing will be necessary for him during his visit -.His conduct since you left us has, I assure you, been perfectly exemplary and his improvement quite satisfactory to me.-

I am sure it will be gratifying to Mrs Smedley and yourself to be informed he has indeed been a very good boy. Trusting he will find you all in the enjoyment of a good state of health, I beg, with Mrs Russell's united compliments to Mrs Smedley, yourself and family

To remain, Dear Sir,

Your faithful friend and wellwisher

(Rev) J. Russell

A letter from Russell dated 5th Feb. 1829, reads:

I beg to acknowledge the receipt of £20 safely brought to hand by your son Joseph, who arrived here about 9 o'clock last night by the Boston Carrier. I am happy to find him looking so well, and to see him return so cheerfully to school. I shall be glad to see you on your way to Alford, we have but one bed at liberty, which I beg to offer you (paper damaged) will be any accommodation on your journey either to you or any part of your family. Joseph sends his love. Mrs Russell unites in best wishes to yourself, Mrs Smedley and the young ladies, with Dear Sir.

Your sincere wellwisher, I Russell

Yet another letter from Russell to Joseph of 8th April 1830, ends with this flattering remark: "I believe the whole of your company speak of Mrs Smedley and yourself as if you were their Father and Mother."

However, one letter dated 17th November 1832, was sent to young Joseph, with a second attached sheet for Joseph Snr., and concerns young Joseph's future:

Richard E. Smedley

My dear Joseph,

Master John Hodson called upon me this morning as bearer of a letter from you. I think you are quite right, as you are Turning your mind to the stage, to take an active part as a performer. If you recollect that is what I advised you to do before you left school, and I quite coincide with your father's opinion on the subject…

A letter from Russell dated 21st October, 1834, reports how sorry he is to hear of the illness of Joseph's two daughters, both of whom "seem to have delicate constitutions." He also averred that: "George is very well indeed, and getting quite fat. With respect to his clothes, Mrs Russell thinks with a little mending he will require nothing before Christmas. He had last week a new cap."

A more or less contemporary engraving of the Spilsby School used as a notelet by Joseph Jnr when writing home

The Life and Times of Joseph Smedley

Just to illustrate how much Joseph's family came to help the family business, the following playbill from Sleaford is offered as an example:

THEATRE, SLEAFORD, 15th March, 1824
WILL BE PRESENTED
An entirely new classic, comic, operatic, didactic, moralistic aristophenic, localic, analytic, terphiscoric, panoramic, camera-obscuric, extravaganza-burletta of
FUN, FROLIC, FASHION, AND FLASH
Written by Charles Dibdin, Esq.
TOM AND JERRY
OR
Life in London

Tom	Mr Neville
Jerry	Mr Major
Old Hawthorn	Mr Bell
Logic	Mr Smedley
Nick 'em	Mr Simms
Shuffle	Mr Ditcher
Floss	Mrs Coppin
Snaggs Master	J. Smedley – only seven years of age
Mr Lustre	Mr Richards
Primefit	Mr Coppin
Paddy Byrne	Mr Ditcher
Dusty Bob	Mr Henderson
Sue, Sister to Floss	Miss Simms
Mrs Lustre	Mrs Neville
Miss Lustre	Miss Smedley
Betty Brilliant	Miss A Smedley

Singing by Miss A Smedley
To conclude with a laughable farce, called the
MIDNIGHT HOUR
OR, WAR OF WITS

The above shows not only the seven-year old Joseph treading the boards, but Helen (almost always billed as Miss Smedley) aged 16 and Annette (Miss A. Smedley), who was good at dancing and singing, only 14.

The eldest daughter, Melinda Brunton Smedley, seems to have had little inclination for the stage, and appears on few playbills. Where she does appear, she is listed as Miss Smedley, Helen as Miss H. Smedley and Annette, as usual, as Miss A. Smedley.

Joseph's main overriding concern, however, and a stipulation laid down for his daughters, was that he absolutely forbade any of them to marry an actor!

8
The Robertsons – Again

In 1816, Thomas and the Lincoln Circuit, got into financial difficulties, and, as a result, Thomas was committed to Lincoln Castle (then a prison) for debt. James came to his rescue. (L.S.M. 13-9-1816 and Lincoln Playbill 18-9-1816): "To prevent his brother's unfortunate situation from causing an interruption in the accustomed amusements of the season" he opened the Lincoln Theatre as usual on 18th September, undertaking to "appropriate any profits which may arise from the performances towards the promotion of his Brother's re-establishment in his Theatrical Circuit."

Indeed, many of his friends in all the towns on the Circuit rallied to his help. In Boston on 29th May,[1] a performance of *Venice Preserv'd* was performed – "by permission of the Worshipful the Mayor and the Magistrates" – and raised £86 for his relief, for which he wrote a letter of thanks,[2] dated 31st May, from Lincoln Castle thanking the people of Boston for their help and "a support and favour, Gentlemen, that has converted the hours of imprisonment and distress into those of hope and resignation."

A similar occasion with the same play by an amateur company was mounted in Grantham on 29th June,[3] and, at Peterborough,[4] Robertson and Manly, of the Nottingham, Derby & Stamford Company performed on 10th – 13th July. At Spalding,[5] amateurs performed 'The Rivals' by Sheridan.

---

[1] GH LSM 24-5-1816
[2] GH Lincoln Public Library, 380136
[3] GH LSM 21-6-1816
[4] GH LSM28-6-1816
[5] GH LSM 12-7-1816

At Newark on 14th and 15th August,[6] a "Committee formed for the purpose of promoting his re-establishment in the Circuit after liberation from his present unhappy confinement," while plays were also performed at Wisbech and Huntingdon.

By November, Thomas Robertson was free again.[7] "A Committee of Gentlemen had purchased his travelling theatrical property which they have placed in his hands and appointed him their Manager. He will open the several Theatres at the accustomed seasons."

After this, business appears to have been quite good for a few years, but by 1830 attendances were declining. Also, in the latter part of that year too,[8] "Mr Robertson has for some time been seriously indisposed and unable to attend to his theatrical management."

On 31st August, 1831,[9] Thomas Shaftoe Robertson, Manager of the Lincoln Company, died at Huntingdon, and, a month later, when the Company opened at Lincoln on 25th September[10] "Mrs T. Robertson takes this opportunity of announcing that the Acting Management of the Theatre will in future be conducted by her nephew, Mr W. Robertson." F.C. Wemyss said of him:[11] "Mr Robertson was regarded more like the father of a family than the Director of a Theatre, and were I asked to point out a strict and justly honest man, Mr Thomas Robertson, the Lincoln Manager, would be that man."

Meanwhile, the Nottingham Circuit continued under the guiding management of James Robertson and Manly. In his *Recollections*, published in 1875, Walter Donaldson had quite a lot to say:

---

[6] GH LSM 2-8-1816
[7] GH LSM 1-11-1816
[8] GH LSM 1-12-1830
[9] GH LSM 2-9-1831
[10] Lincoln Playbill
[11] GH "Theatre Unroyal", L Warwick, Lincoln Public Library

The fate of actors, like statesmen, depends on those in power; but when the tide turns, and a reverse comes, then a new scene of action is necessary; and this scene I found in the neat and compact town of Stamford, under the direction of Manly and Robertson. 'Hamlet' was performed on the opening night, in which his majesty of Denmark, Claudius, was sustained by the writer of these Recollections; while the Prince was represented by a young gentleman, Thomas Serle, since well known in the literary world; and the Queen by Mrs. Sheppard, aunt of Helen Faucit.

Robertson the manager could write a comic song, paint a scene, dance a hornpipe, and do the low comedy. In the latter department he was a prodigious favourite in the Nottingham circuit. This I ascribe to long standing. I have known many comic actors great favourites, having no claim to distinction beyond that of being several years before the public. Robertson's conception of such characters as Acres and Tony Lumkin was decidedly wrong. However, on the whole, I consider he was an actor of utility, and might be called a rough diamond. He was the author of a song, 'Beggars and Ballad-Singers' that became popular in London, Dublin, and in every part of the three kingdoms.

In 1818,[12] James decided to retire and live in Nottingham, returning thanks for 30 years of patronage by the public. A Retford playbill of 3rd November (the opening night there) stated that: "The public are informed that the Property and Interest of Mr Robertson in this Theatre have been by purchase transferred to Mr Manly". Mr Manly, then a member of the Company, had taken over Mr Wrench's interest in 1807.

Upon retirement, , Robertson opened a shop in Nottingham, where he sold all sorts of articles, and placed over his door the following legend in large letters, 'Every thing made here except a fortune'.[13]

Two years later, on 11th November, 1820,[14] was given, at Retford, "Mr Robertson's Farewell Benefit, Mr Manly having favoured him with an opportunity of taking a public leave of his Friends". After the play – *The Battle of Hexham* by George Coleman the Younger, came "A View of Wilford

---

[12] GH NJ 25-7-1818

[13] Recollections of an Actor, Walter Donaldson

[14] Retford Playbill, Retford Public Library

Coffee-House near Nottingham, Boat House, The Ferry Boat Crossing with passengers &C introduced by a new Rum ti iddi iddi Comic Song entitled 'I that once was an Actor a Tradesman have been'."

On 1st January, 1831 the following was reported:[15]

> Died, at his house in Bridge Street, London Road, in the 62nd year of his age, James Robertson, Gentleman, being known and highly respected as a Comedian in the Nottingham, Derby and Stamford Company, of which he was joint Manager for nearly 20 years. He was a native of York, and brother to Mr Thomas Robertson, Manager of the Newark and Grantham Company.
>
> As a performer, he will be long remembered in this neighbourhood, the peculiar cast of his countenance and the formation of his person, combined with the regular bent of his disposition, never failed to give the lovers of fun the most ample opportunities of satisfying their laughing propensities. In private life, he had the esteem of all those individuals to whom he was in any way known, and …small indeed was the number of respectable persons in this town to whom the mirth-loving Jemmy Robertson was unknown
>
> Early in life, he entered the Company of which he afterwards had the joint command, then under the care of Mr Pero, and married Miss Elizabeth Robinson, of the same company, the eldest daughter of the present Mrs Wrench and sister of Mrs Manly. This lady died in 1806, leaving him with a family of six children, two sons and four daughters. The two former, Henry and William, are following, with great promise, their father's profession.

Soon afterwards[16] there was a sale of his many effects, by auction, by J. Hayes, on the 18th and 19th January, on the premises near Leen Bridge, Nottingham, part of the "Household Furniture of the late James Robinson, Comedian, and his original sketches, Drawings, Prints, Books of Songs, Scenery of Goose Fair, a Camera Obscura, a Camera Lucida, theatrical dresses, Printing Press, Types, Tools &C" (N.N.M. 15-1-31)

Thus the two brothers exited life's stage.

---

[15] Nottingham & Newark Mercury, 8-1-1831
[16] GH NNM 15-1-1831

Mr Manly continued to run the Nottingham Circuit on his own account, and who made it a rule never to engage married or old people. According to Walter Donaldson[17]

> this was politic; as the walking in this circuit (I kept an account of it) in one year amounted to 500 miles. Coaching in those days was no trifling matter, and salaries being on the lowest scale, actors were obliged to walk. There was one aged man in the company, Earle, and he had been a member forty four years. He was originally a barber, and cut the hair for the 'stage', thinking it was more aristocratic. By great parsimony, he saved a sum of money, which he deposited in a banker's hands in Stamford. The Peace came, and the banker broke, and Earle's savings were lost; yet still he kept up his spirits, and walked his journeys; but this task he executed alone, as company was likely to drift into expense: all actors, he well knew, in their journeys through life, lived well on the road.
>
> Certainly the means afforded by the manager did not allow of much indulgence either in eating or drinking. The salaries were £1-1s weekly, and for this miserable stipend the actor had to find boots, shoes, buckles, silk stockings, hats, feathers, swords, canes, wigs, modern dress, long hose, gloves, military costume; and those that unfortunately possessed vocal ability, were obliged to furnish the part of their songs for the orchestra; and all these articles out of a guinea a week!

Donaldson continued, and after other reminiscences, he returned to the subject of Mr Manly:

> Manly, well knowing his drawbacks for a London audience, wisely determined to remain in his own charming money-getting circuit, where he contrived to fill his <u>own</u> purse, quite regardless of those who laboured in his vineyard. Yet with all his screwing propensities, he had good qualities. He paid what he agreed for; he instructed the young actor in his profession, and where there was any dawning of genius, he encouraged it. No man on the stage understood the mysteries of the art better than Thomas Wilson Manly. That he was a dramatic despot, there is no denying, and a terror to those novices whom agents sent to fill the positions of experienced actors-his <u>hard bargains</u>, as he called them. Although a splendid actor himself, he studiously kept his children from the stage. One he articled to a lawyer, and another to a doctor. His daughters he

---

[17] Recollections of an Actor

trained for first-class governesses. And well knowing the estimation the dramatic profession is <u>unjustly</u> held in by a section of society not celebrated for sense, judgement, or liberality, he determined his offspring should steer clear down the stream of life unruffled by the quicksands of bigotry and malice and all uncharitableness.

Nottingham playbills of 14th October, 1833, and in 1837 show that Mr Manly was granting an Annual Benefit to James Robertson's widow at least until the latter date, and these are believed to have continued until 1840, when Mr Manly retired from the management of the Nottingham & Derby Company.

Interestingly, the theatre in Retford was originally owned by a Thomas Gauntley of Tuxford (a small market town between Newark and Retford). He leased the theatre to William Pero in 1807 for £100, who then leased it to Robertson and Manly. However, on the theatre's deeds, and repeated on an indenture of 1922, it states:

"Between James Robertson of the Town and County of Nottingham one of the Managers (along with Thomas Hill Manly Wilson hereinafter named) of a Company of Comedians occasionally residing at East Retford…"[18]

This casts doubt on Mr Manly's actual name, although it is likely that the deeds were in error. In Miller's list of theatres and managers published in 1833 his name is given as Manley.

William Robertson

The second surviving son of James and Elizabeth Robertson, William was born around 1798 and probably in one of the circuit towns of Nottingham, Derby and Stamford Company. He made a number of early appearances on the stage:

---

[18] Deeds of the Retford Theatre, Bassetlaw Museum, Retford

19-10-1805 at Retford[19]	as a child in *The Soldier's Daughter*
22-10-1805 at Retford	as Little Bob in La Fille Malgarde
11-6-1806 at Nottingham[20]	By Desire, Master W Robertson in *Giles Scroggins' Ghost*
23-6-1806 at Nottingham[21]	Hornpipe by Master W. Robertson
1-11-1806 at Retfordas	Julio di Rosari in Hunter of the Alps
4-11-1806 at Retford	as a Cupid in *Rugantino*
9-12-1806 at Retford	*Giles Scroggins' Ghost* by Master W Robertson
13-12-1806 at Retfordas	Dickey in *Five Miles Off*, also as Attendant Spirit in *Arthur and Emmeline*
13-11-1807 at Retfordas	Young Mortimer in *Laugh When you Can*
24-11-1807 at Retfordas	Tom Thumb in *Tom Thumb the Great*

After the 1807 season, William disappears from the stage as was usually the case with the Robertson children who perhaps went to school until the age of 13 or 14. Later, he was articled to Mr Whitson, a Solicitor in Derby,[22] but in 1825 left that profession to become an actor in his Uncle Thomas' Lincoln Company. His first appearance at Lincoln[23] was on 28th September 1825, but it is possible he joined the company somewhat earlier, at one of the circuit towns.

In the cast at Lincoln at the same time was Elisabeth Margaretta Marinus, a German girl from the Theatre Royal, Brighton, then about 24 years old. They appeared regularly in playbills and advertisements until early in 1828, then, on 24th September, 1828,[24] at Lincoln, they are billed as 'Mr W. Robertson and Mrs W. Robertson' in the cast of *The Goldsmith*.

In the following January, at Newark,[25] the baptism was recorded of Thomas William, son of William (Comedian) and Elizabeth Robertson, the boy

---

[19] GHRetford Playbill

[20] GH Nottingham Journal; 7-6-1806

[21] GH NJ 21-6-1806

[22] GH Dictionary of Nat. Biog. Thomas William Shaftoe Robertson

[23] GH Lincoln Playbill

[24] GH Lincoln Playbill

[25] GH Newark Parish Church Register

having been born on the 9th. This first of a very large family, became the future playwright. A daughter, Fanny, was born in 1830, apparently in Cleethorpes.[26]

Two more sons were born at Newark[27]: "James, son of William (Comedian) & Eliza Robertson b'tised 9/12/31" and "John Shaftoe, son of William (Player) & Eliz. Robn. Bapt. 8/12/32."

Other children included Elizabeth, Henry Ashton, (who became a captain in the Army), Georgina, Edward Shaftoe (b. 1844), Frederick Crewe (or Craven) (b. 1846), and Madge (b. 18th March, 1849) at Cleethorpes. All of them except Henry Ashton went on the stage, and Madge became famous. During this period, it is interesting to look at the type of entertainment on offer at the Lincoln Theatre under the Robertsons' management, with an eye for comparison on those performed by Joseph Smedley's company:[28]

4th Oct. 1812	*Speed the Plough*
	No Song, No Supper
	The Favorite Duetto of 'Vive Le Roi'
	By Mr Collier and Mrs Brooke
	The Comic Song of 'The Gallimaufry'
	By Mr Cowell
9th Oct 1812:	*Venice Preserved*
	Is He a Prince
26th Oct 1812	*Merchant of Venice*
	Valentine and Orson, or, The Wild Man of the Woods
16th Nov. 1812	*The Rivals*
	Jew and the Doctor
20th Nov. 1816	For the Benefit of Mrs T Robertson
	The Ethiop, or, The Child of the Desert
	Plus *The Sleep Walker; or Which is the Lady?*
13th Sept. 1820 (1st Race Day)	
	The Antiquary

---

[26] GH Lincoln Public Library, UP1911
[27] GH Newark Church Parish Register
[28] All taken from Lincoln Theatre Playbills, now held by Lincolnshire Archives. RS

	A Rowland for an Oliver
	Stage boxes 5s, Lower and Upper Boxes 4s, Pit 2s-6d,
	Half-price 1s-6d,
	Gallery 1s-6d, Half Price 1s
14th Sept. 1820:	
	Hamlet
	Comic Song 'The Humours of Lincoln Races'
	By Mr Rayner
	A Comic Song by Mr Hallam
	The Rendezvous, or, Fright upon Fright
16th Sept. 1820	
	The Rivals
	X Y Z, or, How to Get a Wife
22nd Sept 1822:	
	Tom and Jerry, or, Life in London

For some time it had been the practice for leading actors to tour the provinces, particularly when the Theatres Royal at Drury Lane and Covent Garden had ended their seasons. However, thus far this practice does not seem to have reached Lincoln, until, in 1824, the following announcement was made, and for the first time at Lincoln, a big, or bankable, name was brought in for a week to headline, using the resident company and its manager as a stock company able to support the star from Drury Lane:

MR KEAN

Mr Robertson feels very much pleasure
in announcing to the City and Vicinity
of Lincoln, and the Public in General
that he has entered into an Engagement
with DISTINGUISHED ACTOR,for the performance
of <u>six</u> of his principal characters.
On Monday, April 26th 1824
RICHARD III
SHYLOCK in The Merchant of Venice
Portia – Mrs T. Robertson
OTHELLO
Desdemona – Mrs T. Robertson

Richard E. Smedley

HAMLET
SIR EDWARD MORTIMER in The Iron Chest
SIR GILES OVERREACH in A New Way to Pay Old Debts

The following report appeared in the *Stamford Mercury*:

"We are happy to find that Mr Kean's theatrical visit to Lincoln has proved satisfactory to all parties. The theatre was occupied every night by a numerous and admiring audience; and not withstanding the very heavy expense incurred, we trust that the pecuniary results have not been such as to discourage our worthy manager from offering a similar gratification at any future opportunity.[29]

It is true to say that Kean, by now, was passed his best. He had led a dissolute life and it was starting to take its toll.[30] He no longer had the reserves of strength, and his voice was suspect. He was still at the head of his profession, having seen off such pretenders as Booth and, only the previous year, that of Charles Mayne Young who had been brought from Covent Garden to Drury Lane to act opposite Kean in plays with equally important roles, such as Othello, Cymbeline, and in *Venice Preserved*. This was a ploy by Elliston to foster partisan support among the theatregoers and so increase ticket sales. Elliston's next plan was to bring in another actor who had garnered such favourable reviews at Covent Garden that he had been numbered as second only to Kean. The season at Drury Lane commenced on 18th November, 1823 with William Charles Macready as *Caius Gracchus*, a new play by Sheridan Knowles. This time Kean fled, producing a medical report claiming that he was seriously ill as a means, no doubt, of ducking the contest, and had gone to his retreat on the Scottish Isle of Bute.

By the time he had decided to return to London, Macready announced he was taking a three-month leave of absence to tour the provinces, whereupon Kean reappeared at Drury Lane. It was, perhaps, another clever business ploy, this time by Robertson to have the two greatest tragedians of the age,

---

[29] Stamford Mercury, Fri. 7th May 1824; British Newspaper Archives (RS)
[30] "Kean" by Giles Playfair

appear on the Lincoln stage, albeit nineteen months apart, to allow their audiences to compare them, as announced thus in 1825:

> November 16th, 17th & 18th 1825
> MR MACREADY
> In
> Macbeth
> A Comic Song by Mr Chippendale
> Deaf as a Post

The Robertsons evidently believed that star names would boost ticket sales, and that Lincoln was big enough to support the import of such high profile performers. Certainly it was a bold move to help counter the gradual decline in attendances.

Macready's memoirs noted: "With the end of September I began engagements that carried me to Southampton, Liverpool, Nottingham, Shrewsbury, Chester, Sheffield, Leicester, Lincoln, Newark, and Edinburgh"[31]

He also played Lincoln in 1834:

> Lincoln, November 20th – *Virginius*
> November 21st – *Stranger*
> November 23rd – "At 10, Mr Robertson called, and, having paid my Bill and posted my letters, I got a sight of the gorgeous front of the cathedral and the Heaven's Gate as I passed down to the river............We walked six miles, sometimes turning to look upon the regally-sited cathedral, which alone is worth a visit to this city, and constantly enjoying the freshness of the brisk cool air, the beauty of the morning, and our exhilarating exercise. On getting into the boat, which we did by a small one let out from a windlass, I reconnoitred the cabin and, finding it too close for me, got a seat to leeward and proceeded with 'Eugene Aram;' I read till the light would serve me no longer, and, after paying 3s for my passage, was conducted from the boat by Mr Robertson to my inn at Boston.

---

[31] Macready's Reminiscences (RS)

Macready went on to describe his performance which was conveyed to "the most chilling aspect of a house I almost ever saw" and a couple of days later was informed by Mr Robertson that there were only five in the audience there. While in Boston, Macready went to St. Paul's Church to look upon the spot "where the remains of my beloved mother lie."

Macready was to play Lincoln again in June 1836.

Both Kean and Macready had learned their craft by travelling around the Country, town to town, company to company, before they became famous, but giving these performances enabled them to play before different, although arguably less sophisticated, and less critical, audiences. Neither were they always plentiful, as we've seen.

It is perhaps worth mentioning yet another Robertson who had her beginnings on the stage:

Georgina Robertson

The eldest child of James and Elizabeth Robertson, she was born about 1792/3, probably at one of the towns on the Nottingham, Derby and Stamford Company.

Her first appearances on stage were at Retford, and she became a regular member of the Company as a dancer and singer during the interludes, sometimes teamed in the dances with the Lassells family or with brother William.[32] On 8th November that year she was given a benefit jointly with Miss Chapman.

She continued to appear as an actress and dancer until 1812, but does not appear on any playbills for 1813. An ad in 1814[33] announced "Miss Robertson respectfully informs the Ladies of Nottingham and its vicinity that it is her intention to reside there after the Christmas vacation, for the

---

[32] Retford Playbill (29-11-1806)
[33] GH (NJ 24-12-1814)

instruction of Young ladies on the Pianoforte." Applications were to be sent to an address in Halifax where it seems likely she had been teaching in 1814, but thereafter taught music in Nottingham.

* * *

William Robertson continued to run the Lincoln Theatre with fluctuating fortunes, and appears to have made visits to theatres outside the usual circuit.

In 1844[34] "Mr William Robertson, proprietor of the Lincoln Theatre" gave £16-8s-0d, the proceeds of one night's performance at Sheffield, to the Widows' and Orphans' Fund of the Oddfellows there and in July of the same Year, advertised performances at Stamford –normally on the Nottingham and Derby Circuit.

By 1847, the end of the Lincoln Company was in sight, the financial position being grim, in spite of which, in March of that year,[35] William offered "to donate the whole proceeds of the performance on the 15th to the benefit of the Widows' and Orphan' Fund connected with the Manchester Unity of Oddfellows." This was the last performance of the Lincoln season.

> The Receipts amounted to about £6,[36] and we are informed that the whole was handed over without any deduction for expenses. Through the entire season, the theatre has week after week been a losing affair: there is therefore much practical Christianity in the closing act of the season----One who is ready to extend help in quarters where it is so much needed is entitled to much better public support than he has this season experienced in Lincoln.

Mr Robertson's Company continued in 1847 at Stamford, then back to Lincoln, then at Peterborough and Spalding, but that seems to have been the end; the Lincoln theatre and its circuit collapsed. The theatre was taken over by a Mr Caple who re-fitted it completely.

---

[34] GH LSM 8-3-1844
[35] GH LSM 12-3-1847
[36] GH LSM 19-3-1847

By September, 1848, William Robertson was in a Company managed by Mr Haslewood, 'formerly of the Lincoln and Newark Company' with which he appeared at Lincoln and Newark.[37] He must have been at Cleethorpes in March, 1849, perhaps still with Mr Haslewood, when Madge was born. Later, he was in London, where, in about 1855,[38] he was part-manager with J H Wallace, of the Marylebone Theatre. He died in 1872.

For the sake of completeness, and because he is referred to on occasional Playbills and elsewhere; (see Chapter Six – 1922 advertisement), just a note about:

Frederick Fowler Robertson

Frederick was the son of George Robertson, who in turn was the youngest son of James Shaftoe and Ann Robertson. George was born around 1772, married a lady called Frances, and later opened a printing and stationery shop. Apart from printing a collection of comic songs for his elder brother James, there is no further mention of him, and it is assumed that he lived and died in Peterborough.

Frederick Fowler Robertson was their son, born in around 1798, and who joined the Lincoln Company, appearing on 15th September, 1820[39] as Claudio in *Much Ado about Nothing*, and again in various parts in 1822 and 1823. However, in February of 1824, he attained notoriety:

> Elopement and Happy Union[40] – About a quarter past eleven on Sunday night last, Mr Frederick Robertson, (son of Mr R. of Peterboro' and nephew to Mr Robertson, manager of the Lincoln company of comedians,) and Miss Tindal, only child and heiress of Joseph Tindal, Esq. Of Green-hill, Grantham, started from the latter place on a trip to Gretna Green. The young lady took a lover's leap

---

[37] GH

[38] GH – Savin, Thomas William Robertson

[39] Lincoln Playbills

[40] Stamford Mercury, 6th Feb, 1824 and Bury and Norwich Post of 11th Feb 1824. (British Newspaper Archive) RS

> out of the window of her father's house, into the arms of her swain; a carriage was in waiting, and away they drove, to consummate an ardent attachment of seven years' standing. The lady was not missed until the breakfast hour on Monday: at about ten o'clock, her father, accompanied by a gentleman who is said to wear the willow, set off in a chaise and four in pursuit; but as the young couple had ten hours and a half's start, they arrived uninterruptedly at the temple of Hymen beyond the borders, and were united indissolubly at two o'clock on Tuesday morning. The happy pair were expected back at Grantham yesterday, to receive the congratulations of their numerous friends, and the acknowledgement and benediction of the bride's forgiving and wealthy father.

The sequel came on the following Sunday when: "On Sunday morning was re-married at Grantham, (by the Rev. W. Potchett,) Mr F. Robertson, to Ann only daughter of Josh. Tindale, Esq., whose union at Gretna Green we noticed in our last paper."[41]

Frederick prospered, although not in theatre, for on 1st October, 1846,[42]:

> at a General Meeting of shareholders of the Ambergate, Nottingham & Boston & Eastern Junction Railway, "Frederick Fowler Robertson, Esq.,of Grantham" was re-elected as a Director of the Company, while he was present[43] in that capacity, on 21st June, 1847, at the ceremonial laying of the first brick in Gonerby Tunnel N.W. of Grantham".

---

[41] Stamford Mercury, 13th Feb. 1824 (RS)
[42] British Transport Historical Records (GH)
[43] LSM 25th June, 1847. (GH)

9
The Smedleys – Later Stages

The 1830s saw an increase in stage adaptations of the works of Dickens, and, in particular, of the books of Walter Scott, especially after his death in 1832, when Scottish subjects generally seemed to find favour. Throughout the country there were adaptations of *Macbeth*, *The Heart of Midlothian*, *Rob Roy*, *The Bride of Lammermoor*, *Ivanhoe* and *Guy Mannering*.

On 19th March, 1830, Joseph announced that he was, in a sense, joining the league of the major theatre managers. Firstly, he did so by engaging a 'big name' artist to appear at one of his theatres. It was a fairly recent development to have star billing, i.e. to have the name of an actor's name given more prominence than any other, which, in the opinion of a typefounder, Dr Edmund Fry, in 1828: "a rude, pernicious, and most unclassical innovating system was commenced which in a short time was followed by the most injurious and desolating ravages on the property of every Letter Founder and Printer in the Kingdom by the introduction of Fancy letters of various anomalous forms, with names as appropriate..."[1], and secondly by paying lip-service to the then current craze for lionising young (child) actors, by making the following announcement:[2]

Theatre, Sleaford
By Desire and under the Patronage of the Hon. Mrs. Handley
ON FRIDAY Evening, March 19th, 1830,
CHARLES THE TWELFTH,
DEAF AS A POST,
And other Entertainments
MR SMEDLEY has the gratification of announcing

---

[1] Quoted by Iain Mackintosh in 'The Georgian Playhouse'; 1975
[2] Stamford Mercury, 19th March, 1830; British Newspaper Archive. (RS)

> to his patrons and friends, that he has succeeded in
> forming an engagement, for TWO Nights only, with
> Master BURKE, who has so delighted and astonished
> the crowded audiences of the Metropolitan and Pro-
> vincial Theatres, as to have justly acquired the title
> of "The Prodigy of the Age!"
> On SATURDAY the 20th, Master B. Will appear in
> The Character of NORVAL, in the Tragedy of Douglas;
> And TERRY O'ROURKE, in the Irish Tutor
> Between the Play and Farce, master B. will lead
> the Orchestra in the Overture to Guy Mannering.
> And on MONDAY the 22d, MASTER B.'s last night,
> *The March of Intellect, with other Entertainments.*

This very much fed the vogue of the time for exalting young actors, many of whom were still children, as being prodigies, albeit capable of giving performances of depth; but usually copied in the manner and style of another actor. This, according to Iain Mackintosh,[3] was due to "the impassioned but brief worship of youth and beauty that enveloped Britain during the Napoleonic Wars." It was initiated to a degree by Master William Henry West Betty, a boy from Northern Ireland who had begun his theatrical training in 1803 under William Hough and, after a successful season in Dublin, he burst upon the theatre-going public, as 'The Young Roscius' at Covent Garden, having been given this sobriquet by Hough and Betty's father to invoke the spirit of Garrick, who had also been known thus. Again to quote Iain Mackintosh, "this fatuous connection with the idol of the eighteenth century may have been the masterstroke that was needed to make Betty the paragon he became, juvenile performers being a feature of eighteenth century entertainment though the practice increased after Master Betty's success."

Betty was brought to Covent Garden by John Philip Kemble and his sister, Mrs Siddons, in 1804; shortly after they crossed over from Drury Lane in protest at the policies of Sheridan. Betty was thirteen years old, and became enormously popular, even eclipsing Mrs Siddons, and appeared at Drury

---

[3] Guide to the Exhibition on Georgian Theatre, Hayward Gallery, 1975, devised by him.

Lane nine days later. Apparently, when he appeared as Hamlet Parliament was adjourned, following a motion by Pitt the Younger, so that the members might attend the performance[4]. He was not universally admired, however. Thomas Campbell wrote:[5]

> The popularity of that baby-faced boy, who possessed not even the elements of a good actor, was an hallucination in the public mind, and a disgrace to our theatrical history. It enabled managers to give him sums for his childish ranting that were never accorded to the acting of a Garrick or a Siddons.

On the other hand, Samuel Rogers wrote:

> While young Betty was in all his glory, I went with Fox and Mrs Fox, after dining with them in Arlington Street, to see him act Hamlet; and during the play-scene, Fox, to my infinite surprise, said, "This is finer than Garrick."

As an adult, Betty had no success at all, made several attempted comebacks, unsuccessfully, and lived on into his eighties in complete obscurity. His son, Henry Betty, also attempted an acting career, presumably trading on his father's name, and appeared at Nottingham Theatre on 17th October, 1838 in *Tancred and Sigismunda*. He, too, did not impress. There had also been a 'Female Roscius'" billed as Miss Mudie, who, at the age of five years old had been hissed in a production of *The Country Girl*. She played at the Nottingham Theatre in 1805 as the Young Norval in a production of *Douglas*.

Master Burke was another such prodigy who energised theatregoers; but in his case, a musical one; and like Betty, he too was Irish. With Clara Fisher, he was one of the most "extraordinary musical children" of that time, and among the most celebrated. He was a violin player of great brilliance and precision. Whereas some of the younger actors' talents could be accounted for by precocity, in the instance of Master Burke some genuine signs of talent and artistry must have been present. He made his debut at Cork when aged just five years. At the age of twelve he made his first appearance in New York. He played Richard III and Shylock, and "led the orchestra in operatic overtures,

---

[4] The Theatre, A Concise History, by Phyllis Hartnoll, Revised Edition 1985
[5] Representative Actors, W. Clark Russell, 1883

played violin solos and sang his own songs."⁶ He was a good enough violinist to play at concerts with Jenny Lind and Thalberg.⁷ One writer said:

> His acting was extraordinary; for though a child may be taught to mouth out Young Norval or Cato's soliloquy with effect, it requires an extraordinary aptitude and quickness to enable him to play such a part as the Irish Tutor. This Master Burke did in a highly amusing style, to which a rich native brogue contributed not a little. Children are imitative beings, and almost by nature mimics; but the ease, the vivacity, and the correctness of Master Burke betoken a dramatic instinct which can scarcely be mistaken.⁸

Also on tour in England at this time was another 'Roscius'. This time however not a youthful pretender, but the adult 'African Roscius': F.W. Keene Aldridge, aka Ira Aldridge.

The title of 'Roscius' was a reference to Quintus Roscius Gallus, the most famous Roman actor, a slave who taught Cicero how to speak in public. He was born in around 126 BC and died in 62 BC, and was equally good in comedy and tragedy. The name became a traditional compliment in the English-speaking theatre; Richard Burbage, the sixteenth century actor of Shakespeare's plays, was known as 'England's Great Roscius'.⁹ It was therefore somewhat ironic that Aldridge, descended from West African slaves, should wear the mantle of an actor who was also a slave.

Ira Frederick Aldridge was born in New York on 24th July 1807 to free Blacks, i.e. not slaves but forced to undertake labouring work. Much of his early life is buried in confusion, with different authors giving different accounts, not helped by an early autobiography by Aldridge in which he claimed to be descended from Princes of the Koula Tribe of Senegal, which may or may not be true but followed him around as part of his legend and appeared on his playbill:

---

⁶ Bernard Grebanier; Then Came Each Actor, 1975

⁷ do

⁸ Representative Actors

⁹ Ira Aldridge by Martin Hoyles, 2008

> The ancestors of the African Roscius, down to the Grandfather of the Subject of this memoir, were Princes of the Koula Tribe, whose dominions were Senegal, on the Banks of the River Gambia. The Father of the present individual was sent for his education to Schnectady College, near New York, in the United States. Three days after his departure from his native shore, an insurrection broke out among the Tribe, and the King, the Grandfather of the African Roscius, fell a victim to his mutinous subjects. Deprived of the means of asserting his birthright, and to certain degree cast on the World a cosmopolite, his Father became a Minister of the Presbyterian persuasion, and now officiates in the Zion Church in New York. The subject of this memoir, born 24th July, 1807, was destined for the same profession but prefering (sic) the Sock and Buskin, he departed from his Father's roof wending his way to the shores of Britain. (Copied from the *New York Courier*)

Aldridge certainly found an early interest in theatre on the other side of the Atlantic, though unable to attend most of them because of his colour, but he did become involved in amateur dramatics. Having decided on his career, and reckoning on a better future in England, he set sail for England in 1824, aged seventeen, working his passage as a ship's steward.

By May 1825, he performed as Othello at the Royalty Theatre in London's East End, and later played several other roles there including Gambia in *The Slave* In the October of that year he moved to a larger theatre, the Royal Coburg in south London (now the Old Vic). The month before, he had met Margaret Gill, who hailed from Northallerton in Yorkshire, and was the daughter of a stocking weaver. They were married on 27th November in Bloomsbury, London, a mixed-race marriage which would not have endeared him to the racist elements of London society. He started to receive favourable reviews, although in 1826 he had to appeal for financial help while in Exeter. Nevertheless, in that year his portrait was painted by James Northcote, a member of the Royal Academy, and a former pupil of Joshua Reynolds. In February 1827, he appeared in six plays in Manchester, including *Othello*, and in that year received recognition from the Government of the Republic of Haiti, who honoured "the first man of colour in the theatre" with a commission in the army.[10] His stay in Manchester was part of his first tour

---

[10] Do.

of England, which also included Sheffield, Halifax, Newcastle, Edinburgh, Lancaster, Liverpool and Sunderland.

It is quite possible that Aldridge played at one of Joseph's theatres in 1830, but it cannot be proved either way. Certainly Aldridge continued to act in the provinces at that time, and, amongst Joseph's papers is a cutting he saved of Ira's Farewell Address.[11] For interest, and for the sake of completeness, I am including it here:

The
AFRICAN ROSCIUS
FAREWELL ADDRESS
Delivered by him on the night of his Benefit,
Wednesday, December 1st, 1830

Son of the land whose swarthy race, late knows
For nought but bloodshed and the murdering groan,
Mark'd by the god of havoc and of strife,
To raise the war whoop, wield the murderous knife;
To roam unfetter'd void of reason's light,
Lone tribe of mankind in chaotic night.
Borne on the billows of the trackless sea,
From genial climes came learning's purity,
Bright as the sunflake bursting from the deep-
Severing the bonds of nature wrapt in sleep-
Shone the mild beams, to illuminate the mind
Of him, the Savage, still of human kind;
To mould the soul to Nature's hallow'd sway.
To drive the clouds of darkness far away;
T'array in robes of friendship pure and bright
The fellow brotherhood of Day and Night.
Link'd with the sister arts the Drama's pile
Its beauteous structure tower'd within our isle!
And though exotic was each lovely flower,
Yet still they bloomed through the night and noontide hour

---

[11] Property of Roy Sumners.

'Twas wandering in those bowers of classic bloom,
The Drama's radiance did my heart illume.
Enraptur'd from the hallow'd bower I seiz'd
A blossom that my youthful fancy pleased:
And wonderful to tell, I straight became
A wand'ring son fir'd with ambitions flame.
Though Nature to my aspect has denied
The rose and lily which in you are allied.
"Child of the Sun" with brow of ebon hue,
I stand before you, but with soul as true.
Cheer'd by the zephyrs on the wings of fame,
I to your shores a lonesome wanderer came;
I sought your kindness, and with heart sincere,
I tender to you gratitude's warm tear.
For in this favour'd land where'er I roam
To me has ever op'd the stranger's home.
From you I've caught the warm and kindly ray,
That cheer'd me onward in this world's lone way.
When to my native shores I do return,
On my heart's fame shall your kindness burn.
O'er my lone grove perhaps in desert spot,
Shall wave the lotus and "forget you not!"
More could I say but what would it avail?
To you I've told my true and heartfelt tale.
The moment's come, and sever'd is the spell—
England's kind Children, a long, a last FAREWELL!

We do know that Joseph's daughter Helen had seen him, and was evidently smitten. Perhaps she had even heard his farewell address, for she took up the pen too as she wrote the following account in 1831 while at Southwell, then aged twenty four:[12]

O age whose hearts reject with scorn the child
Of "fiery April" and have deem'd his wild
And untaught mind as all too base

---

[12] Smedley papers; Lincolnshire Archives, LLHS 38/5/8/2

> *To feel the nobler passions of our race –*
> *Behold in Roscius nature sure is freed*
> *From the vile stream of their degrading creed:*
> *They would not deem a soul like thine was form'd*
> *Ne'er by one generous impulse to be warmed*
> *Bertram, from thee doth interest new create*
> *By the stern grandeur of his "mortal hate" –*
> *And in Othello faithfully we see*
> *Depicted all his burning jealousy –*
> *Can we forget the agony intense*
> *Of thy Alambra as in dread suspense*
> *He kneels for life imploring! Or the joy*
> *That in a moment made the negro boy*
> *A changed creature – full of playful glee,*
> *And the no thought remain'd of misery –*
> *Who then shall paint thy Gambia, jealous, kind,*
> *The very being of the poet's mind;*
> *Whose noble sentiments with added force*
> *Come from thy lips, who (such is still the course*
> *Of a base nation's traffic) hadn't thou not*
> *Been early call'd to file a better lot*
> *Some ruffian band might now have made e'en thee*
> *Heart broken mourn for "blessed liberty" –*
> *O may each Briton in thy Gambia hear*
> *A pleading voice for Africa's fate severe!*
> *Ans whilst we all thy wondrous talent own*
> *And listen to thy deep heart-thrilling tone,*
> *O may thy tongue indeed prophetic be*
> *And England loose the chain of slavery,*
> *That long hath bound the negro's energy,*
> *Then shall his mind be like his body – Free!*
>   – Southwell, 1831

This is of interest because it shows that Helen had seen Aldridge act, knew of his various roles, and also wrote with the eye of an actress. She is clearly aware also, of Aldridge's interest in, and support for, the anti-slavery movement. A more professional or experienced view was expressed in a memoir by

Richard E. Smedley

a John Cole, who published his critique of Ira Aldridge's Othello in a limited edition of thirty copies:

A Critique on the Performance of Othello
By
F W Keene Aldridge
The African Roscius

On Friday evening we were called upon to witness a perfect novelty in the department of theatricals, for such may be considered the acting of a man of colour, whether good or otherwise, but the African Roscius is certainly an actor of genius. His complexion is deeply tinctured with Africa's ray of shade; his figure is tall, manly, and muscular; and he is in the very vigour of manhood, being only in his 25th year. His pronunciation of the English Language is as perfectly correct as that of a native, and his voice possesses great power, with intonations of an intuitive order, and which genius only can display: indeed it is our opinion, that for every variety of intonation and inflection of the voice, , there cannot be rules given, for the orator of true genius can throw out from the feelings of the soul such refrangibility of reflection (if we may be allowed to use these optical allusions) as beggars the rule of art . The tragedy selected for performance on Friday evening was Shakespeare's Othello: the hero by the African Roscius. Novel, imposing,, and sublimae was the first sight of the Moor, personated as he was by the sable African. So effective was the commencement before a word was spoken. The intonations of deep and sweet melody were however, soon added to the grandeur of his personal appearance, and every trait of the noble minded and generous Moor was afterward presented in appropriate and conspicuous style – His second entre was princely, and the immediate interview with Desdemona peculiarly attractive: the tone of love was tenderly uttered, and here the African Roscius met with judicious support from his Desdemona, Mrs Edwards. – His acting during the brawl was animated; and the subsequent risings of jealousy were defined in a masterly manner; the dashed and hurried spirits being troublously pourtrayed (sic). His next meeting with Desdemona was of a heart-rending description, and his exit from the scene most piteous

"Farewell the plumed troop"

was pathetically delivered, and the whole of that portion of the tragedy in which this beautiful soliloquy occurs strikingly impassioned. The scene in which arises the contention respecting the handkerchief was acted by the African Roscius in a highly embittered tone of jealous "well painted passion". The internal commotions of despair, displayed in the last act of the tragedy, with the occasional accompanying "fury of words" were pictured with great force and feeling; and upon the whole we consider Othello, as played by the African Roscius, a performance enriched with the brilliancy of genius. We must not in justice omit to observe that the Emilia of Mrs Brooks was very spirited.

– Scarborough, August 9th, 1831

Whether or not Ira Aldridge played one of Joseph's theatres in 1830 or 1831 is relatively unimportant. Ira's big break came in 1833 when Edmund Kean was playing Othello opposite the Iago of his son, Charles Kean, at Covent Garden. Kean Snr was taken ill on stage and Aldridge, who was present, went on. Kean died a few weeks later, and Aldridge was invited to take over, but a concentrated campaign of vicious racism was mounted against him, with the Athenaeum describing it as 'monstrous' for an authentic black to appear in the play[13] Ira played the part for two performances, after which he was effectively banned from playing theatres in London, and so he went on a tour of the provinces. On October 7th, 1833 he *did* play a theatre for Joseph: at Malton in Yorkshire for two nights.[14]

Although Joseph now owned his own theatres and managed a number of others, he still sought to broaden his empire. For instance, the following item appeared in the *Stamford Mercury* of 12th November, 1830;[15]

> We understand Mr Smedley has succeeded Messrs Huggins and Clarke in the theatrical business at Gainsburgh and Horncastle, and purposes opening the former theatre early in the spring, instead of the autumn, as has usually been the practice.

Huggins and Clarke had been rivals of Joseph Smedley for years, and had managed the theatre at Southwell before Joseph took over the new theatre

---

[13] Ira Aldridge; Martin Hoyles, 2008

[14] Playbills in Lincolnshire Archives.

[15] Stamford Mercury, 12th November, 1830; British Newspaper Archive. (RS)

there, and tried to wrestle control of Grimsby away from him. Whether the Clarke of the partnership was the same as Joseph's former partner, I cannot discover, but I suspect he was, given the timing of his dissolved partnership with Joseph in 1806, and his entering a new one with Huggins in 1807. Huggins' former partnership with Collier had been dissolved in April 1805.[16] Their standard of production and acting was none too well thought-of.

According to *The Road to the Stage* by Leman Rode (1827)[17], the Circuit belonging to Huggins and Clarke included Worksop, Pontefract, Horncastle, Gainsborough, Mansfield, Rotherham, Louth and Brigg. All of these shortly came under Joseph Smedley's management. It would seem from the following report in the *Stamford Mercury* of 19th November, 1830, that the Circuit was broken up following the death of Huggins:

> It is in contemplation of the different towns throughout the late theatrical circuit of Messrs Huggins and Clarke, to raise a subscription as an annuity for the aged widow of the late Mr Huggins, who has been for upward of 40 years in that company. Such of her friends as remember the talented performances of her younger days, and all who feel for the vicissitudes of a player's life, will no doubt have much satisfaction in thus contributing to the support of a highly respectable and deserving old servant of the public.

C.M.P. Taylor states[18] that William Huggins had died in 1821, and his son in 1823, and that it was then that Joseph set his sights on acquiring some of their interests. This is only partially correct, and Neil Wright[19], I believe is correct:

> William Huggins ran the company for twenty-five years until he died on 15 November 1821 in Gainsborough. His son Charles was then 28 and had performed with the company all his life, and he took over as sole manager of

---

[16] The Theatre at Gainsborough by G. Hemingway, 1978. Copy in Newark Library.

[17] Included in 'Romantic and Revolutionary Theatre, 1789-1860: Managers and Salaries, by Leman Rode, 1827

[18] 'Right Royal' Wakefield Theatre, 1776-1994; Wakefield Historical Publications; 1995

[19] "Treading the Boards, Actors and Theatres in Georgian Likncolnshire", Neil R Wright, 2016, Pub. The Society for Lincolnshire History and Archaeology

the company for the next nine years... Charles' older brother Frederick died on 14th November 1823, aged 34, also at Gainsborough. Then the *Stamford Mercury* reported in January 1822 that 19-year-old John Huggins of the theatres Gainsborough, Mansfield, etc had also died, but the paper was wrong as John lived until 1865, latterly described as a 'labourer'.

There had been a theatre at Gainsborough since 1772

> erected by Mr Dickinson, Mr Parker and others. It had an arched front, extending 60–70 feet. The entrance to the pit and gallery was in a narrow passage to the Back St., the front of which was made up in the Egyptian style giving two pilasters on each side, with corresponding head. Within this entrance was placed the check-taker, who passed the parties to their respective places.[20]

It was used by the Company of William Herbert, and closed in 1787, becoming a warehouse. At about this time, a Mr West[21] opened a theatre in the Old Hall.

The Old Hall was, and is, a timber-framed medieval Manor House. Built by the Burgh family in about 1460, it was intended as a family home, but also a status symbol, signifying their wealth and importance. However by 1596 they had fallen upon hard times and the house was sold to the Hickman family.[22] Thereafter, the house had several owners and even more uses. One of these was William Hornby who took the lease and tried to establish a coarse linen factory, which failed, so he sub-let that part of the building as a theatre. At the same time, numerous rooms in the west wing of the house served as workshops for carpenters, plumbers, coopers and basket-makers, while the ground floor of the east wing was often occupied by dancers, conjurors and puppet-shows.

John Wesley preached there in 1759 (in the Great Hall), 1761 and 1764. In 1773 the first floor room was licensed as a place of worship for the Congregationists.

---

[20] The Theatre at Gainsborough by G. Hemingway, 1978, from History and Antiquities of Gainsborough, 1843.
[21] Lincolnshire Notes and Queries
[22] Lincs. County Council, History of Gainsborough Old Hall

In October 1796 Collier and Huggins from Theatres Scarboro', Durham, Shields and Sunderland purchased the lease of the Gainsborough, Louth, Brigg, Mansfield and Worksop Theatres. Their opening plays at Gainsborough were *The Grecian Daughter* and *Bon Ton*. It was reported that "the Theatre received material embellishments, both as to Decorations and Painting".[23]

On 1st December 1800 there was a fatal accident at the theatre. "A boy was attempting to get from the gallery to the balcony when he unfortunately lost his hold and fell down upon the spikes near the orchestra." He fractured his skull and died on the following Wednesday.[24]

In the harsh winter of 1816–17 when there was much unemployment, the kitchen was opened as a 'soup kitchen' for the emergency feeding of the impoverished and some 20,000 free meals were served in a period of six weeks.

The theatre at Gainsborough was opened to coincide with the 'Marts'. These were a type of fair held annually; one on Easter Tuesday and the other on the Tuesday after the 20th October, each for nine days – except Sundays –"for the sale of cloth, pedlery, and other merchandise, but horses, cattle, and swine are exposed for sale only on the Wednesday;…The horse and cattle fair is held on Bridge hill; the cheese on the first two days of each fair in the market place; and the mart for cloth, toys, etc., in the Mart Yard".[25]

The Grand Hall which served time as a theatre is still interesting to the theatre historian today. At the end of the Hall where the stage would have been situated there are hatches in the end wall from where the scenery rolls were mounted and operated. At the other end, one can still see where the supports and wall brackets supported the gallery, which would have had about five rows of seating accessed by an external staircase.

---

[23] The Theatre at Gainsborough by G. Hemingway, 1978, citing the Doncaster, Retford and Gainsborough Gazette 22-10-1796
[24] Guy Hemingway, The Theatre at Gainsborough
[25] From White's Directory, 1856, quoted by David Hey in 'Family History and Local History in England'

The players made their entrances through a bay at the side of the stage (used as a 'Green Room'), which was next to a door opening onto the outside where their wagons would have been placed as dressing rooms.

According to a pamphlet published in 1953,[26] and written by Harold Brace, by 1830 the Great Hall had ceased to be a theatre, and became the Corn Exchange. This does not jibe with the playbills of the period, although they, in the fashion of the times, are only headed with 'Theatre, Gainsborough'. It is therefore possible that Joseph had to find alternate accommodation either in a temporary setting or at an inn. However it is also possible, indeed more likely, that Mr Brace was wrong as a note in 'Lincolnshire Notes and Queries' says of Gainsborough Theatre: "The large room in the Old Hall was used for dramatic purposes until some fifty years ago."

Although not published in book form until 1930, there is no date as to when this was written, but the Great Hall was certainly still a theatre until 1839.

Huggins and Clarke closed for the 1830 season on 18th October[27] and less than a month later Mr Smedley succeeded them at Gainsborough and Horncastle. On 4th April 1831, performances of *The Brigand*, *Popping the Question* and *The Illustrious Stranger* were given, "by desire of H.B. Hickman Esq., High Sheriff," and on the 5th – "the first day of the Mart" – *The Bottle Imp* and *The Haunted Inn*. There were performances every night in Mart week. Although, somewhat strangely, the playbills do not specifically name Joseph Smedley's management, he is the most likely, and, indeed on Tuesday 22nd October 1833 Mr Smedley opened for a month's season with *The Two Drovers*, a ballet dance, and *A Fish Out of Water*.

The "Marts" themselves continued until, in 1884, a lion escaped, terrorising the people of the town. No action was taken, however, this being considered to be such a rare occurrence that it was unlikely to repeat itself. Unfortunately, it happened again in 1887 and the license for the fairs was consequently withdrawn.

---

[26] "Former Uses and Abuses of Gainsborough Old Hall by Harold W. Brace, F.R. Hist. S. Lincs Archives; R Box L Gain. 728.83 BRA (unbound pamphlet)
[27] GH Newark Times 13-10-1830

Gainsborough was to be portrayed as the fictional St Ogg's in *The Mill on the Floss* by George Eliot (Mary Ann Evans), published in 1860.

There is a theatre at Horncastle in an outbuilding at the rear of the Red Lion Inn, where it still stands (called the Lion Theatre), which was certainly then in existence, and is still used today for community theatre. There is some doubt as to whether it was this theatre that had been operated by Huggins and Clarke, who counted Horncastle as one of the best dates in their circuit, and whose season there in 1829 lasted six weeks.[28] Neil R. Wright suggests[29] that this was another building, sited in Dog Kennel Yard off St Lawrence Street, a converted barn, on the site of which now stands a supermarket.

This is supported by a study by Heritage Lincolnshire into the archaeological impact of the proposed development of the site:[30]

> A theatre dating to the 18th & 19th centuries had been located adjacent to the investigation area at the bottom of St. Lawrence Street in Dog Kennel Yard. The building had operated as a barn, threshing floor and finally a warehouse, prior to its use as a theatre. In 1859 the theatre was purchased to serve as the new British School, and subjected to rebuilding and decoration for that purpose. The school was closed in 1877 and sold for use as a malt kiln. A century later the building was functioning as a vehicle repair shop...."

In about 1830 or 1831, for the relevant playbill is undated, the theatre at Howden appears to be under the management of Joseph Smedley,[31] although we know that he had shares in it as well as nearby Selby. Howden is a small town north of Goole in Yorkshire, which, in 1831, had a population of 2130. Joseph announced a benefit performance for Mrs Carr and Mrs Po; Mr Carr seems to have been the outgoing Manager, who had got into financial difficulty:

> Mr Carr, with the utmost respect begs leave to call the attention of the Patrons of the Drama towards the Theatre, and to give it for a few moments a serious and

---

[28] Neil R Wright; "Treading the Boards".
[29] Neil R Wright, Treading the Boards
[30] Desk-top evaluation for Conging Street, Horncastle, July 1993
[31] Nicoll, Vol IV

kind consideration. Since the opening scarcely sufficient money has been taken to defray the incidental expenses of Bills, Lights, Rent &c. Had Mr C's own situation only been at stake, the Inhabitants of HOWDEN should never have been troubled with the present irksome and unpleasant solicitation; but when he considers the united claims made upon him, together with the sterile prospect he has in view, like a poor Mariner stretching his eyes o'er seas immeasurable, where all is dark and drear, he confidently persuades himself the benevolent feeling of the Ladies and Gentlemen of HOWDEN will not behold the total wreck of his affairs, when their kind Patronage and Support will enable him to steer his shattered Bark into a place of safety; nay, even the prejudiced, he humbly hopes will remove their scruples, and let a liberal feeling occupy their minds; for, "We are all Passengers on Life's Highway, and when a Traveller happens to stick in the Mire on the Road, the next that comes by will surely stretch out his hand to extricate him." An Actor who his (sic) dependant on the Public and is reduced by a train of unavoidable misfortunes, has no resource but to solicit the liberality of a generous and considerate Public, who are ever ready to step forward and encourage the deserving.[32]

It was surely something of a coup for such a small town to be visited by one of the greatest theatrical wonders of the age: an actor said to have been the first to demand and get star billing for every appearance:[33]

Mr KEAN

MR SMEDLEY ever anxious to merit the patronage and support of his Friends and the Public, has the pleasure of announcing, that at an expense unparalleled in this Theatre, he has concluded an engagement with that distinguished Actor,
MR KEAN,
(From the Theatres Royal, Drury Lane, and Covent Garden)
FOR TWO NIGHTS ONLY,
Viz. – Friday and Saturday next

Joseph continued to tour, and May 1831 found him playing at Mansfield Theatre. Mansfield is today a former mining and market town approximately

---

[32] Playbill in Lincolnshire Archives
[33] The Georgian Playhouse, Iain Mackintosh, 1975

14 miles north of Nottingham, and had been managed by Huggins and Clarke prior to Joseph's taking over the license. He presented the usual fare of plays:[34] *The Road to Ruin, and How to Avoid It*; and *The Happiest Day of my Life* and *Wonder! A Woman Keeps a Secret*, and *Perfection, or The Lady of Munster*.

And , on July 14th, 1831
For the Benefit of Miss & Miss A Smedley:
THEATRE, MANSFIELD
ON THURSDAY EVENING, JULY 14th, 1831
Will be presented an entire new Petite Comedy, called
THE MARRIED
LOVERS
Written by the Author of the "Lost Heir." &C
Duc d' Orleans............MR MELLON
Marquis de Menn iville............MR NEVILLE
Sir John Ascot............MR MAJOR
Colonel O'Dillon............MR SMEDLEY
Pierre............MR SEYMOUR
Francis............MR BOWER
Duchess d'Orleans............MISS NEVILLE
Madame de Menniville............MISS SMEDLEY
Lady Ascot............MISS A. SMEDLEY
Annette............MRS O. PERRY
Incidental to the Piece,
MISS SMEDLEY WILL SING
The "Page Troubadour" and "Ill Deceive thee Never".
And the Characters will Dance a QUADRILLE
COMIC SINGING BY Mr O. PERRY.
After which an entire new Farce now acting nightly with increasing attraction and applause called
Every Body's Husband.
Twisselton............Mr MELLON
Bunbury............Mr O. PERRY
Figgins............Mr NEVILLE
Sprigins............Mr MAJOR

---

[34] Playbills in Nottingham Central Library

Dick............Mr BOWER
Mrs Pimpernell............Mrs NEVILLE
Fanny............Miss A. SMEDLEY
Miss Thompson............Miss NEVILLE
Miss Tomkins............Mrs. O PERRY
Miss Twisselton............Miss SMEDLEY
COMIC SINGING BY MR. MAJOR
To conclude with an entire new Farce (never acted here)
called Turning the Tables.
Mr Knibbs............Mr MAJOR
Mr Jeremiah Bumps............Mr O. PERRY
Mr De Courcey............Mr MELLON
Mr Thornton............MR BOWER
Jack Humphries............Mr NEVILLE
Servant............Mr ROSE
Miss KNIBBS............Miss A. SMEDLEY
Mrs HUMPHRIES
Patty Larkins............Miss SMEDLEY
BOXES, 3s PIT, 2s GALLERY, 1s

This shows how, although nominally in charge of the orchestra and musical entertainment, even Mr O. Perry was expected to play a role when needed.

Also, somewhat strangely, amongst surviving playbills in the collection at Nottingham's Local History section of Nottingham playbills, there is a blank playbill, i.e. name of theatre and date of performance left blank for filling in later, which lists Joseph as a cast member. None of the others in the cast is recognisable as a member of the Nottingham company of the time, however, and the theatre concerned only had a Pit and Gallery:

THEATRE
ON EVENING 1831
Will be performed that much admired Play of
LOVER'S VOWS
OR, THE SOLDIER'S RETURN
Frederic, the Soldier............Mr THOMAS
Baron Wildhaim............Mr WOOD

Anhalt............Mr STEVENS
Butler............Mr HODSON
Cottager............Mr SMEDLEY
Agatha............Mrs Wood
Amelia............Miss Weston

* * *

END OF THE PLAY,
A COMIC SONG, BY MR STEVENS
The comic Duett of Polly Hopkins, by Messrs Thomas and Stevens
"The King, God Bless Him" by Mr Thomas
A COMIC SONG, BY MR HODSON
A FAVOURITE SONG, BY MR THOMAS
A Sailor's Hornpipe, by a Gentleman of Bulwell
The whole to conclude (by particular desire) with that much admired
Piece of
THE RED BARN
OR, THE MURDER OF MARIA MARTIN

William Corder............Mr WOOD	Old Martin............Mr STEVENS
Barnard............Mr HODSON	Mr Bobbin............Mr THOMAS
Maria Martin............Mrs WOOD	Nancy............Miss WESTON

PIT 1s Gallery 6d

In December of that year, back at Grimsby, they performed:[35] On Dec. 21st:"*Sweethearts and Wives*", Comic singing by Mr O. Perry, And "*Rival Valets*"

On Dec.23rd: "*Black-Eyed Susan*"; or "*All in the Downs*" (featuring a hornpipe by Master G. Smedley) and Comic Singing by Messrs Major and O. Perry and a Comedy, "*Two Friends*", followed on December 30th, "*Free Knights*", or, "*The Edict of Charlemagne*", Comic Singing by Mr Major, and "*Perfection*", or, *The Lady of Munster*. Also while in Grimsby they played:

Jan. 2nd, 1832: "*The Battle of Waterloo;*" or, "*The Fall of Bonaparte*" and "*William Thompson*"

---

[35] Playbills with kind permission of Mrs D. Whittingham of Grimsby,

Jan. 9th 1832 *"Merchant of Venice"* or, *"The Cruel Jew"* Comic Song: 'The Old Bachelor," Mr Major and *"The Siege of Algiers"* or, *"British Tars Triumphant"*

The prices at Grimsby were: Pit, 2s Gallery, 1s

Throughout Joseph Smedley's life in the theatre, fierce debate and argument raged about the Patent Houses' stranglehold on the performance of drama, both in London, and further afield; the system of censorship under the then current legislation, and its effect on dramatic literature, i.e. the lack of any protection for the rights of the dramatist or the performance of his work.

The Enabling Act of 1788 allowed licences to be granted by magistrates for the performance of certain types of entertainment within a 20-mile radius of London and Westminster, and for the 'legitimate drama' in theatres outside that area, for a period of 60 days.

These discussions took place in the salons, the coffee-houses, the theatres and elsewhere; already the owners of some theatres had been forced to close and the assertion of the rights of the Patent Houses defended by no less an advocate than Richard Brinsley Sheridan, a part-owner of Drury Lane, a dramatist in his own right, and a Member of Parliament.[36]

The controversy was becoming incendiary, and on 31st May, 1832, the blue touch-paper was lit, for Edward Lytton Bulwer rose in the House of Commons to request that a Select Committee be formed for the purpose of "inquiring into the State of the Laws affecting Dramatic Literature, and the performance of the Drama.".[37] In truth, however, even he was not altogether a neutral observer.

Edward George Earle Bulwer-Lytton, 1st Baron Lytton of Knebworth, to give him his full title, was, a politician, a playwright, essayist and poet. Although largely forgotten today, in the first half of the nineteenth century, he was immensely popular, and seemingly ubiquitous. He was born in London in 1776, the youngest son of General Earle Bulwer (1776–1807) and Elizabeth Barbara Lytton (1773–1843), heiress of Knebworth.

---

[36] Romantic and Revolutionary Theatre, 1789-1860, Cambridge University Press

[37] Hansard: State of the Drama; 31 May 1832

Against his mother's wishes, Edward married, in 1827, the Irish beauty Rosina Wheeler (ended in separation, 1836) and he was forced to support himself by writing.

He had a huge output including *Eugene Aram* (1832) – not to be confused with Thomas Hood's poem of the same title much favoured later as a party piece of Henry Irving – *The Last Days of Pompeii* (1834) and *Harold* (1843). Plays include *The Lady of Lyons* (1838), *Richelieu* (1839) and *Money* (1840).

Created a baronet in 1838, he succeeded to the Knebworth estate in 1843 and assumed the surname of Lytton. He re-entered Parliament as MP for Hertfordshire in 1852 and was Colonial Secretary in the Derby government. He was raised to the peerage in 1866.[38]

Edward's older brother became Sir William Henry Lytton Earle, Baron Dalling and Bulwer, a diplomat and author.

The speech given by Bulwer-Lytton on 31st May, 1832, set out the argument fully, together with the questions which, he felt needed to be asked:[39]

> They all knew that there was a patent granted to the two great theatres for the performance of the drama. The extent and power of these patents, with the laws by which they were strengthened, had long been a matter of dispute; but by the late decision of a high judicial authority, it seemed that all performances worthy of the attendance of persons pretending to a reasonable degree of education-all performances, except those of the most mountebank and trumpery description, fit only for the stage s of Bartholomew Fair-were to be considered as infringements of the law, and as subjecting those who assist their many thousand actors, proprietors, and decorators, who depend for support on their existence-without the pale of the law; and the question was, therefore, forced before the public in the following shape: "How far is it expedient for the public, that privileges and enactments of this monopolizing description should be continued?

---

[38] Chambers Biographical Dictionary

[39] Hansard

Lytton went on to say that the original reason for suppressing minor theatres had ceased to exist long ago, and, he contended, the only ground upon which the patents had been given in trust to the metropolitan theatres had not been fulfilled. He went on:

> Why was a patent granted to two theatres alone? There was but one alleged ground-for the preservation of the dignity of the national drama. Now, how had the patents obtained that object? It happened, curiously enough, that no sooner were the two great theatres in possession of this patent, than the national drama began to deteriorate, and a love for scenic effect to supersede it.

Thus, the Committee was to also look into the production standards of the day and the taste of the public in their theatrical entertainments as well as its primary raison d'etre of "inquiring into the laws affecting dramatic entertainments."

Lytton, unsurprisingly, championed the rights of dramatists:

> The instant an author published a play, any manager might seize it-mangle it-act it-without the consent of the author-and without giving him one sixpence of remuneration. If the play was damned, the author incurred all the disgrace; if the play succeeded, he shared not a farthing of the reward. His reputation lay at the mercy of any ignorant and selfish managerial experiment; he might publish a play that he never meant to be acted, that he knew would not bear to be acted; but if, as in the case of Lord Byron, his name alone would attract an audience, he was dragged on the stage, to be disgraced against his will, and was damned for the satisfaction of the manager, and the dignity of the national drama. He had no power-no interest in the results of his own labour-a labour often more intense and exhausting than the severest mechanical toil. Was this a just state of things?

Lytton's motion was seconded by a Mr O'Connell. Mr John Campbell said he "should strongly support the Motion. The laws respecting theatrical representations must be revised" and Mr Hume was "glad to find… there should be a free trade in theatres."[40]

---

[40] Hansard

Despite the objections of other Members, the Motion was agreed to, and the Committee was appointed with 24 members, a number of whom had an interest in the writing of plays

The Committee interviewed 47 witnesses, many of them among the most prominent people in British theatre, including Edmund Kean and William Charles Macready; Charles Kemble and Charles Matthews.

There were a great many questions asked in order to establish exactly what the powers of the Lord Chamberlain were, and how the system of licensing was managed; in practice, however, much of this work was delegated to the Examiner of Plays, who at this time was George Colman, the Younger, and his Deputy, John Payne Collier.

Colman in person was as great a wit as the characters in his comedies, and considered to be great company. Byron wrote of him:

> If I had to choose and could not have both at a time, I should say, let me begin the evening with Sheridan and finish it with Colman. Sheridan for dinner and Colman for supper; Sheridan for claret or port, but Colman for everything. Sheridan was a grenadier company of life-guards, but Colman a whole regiment – of light infantry to be sure, but still a regiment.[41]

In her memoirs of her husband, Mrs Charles Mathews, who knew both Sheridan and Colman personally, wrote:

> Colman perfectly broke him (Sheridan) down by the force of his vivacity. Sheridan had no chance with him in repartee, and he always gave up to his little merry companion after the first attempt, in which he generally failed. His genius seemed to forsake him for the time, and Mr Colman's fire appeared to blaze the brighter for being kindled upon the embers of the splendid ruin before him. He always felt his own advantage, and was more brilliant as he found the other more dull.[42]

---

[41] The Book of Authors by W. Clark Russell; Pub. Frederick Warne & Co
[42] Quoted in the above by the Editor.

Overall, the majority of the witnesses were keen to maintain the status quo, opting on the side of the patent houses as the only theatres that should be able to perform drama as they were the arbiters of good acting and the best drama, even though it was pointed out that they had in many ways abrogated their responsibilities in providing entertainments which were far from worthy, and which did nothing to protect the dignity of the National Drama.

Furthermore, it was reported that the audiences for the Patent Houses were declining, a factor which was also blamed on the 'other' smaller houses. In fact, at this time, attendances had been declining throughout the land, and not just those London patent theatres, but those in the provinces which had also received the Royal Patent; the Theatres Royal.

The majority of witnesses painted a picture of poor standards of acting and production in the provinces; and this would have an overall negative effect on drama as a whole, since regional theatres were largely considered to be training grounds, or acting schools, for those with talent who would go on to play in the major patent houses. In most cases their size could hardly have threatened the larger patent theatres, nor, according to witnesses, could they assail the quality of their dramatic output, and with the size of London growing, restricting the legitimate drama to only two houses flies in the face of common sense. Or, to quote the Covent Garden Theatre Letterbook of H. Robertson 1823–49:[43]

> In the largest and most cultivated metropolis of Europe, where the population is calculated at a million and a quarter, – where, at least, there are an hundred thousand well-educated adults whose pursuits are entirely those of pleasure, or literature and the arts, – where the elegant, the learned and the talented of the whole empire congregate, – where the mass of people are eagerly seeking knowledge, and daily progressing in intelligence, – where are the societies, institutions, and means of all kinds for the dissemination of knowledge, and the enlargement and elevation of the intellect, there are Two theatres, (which having no mean,)

---

[43] Quoted in Romantic and Revolutionary Theatre 1789-1860(The Monopoly Retards Cultural Development in the greatly enlarged London), from Covent Garden Letterbooks of H. Robertson , now in British Library, Add MSS 29643; this transcription by kind permission of the British Library

are empowered to perform the regular and reasonable Drama – and 17 or 18 others, (which are suitably constructed for it), where nothing but Tom foolery-farce-singsong-Dancing-and Dumb show, can be exhibited. This admirable contrivance for the degradation of society is further assisted by the two theatres, where the regular Drama may, but cannot be properly performed, being situated close together, at the farthest possible distance from the circle of respectable suburbs where the most intelligent and best educated portions of society reside, – the Regent's park and the Clapham Road – Kensington and Stratford – are a tolerable two hours journey from either of these emporiums of the regular Sock and Buskin, whilst at the minor Theatre, so conveniently constructed, and well situated for the performance of regular plays, nothing but pieces tending to degrade still more the minds of the people, may be performed. The anomaly is perfectly ridiculous…

As also stated in *Romantic and Revolutionary Theatre*,[44] it was certainly true that

as the populations of the major centres, especially London, began to increase, the monopoly of legitimate drama exercised by the patent theatres and their resolute opposition to enlarging the number of licensed theatres permitted to perform this drama became irksome to entrepreneurs less interested in the preservation of the 'national drama' than in making money.

Nowhere does it attribute the same motivations to the managers of the patent houses.

The report of the Select Committee's findings was, for reasons mentioned above, surprising, though welcome. It conceded that there had been a decline in the Literature of the Stage, and the taste of the public for Theatrical Performances. It acknowledges that some of the reasons for this were outside the scope of any Legislature to control, such as the fashion of dining late, the absence of Royal encouragement, and the indisposition of some Religious Sects to tolerate Theatrical Performances. The uncertain administration of the Laws, the small encouragement given to Literary Talent to lend its

---

[44] Taken from Romantic and Revolutionary Theatre, Ed Donald Roy, by kind permission of Cambridge University Press

talent to the Stage, and the need for better legal regulation with regard to the number and distribution of Theatres were, the report maintained, to be the principal matters to be considered.

It recommended that the Laws should be rendered more clear and effectual by confining the sole power to license theatres in London (and places of Royal residence), to the Lord Chamberlain, and that his sole jurisdiction should be extended 20 miles around the capital. It went on to say that in the interests of fair competition that the Lord Chamberlain should continue a License to all the Theatres licensed at present, whether by himself or by the Magistrates.

Since the Committee had difficulty in defining the meaning of 'Legitimate Drama' and to give an opening to both the higher as well as humble orders of Dramatic Talent, Managers of the said Theatres should be allowed to exhibit such plays as had received, or should receive, the sanction of the Censor.

The number of Theatres so licensed, said the Report, would be sufficient for the accommodation of the public. The Committee also recommended that the Chamberlain should possess the same power to suppress any Theatre exhibiting any Dramatic Representation without a license.

The Committee further advised that the office of Censor should be held entirely at the discretion of the Lord Chamberlain, who could be removed if there was any dissatisfaction in the exercise of his office. This was in order to give weight to the responsibility of licensing plays, for which the Committee recommended a revision in the way fees were paid to the Censor, so that the license fee for a song could not be indiscriminately applied to a play in the same amount.

The Report also concluded that the two patent theatres, Drury Lane and Covent Garden, clearly held privileges that neither preserved the dignity of the Drama, nor, because of the present Administration of the Laws had they been of much advantage to their proprietors. The Committee, while acknowledging the large sum invested in them, believed that the changes they were proposing would not place the Proprietors in a worse financial position than they were in under the existing system.

With regard to Dramatic Literature, it seemed clear that an Author was subjected to an 'indefensible hardship and injustice'. They therefore recommended that the Author of a Play should possess the same legal rights and protection as the Author of any other literary production; and that his Performance should not be legally exhibited at any Theatre, Metropolitan or Provincial, without his express and formal consent.

The Committee opined that the amendments to the current system they proposed would free the Drama from many disadvantages, and left to the fair experiment of Public support. It said that even Actors who had favoured the existing Monopoly would find new schools and opportunities for their art, and that Authors would find a greater variety of Theatres in which to present their plays.[45]

This Select Committee Report was presented on 2nd August 1832. Bulwer-Lytton followed this by presenting a bill to implement the recommendations made therein. It was passed by the House of Commons, but was defeated in the House of Lords (2nd August 1833). Nevertheless, it resulted in the Dramatic Copyright Bill of 1833, ensuring the rights of authors of books and plays, farces, or any piece of Dramatic Entertainment.

The changes recommended in respect of theatres were not enshrined in Law until the Theatres Act of 1843 was passed. These Acts caused a sea-change in the world of theatre, and the way in which theatres were managed.

In the same year that Charles Kemble gave evidence to the Committee (1832), he sailed for America, taking with him his daughter, the beautiful and talented actress Fanny Kemble. She had made her debut at Covent Garden three years earlier where her Juliet had been a huge success; so much so that she managed to save Drury Lane, and her father, who was then running it, from bankruptcy.

His son, and Fanny's older brother, John Mitchell Kemble, born in 1807, was, then, if only briefly, in Farnsfield, a small village near Southwell in Nottinghamshire where Joseph managed the theatre.

---

[45] Taken from Parliamentary Papers and reported in Romantic and Revolutionary Theatre, 1789-1860, 2003; and paraphrased by author.

Despite having spent his early years in theatres, J.M. Kemble's ambitions did not lie in that direction. He gained an early love of grammar and language which was fostered while at school in Clapham by its head, Charles Richardson, a lexicographer. He went on to King Edmund's Grammar School in Bury St Edmunds under Dr Benjamin Heath Malkin, where, among his contemporaries were Edward FitzGerald, James Spedding, (who later wrote a biography of Bacon), and William Bodham Donne, who became a lifelong friend and whose son married Mildred, one of JMK's daughters.

While at Cambridge, he became a member of the Apostles, a sort of debating society. His friends there included Alfred Tennyson and William Thackeray. He became passionately involved in radical politics, and then developed an interest in law, particularly as it pertained to illustrated history or ancient customs.[46] He then went to Germany where he began a serious study of German Philology, but had to return in 1830 to witness his sister's success at Drury Lane, and because his father had secured him 'an opportunity in the Church'.[47] JMK took his degree in the February, and determined to take orders, but had to wait for divinity lectures until the following Michaelmas term (early October to early December). In July 1830 he joined an expedition to Spain to attempt to topple Ferdinand VII. The attempt ended in abject failure, and he returned to London on 21st May. Hence, therefore, Tennyson's description of him in his sonnet "to JMK", published in 1830:[48] "My hope and heart is with thee-thou wilt be / A latter Luther and a soldier priest."

Kemble then abandoned his clerical ambitions and spent the period from Michaelmas 1832 to the summer of 1835 mostly in Cambridge studying manuscript sources for Old English literature and history. This does not, however, account for his presence in Southwell, as the Minster Library, its historic collection of material notwithstanding, was not considered a centre of study by philologists at this time.[49]

---

[46] Oxford DNB entry by John D. Haigh, accessed 24th Aug. 2016

[47] do

[48] Taken from "Tennyson, a Memoir" by Hallam Lord Tennyson, Pub Macmillan and Co, 1897

[49] E-mail from Southwell Minster Hon. Librarian, 7th September, 2016

His note to Joseph Smedley, however, contained practical advice on how to "scour silver and gold lace, so as to restore it to its first lustre," doubtless gleaned from his long associations with those who worked in the theatre, and his formative years being spent there. This is his advice:

> Take the lace and lay it as smooth as you can on a dry woollen cloth then burn Allem (sic) and beat it to powder, sifting it afterwards through a very fine sieve, then with a brush, brush it gently over the lace, and by so doing, and often turning it, the business will come to perfection.

If nothing else, it serves to confirm that Joseph and Melinda continued their contacts with the Kemble family, given further credence by the surviving etchings of Charles Kemble amongst Joseph's collection of memorabilia and papers.[50]

Perhaps the most important theatrical event of 1833 was the passing of Edmund Kean, who died at 9.20 am on the morning of Wednesday, the 15th of May, in the house adjoining his own theatre in Richmond, Surrey.

Much has been written elsewhere about Kean's life, but his death cannot go unremarked upon. The following is an account of the funeral:[51]

> The obsequies of this eminent actor were performed with a befitting solemnity, and with due honour, on the 25th of May. The coffin, while it lay at Mr Piggott's, the undertaker, in Richmond, was visited by great crowds of the inhabitants; upwards of a thousand, it was calculated, passed through the rooms during the preceding evening. At half past ten o'clock on the morning of the funeral, Mr Kean's house was opened to the public. Within a few minutes of three o'clock, the procession moved in the following order:

---

[50] Property of, and reproduced by kind permission of, Roy Sumners.
[51] The Annual Biography and Obituary of 1833, Pub Longman, Rees, Orme, Brown, Green &Longman, 1834

Two Beadles
Two Mutes
A Page   Plume   A Page
The Undertaker
Pall Bearers   Pall Bearers
Mr Braham   **THE**   Mr Macready
Mr W. Farren **BODY**   Mr Harley
Mr Cooper   Mr Dunn
Chief Mourner, Mr Charles Kean,
Supported by Mr John Lee
and Mr S. Knowles
Theatre Royal Drury Lane
Fund Committee.
Members of the Theatres Royal Covent Garden,
Haymarket, and English Opera,
Sadler's Wells, the City theatre, Surrey Theatre, and the Queen's Theatre.
Members of different Professions.
Inhabitants of Richmond

The Rev. Mr Campbell read, in a most impressive and emphatic manner, the burial service; and a requiem, ably conducted by Mr Hawes, was sung, consisting of two psalms to Purcell's chant in G minor. After the lesson, Handel's anthem, "When the ear heard him," and the chorus, "He delivered the poor that cried," were finely executed; and, immediately before the parting blessing, Handel's heart-moving composition, "His body is buried in peace, but his name shall live for evermore," was beautifully sung.

It has been estimated that the sums received by Mr Kean since the year 1814 amounted to £176,000. Nevertheless, his worldly affairs were so deranged at the time of his death that his executors declined administering to his effects.

*　*　*

We do not have many of Joseph Smedley's playbills for the year 1833. However we know that he and his company continued to tour, and in Barton, in June, he presented *Education*, which featured Mr Reeve as 'Damper', and his daughter, Miss Reeve as 'George, son of Broadcast' and, in addition to Mr Smedley, Miss A. Smedley, Miss H. Smedley, and

Miss Smedley (Georgiana). Mrs Howell sang 'Away to the Mountain's Brow', with Comic Singing by Mr Major, followed by a "Great New Comic Pantomime; got up expressly for the occasion, with new Scenery (painted by Mr Reeve) Tricks and Decoration, called HARLEQUIN And The Three Wishes."[52]

Mr Reeve had acted in Joseph's company before, but had not appeared on any Smedley playbill since 1826 owing, in part, to illness, with a subsequent downturn in his luck, which from correspondence in the Smedley archive[53], written from Newport in November 1826, Joseph had tried to assuage with a loan:

My Dear Sir,
   You are no doubt much surprised not having heard from me at the time stated, but I trust when I say I have been extremely ill you will receive it as sufficient excuse. This with want of necessary articles for wear has been so great a drawback on my saving fund that however strongly I wished to return at the time specified, the great obligation which your kindness has impressed me with I have not been able to do so. I merely hope you will not think the worse of me for this failure, unavoidable, or detract the high Character you in your own mind hold of me. In a month or 5 weeks…should nothing unforeseen happen I shall be enabled to relieve myself from the anxiety which this has caused me. I am now enjoying perfect health. I have given every satisfaction to Mr Parson and no doubt shall receive a continuance of his favour. I have hitherto played but little stage business, the company has been too full, when I joined it had been made up but a fortnight and many of them very bad actors and great dissension and strife is continual and frequent among them with regard to the casts;…
   I blush to think I cannot make good my promise to you as the kindness you rendered me was of that nature which I in gratitude never can enough repay. It has been themeans of advancing me in life more than might have been expected…

When I get to Salisbury I shall have no lien on me in any way and shall not fail to make good the payment of your kind loan.

---

[52] Playbill, Lincs. Archives (LLHS 38/5/4/2ci)
[53] Lincolnshire Archives; LLHS 38/5/3/12

In Grimsby on 14th August, 1833 it was announced: "W R Grossmith (the *celebrated* young Roscius') and his brother Master G. Grossmith now 6 years old will appear in 23 characters".

In Nottingham, meanwhile, at the theatre then in St. Mary's Gate, on September 30th 1833, to coincide with the famous Goose Fair, the Nottingham Company under Manly's management presented:

MR WALLACK
Late Manager of the Theatre Royal Drury Lane
(just returned from his tour in America) is engaged for 3 nights.
PIZARRO
Or, The Spaniards in Peru
ROLLA, Mr Wallack
Atalibe   Mr Lacy   Alonzo   Mr Nantz   Pizarro   Mr T. Manly

This was presumably James Wallack, born in London in 1795, whose brother, Henry John Wallack had been lessee at Wakefield in 1820, and whose parents were leading players at Astley's Amphitheatre in London.[54] James's talents are often described as being imitative of J.P. Kemble, and he alternated appearances in the cities of America with those in England.[55] He went on to become manager of the National Theatre in New York, and, with his son, Lester, he opened the third of the Wallack Theatres in New York City at Broadway and 13th Street, in 1861.

Fanny Kemble, whose uncle was, of course, J.P. Kemble, wrote:

> Wallack was to act in the "Rent Day"… I cried most bitterly during the whole piece; for as in the very first scene Wallack asks his wife if she will go with him to America, and she replies, "What! Leave the farm?" I set off from thence and ceased no more. Wallack played admirably; I had never seen him before, and was greatly delighted with his acting. I thought him handsome of a rustic kind, the very thing for the part he played-a fine English Yeoman."[56]

---

[54] CMP Taylor; Right Royal, Wakefield Theatre 1776-1994; 1995
[55] Concise Dictionary of American Biography 1964, Pub. Scribners
[56] Quoted in Representative Actors, W. Clark Russell 1883, Pub. Frederick Warne and Co.

Richard E. Smedley

In November of that year, again at Grimsby, where, for Joseph and his wife's Benefit evening, he returned to the well of infant prodigy once again, with the aforementioned Miss Reeve:

THE INFANT PRODIGY.

Mr Smedley has great pleasure in announcing the appearance of MISS REEVE. An INFANT PRODIGY, (being only Eight Years of age) who has been Received in every theatre where she has had the honour to perform, with a degree Of enthusiasm equal to that which attended the celebrated
MASTER BURKE
FOR THE BENEFIT OF
MR & MRS SMEDLEY
THEATRE, GRIMSBY

— o o o —

ON FRIDAY EVENING, NOV. 29TH, 1833
Will be acted the New and Popular Play (for the first time here) of
THE WIFE
A Tale of Mantua

Written by James Sheridan Knowles, Author of "Virginius," "William Tell," &c. The sun of Mr. Knowles' genius has once more burst through the clouds which lowered on The dramatic horizon; and every Theatre in the kingdom is receiving a new impulse from the performance of this beautiful and successful Play

"A woman hath in every state
"Most need of circumspection; most of all
"When she becomes a Wife! She is a spring
"Must not be doubted; if she is, no oath
"That earth can utter will so purge the stream
"That men will think it pure."

Leonardo Gonzago {Princes of Mantua} MR CHILDE
Ferrudo Gonzago {   } MR MOORE
Count Florio, MR REEVE   Julian St. Pierre, MR SMEDLEY
Antonio, (a Curate) MR MAJOR   Lorenzo, (an Advocate) MR SEYMOUR
Bartolo MR FRIMBLEY   Carlo Master SMEDLEY
Bernado MR ROSE   Marco MR SHORT
Guards &c by supernumeraries

Marianna, *(the Wife)* Miss SMEDLEY   Floribel, Miss A. SMEDLEY
Inez, Mrs. FRIMBLEY   Ladies, Miss WATKINSON, &c
COMIC SINGING BY MR FRIMBLEY
Dancing by Master G. And Miss G. Smedley

* * *

After which an entire new Farce, never acted, called
THE EMPTY HOUSE
WRITTEN BY MISS H. SMEDLEY
Mr Von Walthal, Mr FRIMBLEY   Hans Bruhman Mr MAJOR
Henry Bryan, Mr UNDERDOWN
Lestelle, Miss A. Smedley   Mabel, Mrs FRIMBLEY
Fanny Merton Miss REEVE!
Assuming the characters of
Master Ernest Augustus Constantine Biggs,   Miss REEVE
Master Nimrod Dashington   Miss REEVE!
Jack Seasprit   Miss REEVE!
PIT, 2s GALLERY, 1s

By 1827, attendances at the Apollo Lodge in Grimsby had dwindled. This was largely due to a dispute between a member and George Oliver, and the attitude and behaviour of some more recent members which caused many of the established members to stay away. As a result, membership subscriptions fell into arrears, the Treasurer was without funds and the Lodge was in serious trouble, so much so that on the 20th July, 1827, Mrs Kitching, circulated the following notice:

> Mrs Kitching having given notice that she will close the Lodge and seize for rent, your attendance is requested at the Lodge on Monday the 23rd inst., to inspect the treasurer's account, and to make arrangements for the payment of it.
> By order of the W.M.
> Yours fraternally,
> W. Skelton, Secretary

Stephen Kitching had drowned, with five others, in the Humber on December 20th, 1820, and Mrs Kitching was his widow. Under the terms of her husband's will, one of the trustees for its administration being George Oliver:[57] "All that Mansion or building, used as a Freemasons' Lodge, with the two lots or parcels of land whereon, or on some part of one of them is erected, known by the numbers 17 and 18, in the said East Marsh".

The meeting took place and an accommodation acceptable to Mrs Kitching was agreed.[58]

The Lodge eventually became dormant; the last initiation having taken place in February, 1827, and after 1829 no further returns, reports or payments were made to Grand Lodge.

Dr Oliver left Grimsby in 1831. In 1833 the Lodge was closed for good.

At the final meeting of the Lodge, the Brethren declared the necessity of annihilating their records to prevent the eyes of the outer world prying into their proceedings. This was duly carried out by fire. Then the following notice was displayed:

> To be sold by auction by Mr Judd, at the Apollo Lodge, Grimsby, this afternoon, Friday, July 19th 1833 the following Masonic furniture viz: 4 mahogany arm chairs, 4 Forms with backs, 2 long deal tables, Portable Writing Desk, Pair of globes, 3 cushions and boxes, Pulleys and Weight, 2 brass chandeliers, 3 candlesticks, 16 Tin Candlesticks, Balloting Box and Balls, 5 Boxes, Stove, 4 Pictures in Gilt Frames ,Copper Boiler, Pedestal, Piece of Painted Canvas, 14 Punch Glasses, Punch Bowl and Ladle, 2 Bibles, 4 Swords, 4 Spittoons, 9 Silk Collars, Drawing Board, 7 Mallets and Hammers, Ebony Inkstand, Waiter, 30 White Wands, Emblems, &c., &c.
>
> Sale to commence at 4 O'Clock

* * *

---

[57] History of Freemasonry in Grimsby, 1802-1938; F J Chapman, 1939, Pub. by request by A Windle & Co

[58] History of Freemasonry in Grimsby, 1802-1938; F J Chapman, 1939, Pub by request by A Windle & Co

We don't know if this affected Joseph, or to what extent he was saddened by the Apollo Lodge closure. Perhaps he understood that changes were afoot and that Grimsby was gradually changing in other ways too.

By coincidence, also in 1827, the ownership of the land on which the theatre stood changed hands, and was bought by the Revd David Blow. He had plans to demolish the theatre in order to build some cottages on the site. This led to Joseph heading his bill for the Masonic night in Grimsby *("Free Knights")* as follows:[59]

> Mr Smedley having been discharged from the present Theatre, (after Twenty-five Years Occupation) proposes erecting a NEW THEATRE, in shares of £10 each, to be ready by the autumn of 1833. Subscribers' names will be received by MR SKELTON, bookseller, at whose shop the prospectus and plan is left for inspection.

We can assume that this venture was undersubscribed for the new theatre wasn't built. Instead, on Joseph's next visit to Grimsby he presented another young prodigy, 'The Infant Kean', on June 18th & 19th 1834 at – The Apollo Lodge! This seems to have been adapted as a theatre for some time after. Incidentally, 'The Infant Kean', who also played the Clarence Theatre in Hull in the same year, was nine years old and said to be the "exact image of the celebrated actor Kean" and with his two brothers and sister formed a juvenile company.[60] The timing could have hardly been better!

In 1835, the touring went on: Billed "for a few nights only" at Howden, Mr Smedley ("with a company of Eleven Male and Seven Female performers and at an expense unparalleled") opened on 1st July with *George Barnwell* and *Spectre Bridegroom*.

In a Benefit for Joseph and Melinda also at Howden on July 3rd, they performed *Ivanhoe, or The Jew's Daughter* with *Milliners Revolt* and, later in the month played *Heir at Law*, with Inkle and Yarico; *A Bold Stroke for a Husband*; and *Wives as They Were* (for the Benefit of Miss and Miss A Smedley).

---

[59] From a playbill kindly supplied by Mrs D. Whittingham of Grimsby
[60] Playbill in the Cornell University Library Collection of James H Brown

In August they opened in Selby where they played in *Heir at Law* with *Simpson and Co*; *Pizarro*; *Heart of Mid Lothian* with *Happiest Day of My Life*; *A Bold Stroke for a Husband* with *Blue Beard*; and *John Bull* with *Rosina*; and for the Benefit of Joseph and Melinda they decided to play *Macbeth* with *Neighbours and their Wives*.

In Pontefract in September they enacted *John Bull* with *Uncle John*; *Heart of Mid Lothian* with *Happiest Day of My Life*; *Married Life* with *Lady and the Devil*; *Poor Gentleman* with *Raising the Wind*; *Heir at Law* with *Simpson and Co*.

Later on in September, at Malton, they repeated their performance of *Macbeth* with *Neighbours and their Wives,* and continued with *The Heart of Mid Lothian* with *Wanted – A Valet* and into October with *Married Life* with *Wags of Windsor*; *The Stranger* with *Timour the Tartar* and for "the first fair night, and the last week of performing" *John Bull* with *Sleeping Draught, or, Love and Laudenum*.

The second fair night, 13th October, 1835, the programme was *Green Man* and *Lady and the Devil*.

Almost two weeks later, in Gainsborough, and to the announcement of "Reduced Prices! Boxes 2s.6d.; Pit 1s.6d. and Gallery, 6d. During the Mart."

Opening on 26th October 1835, they presented *A Bold Stroke for a Husband* with *Milliners Revolt* (written by Miss Smedley); followed on 27th October by *Pizarro and Sharp and Flat*.[61]

Their next stop on the tour was a new departure entirely for Joseph, his family and his Company, for Joseph took on the lease of the Wakefield Theatre. The consequences of this and its subsequent ramifications would considerably affect them all.

---

[61] All above from playbills in Lincolnshire Archives.

10
Family Matters (2)

On 22nd April, 1834, Joseph and Melinda's eldest daughter, Melinda Brunton Smedley, married Joseph Tindal Young, a wealthy farmer from Gayton-le-Marsh in Lincolnshire. They were married at Sleaford.

Joseph Tindal Young was the first son of Richard Young (1775–1813), and his first wife, Charlotte Spicer of Alford, who went on to have six more children; John, William, Richard, Tom, Mary-Anne and Charlotte, as well as an infant daughter who died and was buried with her mother, in 1810, in Alford. Richard Young married, secondly Mary, but there was no issue from this marriage.

Almost a year after her marriage, on 10th April, 1835, Melinda gave birth to their first child, a son, whom they named Joseph Smedley Young, and who was christened at Gayton-le-Marsh on 12th April.

Their second child was a daughter, born 20th March, 1837, and named Melinda Bullen Young. She too was christened at Gayton-le-Marsh on 2nd April that year; and, on 17th October, 1838, another daughter, Helen, was born.

Gayton-le-Marsh is a small village not far off the main road from Grimsby, via Louth, to Alford and, as such, was very much on the route of Joseph and Melinda's regular tour schedule, and no doubt a handy place to visit to break up the journey. It was also somewhere that George and Georgiana liked to visit as part of their school holidays.

By now, Helen, Joseph and Melinda's second surviving daughter, was in her twenties, and proving an enormous benefit to the Smedley Company. She was able to act, perform comic songs – some of which she wrote – dance, and was gifted in writing farces, which her father presented on stage. One of these, *The Empty House*, was performed at Grimsby on November 29th 1833. According to a memoir written by one of her nieces, Helen was very clever, "excelling at Greek and Hebrew, and wrote several books."

11
The Smedleys – Final Stages and Further Family Matters

Joseph Smedley's first visit to Wakefield was in November, 1835. His company was to appear there for a season of eight weeks, longer than was usual for that theatre, and, therefore, something of a risk.

The local newspaper, the *West Riding Herald*, gave him a huge welcome, which must have been gratifying to Joseph, and presaged a successful season:[1]

> The lovers of the drama in Wakefield will be glad to hear that our theatre has been taken for the season by Mr Smedley, whose companies of performers have earned for themselves such deserved marks of public approbation in Lincolnshire and other parts. It has been frequently stated that the drama has declined in Wakefield; and appearances have certainly seemed to sanction the statement. If such be the case, we can only trace it to the lack of talent which has been exhibited on our boards; and we feel confident that the visit of Mr Smedley will give a new impulse to the dramatic cause in this town, and raise it again to that estimation in which it was formerly held, as a means of public instruction and amusement, by the respectable inhabitants of Wakefield.

Unfortunately, the opening night on 9th November didn't live up to it. They opened with a tried and tested favourite, *The Tragedy of George Barnwell*, followed by the farce *The Wags of Windsor*. The house was poor, and before the play had even started Joseph had to quell some rowdy youths who caused a "disgraceful clamour." The only part of the theatre which could be said to be busy was the gallery, while the boxes, which had been especially redecorated, remained empty.

---

[1] West Riding Herald, 30th October 1835; Wakefield Library and Museum

The newspaper, however, remained optimistic and congratulatory:[2]

> On Tuesday night, the Theatre in this town was opened (after an interval of near two years had elapsed) by Mr Smedley, the enterprising manager of the theatres at Beverley, Pontefract, Gainsborough, &c. Though we were aware of its being in progress of repair and of preparation for some time, we did not expect that it would be properly fitted to receive an audience before the expiration of another fortnight. We were, however, agreeably surprised on Tuesday night, to find it neatly and commodiously fitted up, and suitably decorated. The painting and varnishing of the interior sides of the boxes representing curtain drapery, and the devices on the external side are tasteful and light in their effect. The front seats of the pit are, as it struck us, not sufficiently raised; the level of the spectator's eye being, if we mistake not, much below the level of the stage, and the orchestra intervening between both. This might easily be remedied, as the benches rise rather abruptly from the front bench to the back one of all. If the front bench did not sink below a just proportion with the stage, this abrupt gradation of ascent in the benches of the pit would be a decided advantage to the audience of the pit. The defect we notice in the front seats may not, however, produce the inconvenience to others that it would to us, and we mention it rather as an opinion of our own as a suggestion for its alteration, without the declared sense to that effect of those who may feel inconvenienced by it.

This is as close as we can get to an idea of what the interior of the theatre looked like, and with particular regard to the raking of the seats to improve sightlines, even if only partially successful. We do not know whether Joseph took the advice or not. About the performance aspects, the article went on:

> Mr Smedley certainly deserves encouragement from the people of Wakefield, in his praiseworthy exertions to afford them amusement – of, at least, a harmless kind when confined to a representation of the humorous peculiarities of character and manners; and instructive when representing the just retribution which vice is almost sure to meet with, even in this world, and the reward which virtue enjoys in its own consciousness, though vice should for a time prevail against it in worldly considerations. The Tragedy of George Barnwell was the opening piece. Much of censure and much of praise has been bestowed upon this tragedy,

---

[2] West Riding Herald, 13th November 1835; Wakefield Library and Museum

by critics who tested it according to its moral effects in representation. We are not now disposed to repeat what has been on both sides advanced. We never saw it acted that it did not produce from the audience a testimony of its power over the feelings; and we are inclined to think, that when the feelings are affected, and brought into sympathy with the moral sense, some benefit may accrue therefrom. The part of George Barnwell was sustained by Mr Mosley, who is a very young man, and who has a good conception of the part. The contending feelings of a young and virtuous mind, seduced from its integrity, and at last plunged through a fatal passion for a meretricious female, and by the seductive arts of that female, into an abyss of guilt, still struggling with the consciousness of guilt, and suffering all its mental horrors, were well rendered. In the prison scene, when the repentant murderer, deriving hope from the gospel, is interrupted in his meditations by the successive and most trying visits of his old master and his young friend, and lastly by the virtuous daughter of his master, who then for the first time he discovers to have been enamoured of him, Mr Mosley certainly betrayed much knowledge of theatrical effect. His voice, moreover, is sonorous, and his enunciation clear, distinct, and measured. Mr Neville (Thorogood) was well received. Miss Neville (Millwood) had a most difficult part to perform.

Again, this is one of very few reviews of the time that give us a sense of the perceived calibre of the actors in Joseph Smedley's company. More often, such pieces may remark on who acted which part, but little more; here we have a fairly detailed critique. We do not know how well qualified the reporter was to remark upon it, but from the reference to the London Theatre, and comparisons of scenery and props, it suggests a more cosmopolitan approach. The piece continued:

Few women can personate the meretricious Millwood. It is a part, we think, the most objectionable in the play, and if Miss Neville has failed in its representation, she has done so with every actress who has attempted the performance of the part. The after piece, the Wags of Windsor, was humorously performed. The Irishman seeking for service, by Mr Frimbley, and the Yorkshire boy in the same pursuit, by Mr J. Smedley, were not bad representations. The Yorkshire boy was the best of the two, but he had the advantage of being 'at home,' the Irishman had not.

The gallery was completely crowded, the pit was thin, and the boxes were comparatively empty; but this, on the first night, was to be expected.

...On Wednesday night, the comedy of 'Speed the Plough' was performed, and

the characters of Sir Philip Blandford by Mr Neville, Morrington by Mr Rogers, Henry by Mr Mosley, and Farmer Ashfield by Mr Smedley, were well represented. Miss Neville as Susan Ashfield, was much applauded. After this followed the melodrama of the Wandering Boys, in

Which the two Misses Smedley represented the Wandering Boys, and were greatly applauded. On the whole, the performances of both nights were good, and the company deservedly received the applause of the audience.

Indisposed to criticise or to censure where the object is to please the public, and where every effort is made to effect that object, we cannot however refrain from suggesting to Mr Simondson, that it would be not injurious to him to speak his part with less rapidity, and with more attention to its performance than to the jokes of the gallery, or to whatever there is of risible on the stage. It is for the audience to laugh at the laughable. He should recollect that he is an actor, not an auditor or spectator. The gallery was full, the pit and boxes comparatively empty. This may be owing to the impression that the house was not sufficiently prepared for the reception of an audience. This impression will be removed by the concurring statement.

Of all who visited it with ourselves, and we with them can assure the ladies and gentlemen of Wakefield, that not only are the boxes neatly and tastefully fitted up and accommodated, but the acting, taking it generally, is as good as provincial acting usually is, and that it requires not a star *of the London stage to please those who are, albeit, familiar with that stage and its stars. We should have mentioned, that the scenery and, indeed, all the properties of the stage of Wakefield, are to our thinking superior to many theatres of more note than it has been our fortune to visit in the provinces, as our brethren of the critic-craft in the metropolis denominate the country, when talking of it with reference to theatricals…*

Last night the performance improved in our opinion; and the audience seemed sensible that, from being, as on the two previous nights, good, it was better. The applause was great, and we again say, well deserved. The house in the gallery was full, in the pit pretty nearly full, in the boxes thin though better filled than on the previous nights.

As the theatre had been closed for almost two years before Joseph took the lease, it naturally took time for the theatre-going public to discover that it was open once again. At least there *was* a theatre-going public, for Wakefield had a considerable past record in this regard, having been visited by the likes of Kean and Kemble. It had been part of Tate Wilkinson's York Circuit at one time, and had, since then, had a chequered past under various managements, even though the lease was actually held by Tate Wilkinson's son, John, for a while. It had also been, during Wilkinson's tenure, one of the worst areas for hostile attitudes toward stage performers and unruly behaviour such as hissing and heckling. Actors had to be brave, defiant and not subject to intimidation. They had to learn to deal with such behaviour and turn it back on the audience.

The theatre had been in the ownership of James Banks, who had been responsible for its construction, but he died in 1814, and the ownership passed to his widow, Mrs Mary Banks. Most of the other theatres in the Wilkinson circuit had been taken by Thomas Downe. Doncaster, however, was under the management of W. J. Hammond, who had also leased the Wakefield Theatre – for the final time in September of 1832, when he presented, for one night only, Frederick Henry Yates and his wife, who, prior to her marriage, had been Elizabeth Brunton. In early 1833, the theatre at Hull had been taken by one Orlando Eli Read, who then opened at Wakefield on 18th November 1833 and extended the season past Christmas and New Year. According to C.M.P. Taylor[3], he was an "uncertificated bankrupt, just released from prison."[4]

Perhaps out of respect for the late Mrs Banks, who had passed away in January, 1834, the theatre had closed in that month, but Read then reopened it on 4th February with a partner, a Mr Ingleton, "of the Royal Pavilion Theatres, Leeds and Hull." However the death of Mary Banks effectively broke the ties with Wilkinson's York Circuit. Read closed his season on 27th February and was followed a week later by a visit by Mr Charles Mathews in his popular one man show *At Home*, for which the prices were increased. Eighteen months later, Joseph Smedley took the lease. Although Read had exercised a policy of presenting novelty acts and spectacle, along with a diet of melodrama and farce, Smedley chose to continue his usual presentations of a melodrama and a farce interspersed with dancing and comic songs, with a different programme nightly, usually lasting about four hours. The dramatic content, however, was mainly Shakespearean, i.e. *Hamlet, Othello, King Lear, Macbeth, Romeo and Juliet* and *Richard III*, in addition to his usual repertoire of favourites such as *Jane Shore, Pizarro*, et al. Joseph was to find that

---

[3] Right Royal, A History of the Wakefield Theatre, 1776-1994,

[4] Do – quoting an anonymous letter in Hull Central Library addressed to a firm of York solicitors.

Wakefield audiences were more sophisticated and worldly-wise than those in the towns and villages of rural England that he usually visited.

Joseph's policy, he helpfully informed the public, was that "Monday Evening's performance will be appropriated to opera, Wednesday, legitimate comedy (and set apart as the Fashionable night) Fridays to melodrama and spectacle, and Saturdays, to Tragedy."

It has to be said, though, that Joseph and his company did not find it easy to make their mark. Despite the good press his arrival in the town had been given, it also attracted a great deal of opposition from the evangelists. As was noted earlier, the 1820s and 1830s signalled a decline in theatre attendances countrywide, especially outside London, partly as a result of the effect of Methodism on the middle classes, and partly due to low wages, but also rival entertainments such as musical concerts which were also drawing from the same well.

Despite the somewhat faltering start, by November 27th, according to the *West Riding Herald* of that date, audiences were increasing nightly, and during his first season at Wakefield, Joseph and his company presented *Romeo and Juliet* and *The Two Drovers*; *Rob Roy* with *The Irish Tutor*; *A Bold Stroke for a Husband* with *Wanted a Valet*; *The Wood Demon* with *We Fly by Night*; *Jane Shore* with *Inkle and Yarico*; and *Macbeth* with *The Spectre Bridegroom*.

On a playbill for the 28th November, Joseph pronounced the following, being, no doubt, in a philosophical frame of mind:

> The Perpetual Comedy
> The World is the Stage – Men are the Performers –
> Chance composes the Piece – Fortune distributes the Parts –
> The Fools shift the Scenery – The Rich occupy the Boxes –
> The Powerful have their seat in the Pit, and the Poor sit in the Gallery
> – The Fair Sex present the Refreshments – The Trusty occupy the
> Treasury Benches (!) and those forsaken by Lady Fortune snuff the
> Candles – Folly makes the Concert and Time drops the Curtain.

Joseph attempted to encourage attendances by visiting and talking to as many of the worthiest citizens of Wakefield as possible, as well as sports clubs, social organisations and businesses and trying to gain their patronage. He would offer them a list of attractions in his company's repertoire and request them to choose the programme for a particular evening, in the same way that an actor's benefit night may be chosen by him, and was called a 'bespeak'. This gave them the opportunity to invite their like-minded friends and relations to an evening at the theatre in the knowledge that the entertainment had been chosen by them,, that they were wealthy enough to do so, and that they were 'Patrons of the Arts'.

Hence on the 5th December, a programme containing *Heir at Law* and *Love Laughs at Blacksmiths* was presented "by Desire of the Young Gentlemen of the Proprietary School," and on 7th December the Patron for the evening was the then constable of Wakefield, John Barff, for which there was a full house.

The next month, the following announcement in the West Riding Herald appeared:

> On Saturday Evening, January 2nd, 1836
> By Desire and under the Patronage of
> THE GENTLEMEN OF THE CRICKET CLUB.
> THE WIFE, AND UNCLE JOHN.
> On Monday, the 4th,
> THE MUTINY AT THE NORE,
> AND
> SIMPSON AND CO.
> On Wednesday, the 6th,
> THE WATER WITCH, & MERRY MOURNERS.
> On Thursday, the 7th,
> THE MAID AND MAGPIE, IS HE JEALOUS,
> AND
> POPPING THE QUESTION,
> On Friday, the 8th,
> FOR THE BENEFIT OF THE 'MISS SMEDLEY'S,
> AND THE
> LAST NIGHT OF PERFORMING.
> THE GREEN MAN, AND MY SPOUSE AND I

After their season at Wakefield ended, the company moved the short distance to Beverley where they performed *Ivanhoe* and *Plot and Counterplot;* and, at the beginning of February, they were back at Grimsby with *John Bull* and *Raising the Wind*. Here the company was led by Mr J. Smedley (i.e. Joseph's eldest son, also called Joseph). Others in the cast were Mr Montague, Mr Fitzroy, Mr Rogers Mr Lockwood, Mr Granville, Mr Rose, Miss Smedley (Helen), Miss A. Smedley, (Annette), and Mrs Lockwood.

While in Grimsby they also played *To Marry or Not to Marry* and *Miller's Maid*; *Orphan of Geneva* and *Irish Tutor*; *Heir at Law* and *Uncle John*.

They then moved on to Spilsby where they performed *Wives as They Were and Maids as They Are* and *Miller's Maid*. They also performed, for the Benefit of Mr J. Smedley, *Point of Honour* and *Sharp and Flat* with the company comprising:

Mr Mosley (from the Nottingham Theatre)
Mr Rogers	Mr Webb	Mr Montague
Mr Lockwood	Mrs Lockwood	Mr Jones
Miss A Smedley	Mr Fitzroy	

While in Spilsby, Mr and Mrs Tannett's Benefit was *Ivanhoe*, and on their last night there, 'The Misses Smedley" chose for their Benefit *The Soldier's Daughter* with *Weathercock*.

The following month, April, 1836, found them back at Beverley. Here they performed *Gipsy Chief* with the following cast:

Mr Jones	Mr Lewis	Mrs Hamerton
Mr Wallett	Mr Jackman	Miss Neville
Mr Vining	Mr Neville	Mrs Skerrett
Mr Wafford	Mr Smedley	Mrs Jackman
Mr Skerrett		

As an afterpiece they performed Colman's comedy *Ways & Means*.

Three days later, on April 11th, 1836, the Smedley Company opened in Pontefract… and Gainsborough – simultaneously!

Joseph chose at this stage to divide his company into two. This may have been in order to honour his existing commitments, particularly to those towns whose theatres he had managed and visited for many years. It may also have been in order to be able to expand his theatrical empire even more, and this, in light of forthcoming events is the likelier. It was an incredibly difficult time to take such risks, with falling audiences and theatres everywhere either folding or changing hands repeatedly. It also placed considerable responsibility on the shoulders of Joseph Jnr who had just turned 20 years of age on 4th March.

As it turned out, it was not a permanent arrangement, but certainly a contingency to be drawn upon when convenient and when exigencies demanded.

We do not know whether this had always been a plan of Joseph's or whether he had perhaps got the idea from other companies. In 1827, for example, Mr Manly of the Nottingham circuit, which at that time included Stamford, had divided his company when it became clear that the Chesterfield Races coincided with Nottingham's Goose Fair.

Whatever the reason, Joseph had already decided to return to Wakefield in November for a season, and this may have been a trial run, as we shall see.

Then on to Pontefract, one of the theatres formerly managed by Huggins and Clarke. According to the History Directory and Gazzetteer of the County of York, by Edward Baines in two volumes (Vol 1 – West Riding; 1822, "the theatre is a neat building erected a few years ago by public subscription, and is open twice in the year by a company of comedians under the management of Huggins and Clarke". Here, (for "the Sessions week only"), they presented *Green Man* with *Wanted A Valet*; the cast being as follows:

Mr Green: Mr Smedley *Lord Rowcroft*: Mr Jones
Sir Geo Squander: Mr Wallett *Mr Crackley*: Mr Wofford
Closefit: Mr Jackman *Pinfold*: Mr Vining *Bibber*: Mr Lewis

While at Gainsborough they produced *Ivanhoe, or, The Jewess* with *Weathercock*. The cast was:

Normans
Mr Sheldon   Mr Rogers
Mr Mosley   Mr Webbe
Mr Montagne

Saxons
Mr Tannett   Mrs Lockwood
Mr J Smedley   Miss Smedley
Mr Lockwood   Mrs Fitzroy
Mr Sheldon

Jews
Mr Fitzroy
Miss A Smedley

On the following evening at Gainsborough *Castle Spectre* was performed, and at Caistor, on 23rd April *Ivanhoe* was again performed with similar cast.

On April 26th 1836, with the company reunited at Market Rasen, the programme included *Poison Tree* with *Irish Tutor*, the cast including:

Mr Lewis   Mr Vining
Mr Skerret   Mr Jones
Mr Neville   Mr Jackman
Mr Wafford   Mr Hudson
Mr Smedley   Mr Holland

Unfortunately, we do not have a first name for Mr Vining. His surname is that of a well-known family of actors, mostly associated with Bath and London theatres. Whether this Mr Vining is a member of this family I am unable to discover.

Similarly, we know little about Skerret, although he did eventually go into management himself, and brought a company to Bradford in 1841.

On 28th April they presented Mrs Inchbald's comedy of *To Marry or Not to Marry*, in which Joseph Snr acted; a Comic Song 'The Ladies' Tongues' performed by Mr Lewis, and a Melodrama called *The Wandering Boys*, one of whom was played by Miss Smedley (i.e. Helen). On 30th April they performed, for the Benefit of Messrs Lewis and Vining, *The Merchant of Venice, or, The Cruel Jew*, with Mr Jones as Shylock, Miss Neville as Portia, and Joseph Jnr as Gratiano (Joseph Snr did not appear). In addition there was a Comic Song 'Werry Pekoolier' performed by Mr Vining, and another 'My Grandfather' by Mr Lewis, and followed by another comedy, Mrs Inchbald's *Wedding Day*.

Next, still at Market Rasen, they performed "by Desire and under the Patronage of the White Hart Inn Ordinary" *Ivanhoe* again with *The Jew & Doctor*. The cast included Mr Vining, and "Mr Mosley and Mr Rogers, both from the Caistor Theatre."

On May 7th, now at Caistor, the Company presented *Man & Wife, or, More Secrets Than One* with a cast list as follows:

Mr Montague	Mr Fitzroy	Mr Rogers
Mr Mosley	Mr J Smedley	Mr Lockwood
Mr Sheldon	Mr Tannett (as Cornelius O'Dedimus)	
Mrs Lockwood	Miss A Smedley	Mrs Fitzroy
Miss Tannett		

This was followed by *The Cork Leg*, a farce by Mr Lockwood; Comic Singing by Mr Tannett, and ending with the farce of *The Bee Hive, or, Lots of Fun* featuring Miss A Smedley and Miss Smedley.

On 14th May they performed Sheridan's *Pizarro, or, The Conquest of Peru*, again without Joseph Snr, although this demanded the doubling of roles:

<u>Spaniards</u>

Mr Fitzroy	as	Pizarro
Mr Mosley		Alonzo
Mr B Tannett		Valverde
Mr J Smedley		Sentinel

Mr Tannett	Las Casas
Miss A Smedley	Elvira

Peruvians

Mr Rogers	as	Rolla
Mr Lockwood		Orozembo
Mr Montague		Ataliba
Mr Lockwood		High Priest
Mrs Fitzroy		Cora
Miss S Tannett		Cora's Child

Mesdames Lockwood, Tannett, Miss Tannett, as Virgins of the Sea

Despite the doubling up, this displays a pressing attempt to find people to fill roles, with the first appearance that I can find of Mr B Tannett and Miss S Tannett. These were two offspring of Mr Tannett (the company's scenic artist) and his wife Ursula. (Benjamin, the youngest, born in 1820 at New Malton, and christened there on 1st March of that year; and Sarah, his sister, born in July of 1817.) There were two other sisters, Mary, born 1814, and Betsy, born in 1816.

Two days later, and for the Benefit of Miss A Smedley, was performed an adaptation of the story of *The Hunchback of Notre Dame* by J.S. Knowles, called *Hunchback*, with the following cast:

Mr Smedley	Mr Mosley
Mr Rogers	Mr Fitzroy
Mr J Smedley	Mr Montague
Mr Lockwood	Mr Tannett
Mr Sheldon	Mr B Tannett
Miss A Tannett	Miss Smedley
Mrs Fitzroy and Miss Tannett	

… after which was presented *No!* with: Messrs. Montague, Mosley, Lockwood, Rogers, Fitzroy, Tannett, Sheldon, Charles, Miss Tannett, Mrs Lockwood, Mrs Fitzroy.

They then continued to Sleaford, where they opened on 6th June, 1836, with *Heart of Mid Lothian* and *Uncle John*.

That summer, Joseph announced that Bradford and Huddersfield had been added to his West Riding theatres. This may have been a deliberate policy in order to form a separate small circuit of South Yorkshire venues, and again may have had a bearing on his plans for the future.

Certainly, throughout the current touring season, Joseph could be seen to be recruiting actors and assimilating them into his company, indeed in his first season at Wakefield he had added Messrs Thornhill and Fishwick to the cast. Then, according to existing playbills, at Grimsby in February Messrs Montague and Granville joined the company; Mr Webbe at Spilsby; Mr Mosley from Nottingham at about the same time; and Vining, as well as Mr and Mrs Skerrett joined at Beverley. Mr Sheldon came aboard at Gainsborough; while Messrs Wofford and Holland had joined at Caistor. At Grimsby, Mr Wallett joined the company, as well as Mrs Hamerton ("from the Sheffield Theatre") and Mr Vernon ("from the Scarboro' Theatre").

Bradford was in some ways a bigger risk than Wakefield had been the previous year. There was not a very strong theatre-going culture in Bradford. In fact, thanks to the opposition of evangelical groups, there hadn't been a theatre of any kind since 1820. There had been long-held prejudice against theatrical entertainments, which was inherited by succeeding generations. They regarded theatres as being places where honest folk shouldn't be seen. Neither was there a Mechanics' Institute, or lecture or concert hall either; although Doncaster, Wakefield and Halifax did have a history of theatre-going and those towns had welcomed some of the biggest theatrical 'names' in the country.[5]

Not so Bradford. The first theatre there had been opened in 1810 by L.S. Thompson in a converted barn in Southgate, later Sackville Street, off Westgate, a site he later left in favour of an upstairs room at the King's Arms Inn in Westgate. In 1820, he left there and started a theatre over the butter-cross in Market Street which could hold 700–800 people, and was apparently well-fitted with stage and scenery.[6]

---

[5] William Scruton – "Pen and Pencil Pictures of Old Bradford", 1889. Reprinted by Mountain Press, Queensbury, 1968

[6] do

Thompson was himself an actor, and a good mimic, particularly of Yorkshire characters, as was his son, Lysander Thompson, who later became quite famous.

The theatre was then taken over for a couple of months by 'Jemmy' Wild who normally used a travelling booth to present a programme of conjuring tricks, acrobatics, and the antics of a performing pony, called 'Billy'. Wild was not at this point an actor, and it was 14 years before a theatre worth its name arrived in the guise of 'Smedley's Theatre'.

His theatre was, in fact, a large wooden structure capable of holding up to twelve hundred persons. It was a much stronger and more superior edifice than the usual wooden structures of the day, and it stood upon the site of Messrs. McKean, Tetley & Co.'s warehouse in Peel Square. It stood practically alone, and the space around it was used as a fair ground.[7] In his book,[8] Mr Scruton gave us a vignette of Joseph:

> Mr Smedley came from Sleaford in Lincolnshire. He was a tragedian *on* the stage, but *off* it, a dandified gentleman, full of self-confidence and importance. He was proud of his establishment, and very enterprising, and certainly *deserved* success, if he might not always command it.
>
> [...]
>
> His theatre was "highly respectable", comfortable, well arranged throughout, and possessed good scenery, some of which was from the brush of J. Wilson Anderson, a local artist of considerable ability. The company, though not large, was select and good. In his play-bills, Mr Smedley states that "It is quite certain the town of Bradford is entitled to amusements on the scale of talent and respectability equal to any in the country, *but if so, they must be paid for at the same rate*" [Italics by Mr Scruton]. Accordingly he fixed his "bill of fare" at "*Boxes, 3s.; Pit, 2s.; Gallery, 1s.*". This scale he sustained throughout his stay in Bradford, and had good houses too, his best patrons, however, being the "gods" of the gallery".

---

[7] do

[8] Pen and Pencil Portraits of Old Bradford, William Scruton, 1889

Bradford, as a town, was growing and becoming more and more prosperous. In 1811 its population was 7767, but by 1831 this had practically tripled, rising to 23,223 and by 1841 it had reached 34,580.[9]

Joseph's first season there commenced on July 2nd, 1836[10], and the performance of 4th July was heralded thus:[11]

<u>THE LEGITIMATE THEATRE</u>
<u>AND 22 PERFORMERS</u>
NEW
THEATRE BRADFORD
GUY MANNERING, OR, THE GIPSY'S PROPHECY
Colonel Mannering............Mr Mosley   Henry Bertram............Mr Holland
Dandie Dinmont............Mr Rogers   Gilbert Grossin............Mr Lockwood
Gabriel............Mr Wofford   Dominic Sampson............Mr Smedley
Jock Jabos ....Mr Charles   Baillie Mucklethrift............Mr Neville
Dirk Hatteraik............Mr B Tannett
Gipsies, Farmers &C............Messrs Webbe, Jackman, Sheldon, Hutson &C
Franco............Master G Smedley   Sebastien............Mr Lewis
Julia Mannering............Mrs Jackman   Meg Merrilies............Miss Neville
Lucy Bertram............Miss A Smedley
Mrs M'Cavendish............Mrs Lockwood   Flora............Miss Smedley
Gipsy Girl............Miss Tannett
Comic Singing by Mr Lockwood
THE WEDDING DAY by Mrs Inchbald
Boxes 3s. Pit 2s Gallery 1s

This was followed on 13th July by *The School for Scandal* and *Three Fingered Jack*; and on 14th July by *The Rivals* with 'a musical entertainment' called *Paul and Virginia*.

On August 3rd *Hunchback* was performed with *Turn-Out*; August 10th was *The Merchant of Venice* with a farce called *Widow's Victim*. On 26th August,

---

[9] Bradford Observer, 27th October 1859 (British Newspaper Archive)

[10] According to CMP Taylor, "Right Royal".

[11] Playbill in Lincolnshire Archives.

"By Desire of United Ancient Order of Druids," and for the Benefit of Messrs. Rogers and Mosley, *Richard III, or, The Battle of Bosworth Field* was performed, "Featuring the Murder of King Henry, the Funeral Procession, The Council Chamber, The Young Princes are smothered in the Tower, & Battle of Bosworth Field where Gloucester meets his death." This was followed by ... *Robinson Crusoe*!

On August 27th, for the Benefit of Mr J Smedley, was chosen *The Dream at Sea* followed by *A Variety of Singing* and *Fly by Night*, while on August 29th, *To Marry or Not To Marry* was the main attraction, with *The Toast be Dear Women*, by Mr Holland, and a new farce called *Popping the Question*, followed by another new farce called *Catching an Heiress*.[12]

August 31st, 1836, saw the last night of the first Bradford season, as announced on a playbill with a lengthy discourse from Joseph in his usual, somewhat lofty, moralising, and, by modern-day standards, obsequious tone:

<u>BENEFIT OF MISS AND MISS A. SMEDLEY</u>
<u>THE LAST NIGHT OF PERFORMING</u>

Mr Smedley begs to return his sincere thanks to each and all (but in an especial manner to the patrons of the Drama his thanks are due) for the kind support with which he has been honoured, and he trusts that his own individual exertions, the rectitude and good conduct of his company, together with the great good that <u>may</u> be, and is derived from a well conducted Theatre, will be a sufficient stimulus for the advocates of its amusements to come forward and support his efforts to erect a permanent Building, that shall be worthy of a town so highly respectable in wealth, intelligence, and population. At all events, and under any circumstances, it shall always be his study to make the Theatre, both by precept and practice, what its advocates contend for, "A school of eloquence, the temple of the arts, the shrine of the muses, the chastener of our morals, and the mild, but persuasive monitress of our duties."

---

[12] Playbills in Lincs. Archives.

WIVES AS THEY WERE
AND MAIDS AS THEY ARE
Mr Lockwood will sing the 'King and the Sailor'
Mr Holland 'The Horn of Chase'
Mr Lewis 'Out A Shooting'
WANTED A VALET
A farce written by Miss Smedley

The remarks at the top of this playbill include a suggestion that a more permanent building should be built as a theatre for the people of Bradford.

Indeed, he took this further, and proposed that a theatre be erected, in his usual way, by public subscription. He estimated the cost to be £1200 which he proposed to raise by offering shares of £25 each, with Joseph himself taking eight shares, and to subsequently lease the theatre on terms guaranteeing a 5% return to subscribers.[13]

By the start of September of that year there were almost enough subscribers, and by the end of October all of the shares had been taken. However, nothing further, apparently, was done, and no reason for this can be found. Indeed in the following June of 1837, another wooden building was erected for him in Bradford, this time in Hall Ings. This is still a major thoroughfare in Bradford today; 'Ings' being a term for marshland in Old English.

It seems that the Smedley company's next stop was Huddersfield, where, on the fourth of the month, they presented *Richard the Third* and *The Invincibles, or, The Female Soldiers*. This is the first playbill that I have been able to find with another new member of the cast, a Miss Desborough. She had joined Joseph's company from the Leeds Theatre where she had been appearing until recently. In July she acted Regan in a production of *King Lear, and* on 2nd September 1836, she had appeared there in *Rockwood* as Lady Rockwood, and, on the same bill, in a farce called *Admirals Daughter* as Eliza Thunder. The only other reference to her prior to this is in the *Suffolk Chronicle* where an advertisement appears of a performance of *Pizarro* at Framlingham on

---

[13] Bradford Observer, 30th June, 1836, and quoted by CMP Taylor in "Right Royal"

21st November, 1836, where she played the part of Elvira.

On 6th October, she featured in Smedley's production of *Married Life, or, Fireside Sketches*, and, for her benefit on October 22nd, she chose *(A) Cure for the Heartache*, which also featured Mr Chute ("from the Leeds Theatre and for this Night only!"), as 'Young Rapid'. This was followed by *Luke the Labourer, or, Lost Son*.

On 24th October, she appeared in *Heir at Law* followed by the farce *My Uncle John and his Cousins*. On 29th October, for the Benefit of J. Smedley, they presented *The Iron Chest, or, The Mysterious Murder*, a new song called 'Analysation' performed by Mr Lockwood, followed by *A Bohemian Dance* by Miss Desborough. The evening was finished off with the farce *Two Strings to Your Bow*.

On 31st October, the programme included *Marry or Not to Marry*, *Popping the Question*, and *Catching an Heiress*.

From here they returned to Wakefield, where they opened their season. William Senior remarked[14] that

> of Smedley's two daughters, the younger, Miss Annette Smedley, had the greater liking for the stage, and played more important parts than her sister. Ophelia, Belvidera, Rebecca in Ivanhoe, and Lady Teazle are amongst the characters she sustained during the season of 1836. Miss Smedley, the elder sister, played boys' part, such as The Prince of Wales in Richard III, and Paul in The Wandering Boys, or girls masquerading as boys, such as Viola.

However these roles were now to be shared with another new addition to the company. A lady of "great vivacity and versatility," a Miss Desborough, now joined Joseph's company to play the second boys, dance the hornpipe in between pieces, and to impersonate such roles as Mrs Rattleton and Louisa Lovetricks in farces.

This season commenced on 4th November, and, strangely, there are no extant

---

[14] "The Old Wakefield Theatre", First pub. 1894

playbills for this season amongst his papers, possibly because he didn't want to remember it!

This is what the *West Riding Herald* had to say:

> Mr Smedley, the enterprising manager of this theatre, opened it with a capital provincial company on this night week. Since then he has given four performances, in each of which the prominent piece was some *morceau* of sterling English comedy, ancient and modern. This is as it should be; and he deserves for it the patronage, which no doubt, the discriminating public of this town always so liberally bestows on substantial merit. His opening performance was Sheridan's inimitable comedy of "The Rivals; or a Trip to Bath". On Monday he gave Colman's highly popular play of the "Iron Chest": on Wednesday, "The Deformed; or the Hunchback of Notre Dame" and tonight he delights hid audience with Buckstone's beautiful minor drama, produced last season with such éclat at the Adelphi, "The Dream at Sea". So much for the staple of the performances. The inferior pieces were all lively farces of the first class of that description of dramatic composition. We have said his company is a capital provincial one: we repeat it; and moreover we will add that, in many of the minor theatres of London, especially those "over the water", as the local phrase goes-the Surrey of the Victoria-though, there are some individuals superior to the best of them; on the whole we would look in vain for the coherence and equality which characterise this effective little *corps domestique*. Where the merits of all are so parallel it would be invidious to particularise any; but courtesy compels us to notice one, Miss Desborough, because, as we are given to understand, she is a *debutante*.
>
> Miss Desborough is evidently very new to the stage; but she exhibits, not withstanding, considerable capabilities for high performance. Study-but it must be intense study-of the elements of the histrionic art- may do much for her: but nature appears to have done more. She is, in addition to her mental qualifications for the stage, young, well forged and handsome, no inconsiderable elements of Success in a public profession, where to have beauty is better than the best letter of recommendation; and her manner of acting is *degage* and almost totally free from that stiffness and restraint, which usually characterise young performers. We consider her an acquisition to Mr Smedley's company-indeed she would be so, in our opinion to any provincial company-and we hope ere long to have the pleasure of recognizing her person and applauding her performance

on the boards of "the Garden", "Old Drury", or "the Haymarket" at the least. We were glad to perceive the old favourite of the town, Mr Rogers, again on Wednesday evening. His impersonation of "Quasimodo", in the "Hunchback of Notre Dame" afforded great satisfaction to the audience, and much to admire to all lovers ("we own the soft impeachment") of the Drama.

By all accounts, Miss Desborough was easy on the eye; she was blonde and had a full figure, had a pleasing personality, and, although very new to the stage, she very quickly became a popular artiste with the public and the newspapers. That she courted them is beyond all doubt. It is also likely that in playing the roles she was given, and attracting notices such as the one above, she may have put Annette and Helen Smedleys' noses out of joint, and one can almost feel the backstage angst that this addition to the company caused.

The Dream at Sea and *The Invincibles, or, Female Soldiers*, were enacted on Friday, 11th November, followed on the 12th by *Venice Preserved* with *Past Ten O'clock*. On the following Monday, the 14th, *The Deformed* and *The Spoiled Child* were presented.

The newspaper of 18th November reported:

> We regret that we cannot this week give an elaborate notice and critique of the performances, as well as of the performers of both sexes at out theatre since we last had occasion to comment on both. For the first omission; (forced as it is upon us by want of space) our readers will excuse us when we mention that some of the most approved of our plays, and of our minor dramatic productions redolent of wit and humour, have been most judiciously and with good taste selected for performance by Mr Smedley the manager; and those, it is needless to say, require not the aid of a critic to point out in them the beauties and excellencies already acknowledged by common consent, and applauded by every audience before whom they have been performed. For the second omission-a *critique raisonne* on the performers execution of their respective parts we may, perhaps, be excused by our readers in consideration of the declaration we now make to the effect that if those of them who have visited or who have yet to visit the theatre and will do so do not agree with us in thinking the company a good one; and if they are not like us pleased with its collective performance, then shall we be

content to admit that we are no judges whatever of the style and manner of acting; or of the conception of part or of character in an actor or actress.

So having given its reasons for not reviewing the theatre's attractions and its resident company, it now continues to do just that:

Yet cannot we altogether pass without notice the performance of our old acquaintance on the Wakefield boards-the two Miss Smedleys still increasing in favouritism with the public, and Miss Neville, together with Mr Neville, Mr Smedley, jun. and Mr Mosley; all of whom having had a just meed of praise from us last year require no more from us now than a repetition of it, which we give in those general terms, with pleasure. Mr Rogers "the last but not the least" of those our acquaintance of the past year, is neither "the last nor the least" of those of the favourites of the public of Wakefield, it would seem. Messrs Lockwood, Montague, Lewis, Tannett, and Lacey form a considerable and a strong reinforcement to the company. Miss Desborough is a host in herself; and is determined, it would seem, to carry by a storm of theatrical attractions the combined applause of the gallery, (we give, as in duty bound, the gods the precedence) boxes, and pit. As we said before, Miss D is a young actress of high-rate pretensions in the art. We shall not prophesy, (for no one is a prophet in his own country. In Wakefield we would not be taken as such) but we think Miss D. Will hereafter do no discredit to the favourable judgement that we now form of the taste, facility of manner, ease of execution, and delicate conception of character which she possesses in this attractive, and, in its perfection, most accomplished art. On Wednesday night a Mrs Montague made her first appearance here. Of her, so far as we have seen, we can speak in terms of praise only.

Mrs Lockwood also demands our plauditory notice. In truth Mr Smedley deserves our thanks for his exertions in affording us an an amusement so grateful to us.

We trust the good people Wakefield feel with us, and that they will so testify to Mr S., by giving him a nightly "full bumper".[15]

I don't know what caused the newspaper to publish this puff piece, but it was

---

[15] West Riding Herald, 18th Nov. 1836; Wakefield Library Local Studies.

no doubt pleasing for Joseph to read (if indeed he didn't write it himself, for he was not without a flair for self-promotion when necessary!!) To an actress as new and young as Miss Desborough, however, it would be surprising if she wasn't flattered by such attention, and probably a bit swell-headed too.

That evening, Friday, the 18th November, they presented the play of *The Stranger* with the farce *The Invincibles*, and on Saturday, Shakespeare's *King Henry the Fourth* and *The Dunder Family*. Advertised for the following Monday, the 21st, was *Hamlet* and *The Dead Shot*. On Wednesday, 23rd November, *The Dream at Sea* and *Love and Laugh* were performed.

However, things weren't going quite as well as hoped according to the local paper, which nevertheless continued to give praise to Joseph's company, and, in particular, to Miss Desborough:

> Since our last dramatic notice Mr Smedley has performed to comparatively thin houses, if we except Wednesday night's performance, which was well and fashionably attended. The "Dream at Sea" was, at the request of the ladies of Mr Peterson's family, selected for that night, and much to the credit of those ladies' taste and knowledge of the Drama. This play has a variety of incident both touching and humorous; and it was very well performed. After it followed a farce of infinite fun, called "Love and Laugh." Miss Desborough in the character of Miss Dora, the lively and artless daughter of an old *quid-nunc* (Lockwood), whose rage for news and politics is so great, that he determines she shall be married to no man who is not an M.P., performed with her wonted ease and fidelity of conception of character. The plaudits of boxes, pit and gallery were showered upon her, and liberally bestowed upon Miss Neville, together with Messrs. Lockwood and Moseley. Indeed the performances of the night seemed to give uniform satisfaction to the audience".[16]

The season continued into December, and, on 2nd December, the *West Riding Herald* reported:

---

[16] West Riding Herald, 25th November, 1836; Wakefield Library, Local Studies.

The Life and Times of Joseph Smedley

We were gratified to find during the week past that the theatre was better attended than on any week since it was opened for this season by its enterprising manager, who has done everything with respect to the dramatic arrangementsthat could administer to the amusement of the public. We have before said that Mr Smedley most judiciously selected his plays from those which were, and are most popular and because unobjectionable. So far his theatre not only affords a pleasing, but a profitable recreation. On Wednesday night there were good performances, and a well attended house. The laughter-provoking interlude, entitled "Hunting a Turtle" attracted continued plaudits! Miss Desborough performed with, we think, a more than common power in an actress, so young in years, and so new to the stage, the part of Mrs Turtle, a favourite one, if we mistake not, with Mrs Nisbet and Madame Vestris, two "stars" of the London stage, of the first brilliancy and attraction. Of Miss Desborough's style of acting we have already spoken favourably. We cannot, from some occasional indications of a higher style of acting than that she confines herself to, and which we noticed in some nights of her performances, but think that she would succeed in parts or characters of the higher order of dramatic productions. An occasional harshness in the tones of her voice she should be cautious to correct. However, somewhat more practice, together with proper attention to a correction of this defect, will produce the necessary modulation. It is but occasionally to be detected, and may be easily removed. By a reference to our advertising columns, we perceive a benefit for Mr Smedley is fixed for this night. As he deserves, so, we trust, he will have, a "bumper," as full as possible. On Saturday night Miss Desborough will have a benefit also, and no doubt, a house full to an overflow. Independent of her own acting together with that of the *elite* of Mr Smedley's company, there will be Miss Gilman, Mrs Crouch, and Messrs. Compton and Chute, of the Leeds theatre. Of Mr Compton's high merit the public are already aware, and Mr Chute is an actor, who, as we have never seen him perform, we must judge of by the favourable report we have of him. On Saturday we hope to have the pleasure of judging for ourselves. Miss Gilman as a *danceuse* is a great favourite with all who have witnessed her grace and elegance of movement and agility, and Mrs Crouch is a performer of no inconsiderable celebrity. On the whole we shall, we opine, have a treat.

The writer who penned this was indeed correct, in that on that very evening, for the Benefit of Mr Smedley, was performed the New Tragedy of *ION* with the entertainment of *Two Late for Dinner*; and, on the following evening:[17]

---

[17] West Riding Herald, 2nd December 1836; Wakefield Library, Local Studies.

Richard E. Smedley

THEATRE, WAKEFIELD

* * *

For the Benefit of
MISS DESBOROUGH

* * *

ON SATURDAY EVENING NEXT, December 3rd, 1836 on which occasion Mr COMPTON, Mr CHUTE, Miss GILLMAN, and Mrs CROUCH, of the Leeds Theatre, will lend their valuable assistance for this Night only, when will be presented the Domestic Drama of
LUKE THE LABOURER
Or, the Lost Son
Phillip (the Lost Son) MR COMPTON
Luke the Labourer Mr CHUTE
Clara Miss DESBOROUGH

* * *

Comic Song............"Humours of an Election," Mr Compton

* * *

LA SYLPHIDE,
As danced by Mademoiselle Taglioni, at the Italian Opera,
BY MISS GILLMAN

* * *

After which, the new Farce of
INVINCIBLES;
Or, Les Femmes Soldats
Victoire MISS DESBOROUGH

***

A Character Dance by MISS GILLMAN
Guy Fawkes, to be sung by request, by Mr Compton

***

To conclude with a new Burletta, called
THE UNFINISHED GENTLEMAN;
Or, Jack Ragg out of Place
Bill Downey (the Unfinished Gentleman) Mr COMPTON
James Miller Mr CHUTE
Mary Miss DESBOROUGH

***

The house was indeed packed out. It also speaks highly of Miss Desborough that her former acting colleagues from Leeds, Messrs. Compton and Chute, Miss Gillman and Mrs Crouch, all agreed to act in Wakefield for her benefit. In the following week's newspaper, Miss Desborough placed the following item:

A CARD

***

THEATRE, WAKEFIELD
MISS DESBOROUGH

Takes this opportunity of expressing her gratitude to her Friends and the Public, for the kind, generous, and liberal support with which she was honoured at her Benefit on Saturday evening last, the sense of which she will ever cherish with feelings of the liveliest emotion

It is worth remarking here that Mr Henry Compton was a highly respected comedian. He was born in 1805, he had made his stage debut at Lewes. He had been a member of the Lincoln Theatre's company in 1832 for three years, where he met and formed a close friendship with J.H.Chute, before joining the York circuit.[18] His last season there was in 1837, and he parted from the company in Leeds, and later went on to become one of the most famous and accomplished Shakespearean clowns of his generation, and acted at the Theatre Royal, Haymarket with Buckstone in the 1850s and was still acting to great acclaim at the old Globe Theatre in the 1870s. He started a theatrical dynasty of sorts. His real name was Charles Mackenzie. His father John Mackenzie, had given up his ship-building business and become a preacher; he had married Elizabeth Symonds who came from a long and illustrious line of surgeons. Henry changed his name in order to avoid embarrassing the Puritan sensibilities of his family when he became an actor. He in turn married Miss Emmeline Montague, the daughter of Henry (H.J.) Montague, a well-known light comedian. Their son, Edward Compton, also became a well-known and popular actor who married Virginia, the fourth daughter of the American impresario H.L. Bateman; the man responsible for bringing Henry Irving to the Lyceum as leading man for his third daughter, Isabel. Edward and Virginia Compton had a family of five, one of whom became the actress Fay Compton, enormously popular in the first half of the twentieth century; and one of her brothers was the author Compton Mackenzie.[19] James Henry Chute later married Macready's half-sister, Emily Mazzarina Macready, and, after the death of his mother-in-law he inherited the leases of the Theatre Royal in Bristol and in Bath. He soon built a new theatre in Bristol, designed by C.J. Phipps, which was named the Prince's Theatre, but colloquially called 'The House that Jack Built'. After his death in 1878, his sons carried on the theatrical traditions, although by then stock theatre was no longer in vogue.

***

The following Tuesday, the 6th December, they performed ("by Particular Desire") *The Belle's Stratagem* with the farce *The Happiest Days of my Life*; and on the Wednesday, 7th December for the Benefit of Mr and Miss Neville, *The Tragedy of Richard the Third, Comic Singing &c.* and concluded with the farce *The Honest Thieves*.

---

[18] From 'The York Theatre' by Sybil Rosenfeld; STR, 2001

[19] From the Introduction to "Rosemary", the autobiography of Fay Compton, written by Compton Mackenzie

On the 8th December there was an auction of the property and effects of the late James Banks (the former owner of the theatre) at the George Hotel. On the Saturday, the headline news was: "Wakefield Theatre was put up for sale by auction on Thursday last. When Mr Joseph Smedley, the present lessee, became the purchaser, for nine hundred pounds – said to be a good purchase."[20]

A similar headline appeared in the *Leeds Mercury* of 17th December. Joseph had acquired "all that spacious and substantially built Theatre, with two capital Cellars under the same, (one used as a Cooper's Shop) and a three-stalled stable and Hay-Loft, Yard and other Conveniences behind the same… with a frontage of 36 feet towards Westgate."[21]

On Friday, 9th December, 1836, the company performed *Ivanhoe* and *Catching an Heiress*; on Saturday, the 10th, for the Benefit of Mr and Mrs Montague, *The Wandering Boys*, with *The Innkeeper's Bride* and *The Mutiny at the Nore*.

On Monday, 12th December, for the Benefit of Messrs. Beattie, Lewis, and Cameron, *Othello* and *Where Shall I Dine?* The following evening, and for the Benefit of Mr and Mrs Lockwood, they acted *Speed the Plough*, and *The Tale of Mystery*. On Thursday, 15th, for the Benefit of Messrs. Rogers and Mosley, they gave *Eugene Aram*.

On 29th December, Miss Desborough had a second benefit performance, requested by some of her admirers; an unusual event, not to say remarkable. Afterwards, she was presented with a gold watch and chain as a testimonial "of the high estimation in which the inhabitants of Wakefield hold her theatrical talents."[22] Apparently, "she was dressed in white, and looked magnificent."[23] It was also noted that the Misses Smedley were not included in the cast for the presentation evening.[24]

---

[20] The Leeds Intelligencer, December 10th, 1836. Wakefield Library, Local Studies
[21] Quoted by CMP Taylor in "Right Royal"
[22] From bottom of playbill
[23] Reported by William Senior in 'The Old Wakefield Theatre' quoting someone who had been present
[24] do

The year 1836 had been quite a good year for Joseph and his family and acting company. He probably felt more at home in Yorkshire, and found himself better accepted, being a Yorkshireman too.

Also during 1836, Charles Kemble retired from the stage due to worsening deafness, and, after the death of Colman, who was the Examiner of Plays, in the same year, Kemble was appointed to the position which carried with it a small emolument. Colman had been a most prodigious and successful playwright, and his works formed a substantial part of every theatrical company's repertoire in those times. This was certainly true of Smedley's company, where *Heir at Law* was, as elsewhere, a staple piece. Indeed, after Colman's death an anonymous wag wrote the following epitaph:[25]

> Within this monumental bed
> Apollo's favourite rests his head:
> > Ye Muses, cease your grieving.
>
> A son the father's loss supplies,
> Be comforted, though Colman dies,
> > His "Heir-at-Law" is living.

However, Kemble did not take the duties very seriously, indeed his time in the role was described by J.R. Stephens as "among the most obscure and least documented of all nineteenth century terms of office… he took very little interest in the work… and the major portion was delegated to his son JMK." In 1839, in expectation of the death of Charles Kemble, whose health was failing, Bulwer Lytton offered the position to Macready, who, according to his reminiscences, jumped at the chance. In the event, however, JMK was awarded the title.

It was at about this time that Joseph wrote a letter, or more of a press release, to the owner of the local newspaper, in which he set out his plans for the immediate future:

> Mr Smedley having become proprietor and lessee of the Theatres Wakefield, Bradford, Huddersfield and other places in the county of York, and finding that

---

[25] Quoted in the Book of Authors by W. Clark Russell

the necessary attention in salaries so large and a Company so numerous to be more than he himself could do justice to, he is induced to retain his Oldest son's assistance at least until his second son is old enough to be of the same service. He therefore in the mean time has committed the management of those theatres which have been in his possession so many years to Messrs Rogers and Mosley whom he has selected for their talent, authority, probity and good conduct; and if the public have hitherto thought kindly of Mr S. Of which he is assured by the support he has met with – he can with confidence recommend the Gentlemen he has appointed as every way worthy of their Patronage and support.

This, then may have been behind his long-term plan; already in his early fifties, and Joseph Jnr being twenty years of age and George just fifteen, it appears that Joseph Snr is planning his eventual withdrawal from the stage after ensuring his two sons' future with the birth-right of their own theatrical circuits. His undated copy of this letter was written on the back of a flier advertising the forthcoming Benefit for his daughters:

THE MISSES SMEDLEY

Respectfully announce that their Benefit, under the Patronage of the Stewards of the Ball, is fixed for <u>Thursday</u> next, when they respectfully solicit that support which they will ever endeavour to merit, as well as their private conduct as their professions exertions. The Performance will be Morton's Comedy of

A SCHOOL FOR GROWN CHILDREN
and the farce of
THE ILLUSTRIOUS STRANGER

At the same time, MR SMEDLEY takes leave to say, that having purchased the Theatre (at a price which nothing but the increasing kindness of his Friends and Patrons could justify), it must and will act as a stimulus, and induce him to use every effort in his power to deserve their good opinion.

Richard E. Smedley

The 'Desborough Debacle'

The benefit took place on 5th January, and caused much embarrassment for Joseph and ill-feeling all round. Apparently, Miss Desborough, who was due to act during the Benefit, refused to appear. This occasioned Joseph to go before the curtain to explain her absence to the audience. This is how the newspaper reported it:

THEATRE

This being the last week of our theatrical amusements for the season, we are Rejoiced at being able to state that up to last night (inclusive) they have been kept Up with spirit by Mr Smedley's company, and attended and largely applauded by numerous audiences. We congratulate Mr Smedley upon the support which he has received from the inhabitants of Wakefield. Since our last notice there has been some very good acting in some excellent pieces, wherein the Miss Smedley's, Mrs Reid, Miss Neville, Mrs Lockwood, and Mrs Montague exerted themselves as laudably as usual. Messrs. Lockwood, Rogers, Mosley, Reid, Lacy and Montague performed with increased spirit and received increased applause. Miss Desborough who, in one of our theatrical notices, we characterised as "a host in herself" was on Saturday, Monday and Wednesday nights as effective, and as admired in her style of acting as usual, and received more than her wonted meed of general applause. Last night was a bespeak by the Stewards of the Charity Ball for the benefit of the Miss Smedleys. The house was very full, particularly the boxes. When the first piece, together with the comic singing by Messrs. Lockwood and Reid had concluded, Mr Smedley came before the curtain and stated that Miss Desborough had *unadvisedly* and *ungratefully* refused to act that night, and excused himself accordingly to the audience for her non-appearance. The imputation of ingratitude on the part of this young actress, so highly favoured and applauded by the people of Wakefield, certainly surprised us as it did the entire audience, and produced a universal call for her to appear and answer for herself. This clamour was kept up for a considerable time; but she did not make her appearance, not being, in fact, in the house. Happening to have been told on the morning of Tuesday that Miss D. Could not perform the part cast for her in consequence of her inability to sing in it, we were astonished indeed at Mr Smedley's not stating this to the audience, at least as a palliation of her imputed ingratitude. We saw

Mr Smedley after the play was over, and upon our requesting to know at what time and upon what grounds she refused to act on this night, he showed us a note written by her to him on the morning of Tuesday, and to the effect that it was impossible for her to study the part as it was out of her line, and requesting to be put in a part which she had studied in. To this communication of hers he did not say that he made any reply. Now if this charge of ingratitude on her part to the people of Wakefield be well founded she is little worthy indeed of the favour she received at their hands, whatever may be the amount of her theatrical talents. If it be not, then is Mr Smedley bound as an honest man to make her public reparation for having imputed to her a degree of baseness unparalled (sic) in a young woman , owing so much as she does to public favour and support. We have the authority of one medical gentleman and of two other persons of her acquaintance for stating that Miss Desborough was, in consequence of severe indisposition, advised not to act for the last week and particularly so on last night, owing to her increased indisposition.[26]

This not unnaturally caused considerable comment. The rights and wrongs of the matter as perceived by the theatregoers of Wakefield were discussed and dissected and ultimately divided them. Joseph was asked by the newspaper to afford them a copy of the remarks he made from the stage, something he was unable to do as:

Being as I was behind the scenes prepared to return the <u>usual</u> thanks (which by the bye I forgot to do in the excitement so unexpected as to meet a charge so serious) you may well suppose I cannot give you my speech verbatim on so different a subject. The former I had prepared myself in the latter I could not. It came as you heard it-but if not actually verbatim, I am sure 'tis exactly to the same purport and of which I am not ashamed. I do not mean its language, its rounded (illegible) it has none-but its honesty of purpose. I merely ask for justice to my motives. Honestly and truly do I wish the lady well after all but well it never can be til she has learned <u>gratitude</u> and <u>discretion</u> would you not have considered a Daughter or Sister of yours having acted as she has 'ungrateful and indiscreet-gloss it as you may your convenience would say 'yes'.

---

[26] West Riding Herald, 6th January, 1837. (Wakefield Library Local Studies)

In finishing, Joseph asks for his Respects to be passed to Mr Snow (believed to be the newspaper's owner). The letter is dated 'Rotherham, Jan. 10th, 1837'.[27]

Joseph did give his version of events, and his reasons for saying what he did. The newspaper re-hashed the whole affair and out of fairness, printed the accounts of both Joseph and Miss Desborough.

It is clear that this episode upset Joseph to a great degree, calling into question, as it did, his reputation and his treatment of actors in his company. As we have seen, Joseph was a proud man and jealous of his public reputation for integrity, high moral standards and fair-play. He automatically defended himself against his accuser, Miss Desborough; anxious to be seen as acting in the best interests of all, and correctly in light of someone in his position. Despite a relatively successful season during which he consolidated his management (and ownership) of the Wakefield Theatre, this episode unquestionably cast a shadow over his achievements.

The *West Riding Herald* summed up the season and the Desborough fiasco:

> The theatre closed on Friday night last, after, we have every reason to hope, An advantageous season, so far as Wakefield is concerned, to the enterprising Manager of it, whose property it now is. Independent of our conviction that the Stage may be made a medium of moral improvement, as well as of refinement of taste and manners, we are also satisfied that we do our duty towards our fellow-Townsmen by promoting his success as far as in our power lies, and by demonstrating to the general public the prosperity of this town, of which that success is a proof. Of all public amusements, theatrical performances come most within the cognizance of a public Journalist, and require the closest attention and caution lest they may be diverted from the only rational purpose to which they should be applied…to expose the follies, foibles, and peculiarities of mankind, and to correct them by ridicule-to hold up to public view the vices of mankind, and to cause them to be detested and execrated. Now, we must do Mr Smedley the justice to say that, so far as we have had an opportunity of Observing, he has made the theatre in this town subservient to the purpose above mentioned; and we are pleased, therefore, that he has that encouragement.

---

[27] Draft letter in Family archive; Lincolnshire Archives, LLHS 38/5/3/30

From the inhabitants which such laudable conduct on his part merited.

We should not have written further, but that in our notice of the theatre in last Friday's number, we expressed some surprise at the charge of ingratitude to the people of this town, made against a young actress who has certainly been in a high degree applauded and favoured by them. This conduct on her part, assuming Mr Smedley to be correct in his accusation, we thought unpardonable, particularly in a person so young. On the other hand, if Mr S. Made the charge hastily, and under the impulse of irritated feeling at her declining to act upon that night, we were of opinion that he, as a man in whose candour, propriety, and good feeling we had a perfect reliance, had a right to make her a just reparation, by an acknowledgement of his having misapprehended the cause of her declining to act, as intimated to him by her. With that sternness of impartiality and strictness of justice to all parties, from which, if we know ourselves well, neither threats or entreaties shall induce us to depart, we put the case before our readers; and without giving any decision of our own, we left it to their consideration, well knowing that a just inference as to the charge and defence would, upon explanation, be come to by them. If we used an observation more severe than the case justified, it was in characterising the ingratitude of Miss Desborough as a degree of "unparalleled baseness". The expression was harsh, but under all the circumstances, we thought at the time justifiable. On Friday night, Miss Desborough, who, as her medical attendant informed us, was severely indisposed, and unable, without much danger, to leave her bed on that day, appeared before the curtain (not in stage character) as soon as the first piece of the night had finished, and certainly her pallid face, wasted features, and personal debility, betokened severe indisposition. She was received with rapturous applause, and in a low but distinct, and at times, energetic tone, she delivered the following address to the audience. The reception it met with from the auditory will be judged of by the frequency of the plaudits which interrupted the delivery.

It does seem, from this distance in time anyway, that this is surely a mountain made from a molehill. But if anything, it shows the degree of respect and the regard for good manners that were manifest in mid-nineteenth century life, particularly those in the public eye who were held to a higher account. That the 'indisposition' of an actress and her consequent failure to appear on stage should be regarded as a kind of sleight on the audience, seems alien to us in the twenty-first century. Yet I have lost count of the times that an actor has been 'indisposed' which, as a euphemism, covers a multitude of sins, but these days lends itself to disappointment rather than offence. Quite clearly, however, in the 1830s it seems to have caused both.

This is what followed, quoting Miss Desborough's own words:

> My dear friends, – Thus unattended I come before you; but innocence is bold, and can stand alone with the protection of Heaven over its head. (Applause.)

I know that I am before a discerning and Christian audience, who will listen to me with indulgence, and only suffer their opinions to be guided by the principles of honour. (Applause). In this paper, (holding up the West Riding Herald of the 6th inst.), I find an accusation, made by Mr Smedley against me, of ingratitude towards the public of Wakefield. This is a stigma under which I could not rest; and am now come from a sick bed at the risk of my life to refute the charge here, and before a large audience of my patrons made against me in my absence. (Tremendous applause.) [Miss Desborough then read a paragraph from the paper (printed above), of Mr Smedley's accusation, and then proceeded to address the audience.]

> This statement is perfectly untrue: I did not refuse to act; far from it: it was my most anxious wish to play two of my favourite characters on the two last nights of my appearance here, and not taking into consideration my severe indisposition, and contrary to my medical attendant's advice, I wrote to Mr Smedley to that effect on Tuesday morning before ten o'clock, and stated that I could not study the parts assigned me by him, in consequence of the music necessary to be sung in the pieces, and it being totally out of the line I engaged to play in. (Cheers). I do not profess singing, and I felt myself justified in refusing to play those parts; and in requesting Mr Smedley to select two pieces in which I might perform the leading characters. I told him also that I felt myself entitled to a choice of parts to conclude my engagement with.(Great applause). I knew that the public, whom I had been so fortunate as to amuse (renewed applause), and to whose kindness I am indebted for so many favours, and so high a token of their estimation of my talents as an
>
> actress, humble though they be in my own opinion, would expect me to exert myself in the close of the season (applause); and my object in laying claim to this indulgence was to prove myself as worthy of the high opinion they had formed of, and the great honour they had conferred upon me, as far as my talents and ability would allow. (Great cheering.)

I gave Mr Smedley sufficient time either to comply with my wishes, or to leave my name out of the bills altogether. Mr Smedley never replied to my note, but had my name announced to the public while under the conviction that I should not appear. After what I have stated it is for you to decide what reparation Mr Smedley can make for the wrong he has done me; and, perhaps, the disrespect he has shown towards the public. (Applause.) In everything connected with Mr Smedley I have conducted myself with the strictest honour and propriety, and the return I have met with has been continual persecution, and an attempt to prejudice the minds of the public against me, by imputing to me ingratitude towards those who so kindly patronised me; and I now appeal to the feelings of every father, mother, brother and sister, and I ask whether this conduct be not cruel to an innocent and unprotected female, three hundred miles from her home.

(Great applause.) Many and bitter have been the reports circulated prejudicial to my character, the source of which I have traced, and grieve to say where I least expected it from, and to where I looked for protection. And now I stand forth to court enquiry, and upon the foundation of truth and justice. To defy the power of any one, upon the strictest investigation, to bring ought against me that the Most rigid virtue would not sanction. (Cheers and applause); and it is with this feeling of conscious rectitude of character that I now boldly come forward to claim the protection of Englishmen, from those who seek to throw disrepute upon the character of an innocent girl, when they find her no longer serviceable to their interests. Deeply do I regret being obliged to speak thus of a manager to whom I have always been taught to look for protection (cheers); and such is my disposition of kindness towards him and his family, that I would gladly see him come forward like a man and acquit himself before the public by making any excuse to palliate his treatment of me-any excuse were better than none. (Great applause). Miss D. Evidently much exhausted and overcome by her feelings, after a pause of some moments concluded in the following terms:Pardon me I feel very ill; I had intended to say much more, but feeling myself unequal to the task, I now take my leave of you in the full confidence that there is not one person before whom I now appear who would not stand forward to shield my good name when assailed, and protect me from the cruel lash of envy and jealousy. (Cheers). I know not what effect Mr Smedley's accusation last night had upon the minds of the public; but this I know, that I have but one feeling of gratitude towards you all for your unbounded kindness to me, and I hope, nay I am sure, that you cannot believe for one moment that I am <u>ungrateful</u> to you, and to my other kind patrons in Wakefield. (Cheers and cries of no, no). Accept my heart's best thanks for this fresh token of your approval; and now believe and be assured that I speak with all my soul when I wish you every blessing heaven can bestow. Farewell, Farewell; kind patrons and indulgent friends, farewell; <u>ungrateful</u> you shall find me never. (Miss D. Retired amid shouts of applause.).

The newspaper commentary continued:

The foregoing address-its mode of delivery-and the exhaustion from strong feelings and severe illness, under which Miss Desborough but too evidently laboured, made a deep impression on the audience, and considerable excitement was manifested when Mr Smedley, immediately upon the retirement of Miss D. From before the curtain, came forward to address them. For some time the audience refused to listen to him, but their sense of justice impelled them to give Mr Smedley an opportunity to explain to them how it was that such discrepancy existed between her statement of this night and his of the previous one. He spoke as follows (occasionally interrupted by mingled cheers and hisses).

The newspaper now proceeds to quote, verbatim, the remarks Joseph made to the audience, a draft of which is extant among his papers and is repeated faithfully by the paper. This then, is his explanation of the debacle, which gives an insight into theatre practice and management of the day, and into his own style of it. More importantly, this gives one of very few occasions when we can hear Joseph's own words as though from his own lips:

Ladies and Gentlemen, – I am accused of being tyrannical, oppressive and unjust. Hear my case and judge for yourselves. When Miss Desborough was engaged, I requested one list of the characters she <u>had</u> performed and another which she had not, but <u>wished</u> to do- to avoid, if possible, giving her more study than was necessary and enable her to do justice both to herself and me – now the part in the 'Illustrious Stranger' was in the list of those she <u>had</u> performed and selected by me, for the double purpose of not giving her unnecessary trouble, as well as to accommodate Mr Hayes with a character (in his line) to open in. The part of Fatima although the best in the piece, was as much in her line as any other, and always acted by the first female comic performer-she by her note "positively refused to act as being too insignificant;" now as it is the <u>best</u>, surely it cannot be the manager's fault that the author has not made it <u>better</u>. But managers and authors seldom can come up to the standard aimed at, by ambitious performers—as to its being a singing character (to which the lady had no pretensions) so is the character in the Invincibles which she has by her own choice, <u>twice</u> repeated—the music of it was dispensed with and why not <u>this</u> which is really of so much less consequence to the piece—again her note says "that unless you give me two of my favourite characters to close the season with, <u>without study</u>, I shall make tomorrow evening my last." Now the character in the 'Illustrious Stranger' (so much did I consult her convenience) was positively the <u>only</u> one except Grace Gayrose, on the list of those in which she was <u>studied.</u> Talk of tyranny and oppression—what tyranny can be greater, if managers are to be thus managed, and threatened by their <u>performers</u>! How is it possible they should do justice to the public. 'Tis clear she would <u>not study</u>—nor act a part in which she <u>was</u> studied, except such as had been so frequently done before, as to have lost their attraction—novelty an audience requires and have a right to expect. "If we live to please, we must please to live."

To the best of my ability and judgement I have catered for your amusement—I boast not of the <u>extraordinary</u> talent of my company—but this I <u>can</u> boast, I <u>have</u> fulfilled and will fulfil the pledge I made at the head of the first bill I ever issued in the town—"That the stage by me should not be perverted from its original purpose—that it should be made a school of morality"—'tis true I might unconsciously meet with those whose practice was not in unison with their precept ("for where is the place into which foul things will not sometimes creep") but when it did so happen and I knew it, I never yet hesitated to cast them off as worthless. For by the purity of the profession (which I embraced by choice) have I <u>lived</u> and hope to die—when I cannot do this, at once I'll make my exit and retire from it altogether.

The paper then published the full text of the note that Miss Desborough had written to Joseph, which is substantially what she had quoted in her speech from the stage. It went on that it had asked both parties for copies of their addresses which they had received and inserted verbatim and believed from memory to be correct, but declined to comment further upon them, and that the public should draw its own inference.

Despite this assertion, the article continued:

In our opinion the letter read by Mr Smedley, and which he received from Miss D. On the Tuesday morning, was explicit enough with respect to her <u>reasons</u> for not acting on the night in question; and certainly wears not towards the inhabitants of Wakefield any, the least, appearance of <u>ingratitude</u> on her part. So far we are bound to give an opinion. What differences may exist between that young lady, as an actress, and Mr Smedley, as a manager, it is not for us to inquire. Of her as an actress we have already stated our notions. Did we and other gentlemen of this town not consider her not only possessed theatrical talents, but also of that moral character which can never be forfeited without the forfeit of general support from the public, we should not have presented her with the testimonial, however small it is, which she now possesses, as a remembrance to her of the estimation in which we held her theatrical talents.

Ironically, the remainder of the piece is given to a defence of the newspaper itself against a charge brought by "a person moving in the society of gentlemen" that the conductor of the *West Riding Herald* was guilty of *"thrusting down the throats of the public what was not the truth or fact"* with reference to the theatrical proceedings of the town. Clearly, this was a gentleman who disagreed with the papers theatrical correspondent's view of Joseph's company and work, and their response was to hold it in "light estimation." The item concludes by saying:

> We apprehend Mr Smedley may have just cause to complain should he be apprised by us or others, that an attempt to patronise him and to vouch for his respectability has been made by our critical, most learned, most enlightened, and doubtless, most respectable correspondent.

Needless to say, Miss Desborough was not invited to remain with the company and she said her goodbyes to Wakefield thus:

<u>THEATRICALS</u>

> MISS DESBOROUGH, in taking her leave of her Friends, the Inhabitants of Wakefield, begs to express the deepest sense of gratitude for all their kindness and liberality of feeling so unceasingly bestowed upon her during her stay among them, the recollection of which she will ever cherish with that warmth of esteem which can only cease with life; and, should her health permit her to pursue her Theatrical career, she will look forward with inexpressible pleasure to again visiting the Town of Wakefield, when it will be her greatest pride, and highest ambition, to merit and receive the smiles and approbation of those kind friends,

to whom she fervently wishes every happiness, and, for the present, gratefully and affectionately bids ADIEU.

Where Miss Desborough went from here is questionable. We do know, however, on 9th March she appeared at the Royal Victoria Theatre in London in a piece called *The Peasant Duke*, and again on 13th March, in *The Tyrant of Algiers*.[28] Then, in the autumn of 1837, she took over the management of the theatre at Richmond in Surrey, where she immediately announced that the stage would be "brilliantly lighted with gas"; probably for the first time. During the season, she presented a varied programme featuring Mr Butler, a Covent Garden tragedian; Mr J. Lee of the Theatre Royal Drury Lane who performed the role of Jeremy Diddler; and Tom Matthews, a popular clown.[29]

Her management there was short-lived, according to the following newspaper report:[30]

QUEEN'S THEATRE

Last night this theatre opened under the management of Miss Desborough, late lessee of the Richmond Theatre. The house has been thoroughly cleaned, and decorated with considerable taste; and we sincerely wish this lady success in her undertaking. After a short but sensible address from the fair manager, "God Save the Queen"** was sung with great spirit and effect by the company. The bills announced as the first piece the comic burletta of *Bachelor's Buttons* which it will be remembered was produced at the Strand Theatre during the season just closed; but on entering the theatre we found a notice exhibited announcing that the author, Mr Stirling, had prohibited its representation; and the *Married Rake* was substituted, which, considering the short time allowed for preparation, was exceeding well performed. A comic interlude, entitled *The Miniature Painter*, followed; the plot of which is founded on some amusing incidents arising from the mistakes occasioned by a similarity of name between "an elderly gentleman with a

---

[28] The Morning Advertiser of 9th & 13th March 1838; British Newspaper Archive.

[29] Quoted from 'A Celebrated Old Playhouse: The History of the Richmond Theatre, 1765-1884' by Frederick Bingham, 1886

[30] Public Ledger and Daily Advertiser of 17th October 1837; British Newspaper Archive.

young wife", and his "first-floor lodger." This piece, which possesses some humour, was favourably received; it may, however, be much improved by a little judicious curtailment in some of the scenes. An allusion was made to the new Parliament, which was loudly cheered by the audience: one of the characters says -(speaking of that kind of gingerbread called "Parliament")-"we are going to have a new batch of Parliament- I hope it will be better than the last- some of which was so soft it would bend any way." We cannot however help remarking that this practice of introducing political allusions upon the stage, which has lately appeared to be gaining ground, would be much better avoided. The entertainments were concluded by the well-known piece called *Esmeralda, or, The Hunchback of Notre Dame*, which was well got up. In the course of the evening several songs were sung by the Messrs. Jean and Turner, and some clever dances were executed in very good style, especially a morriss dance and a Turkish dance, by two young ladies (Misses Florence and Brier), which latter was encored. The house was well attended.

** It is worth remembering here that Queen Victoria had come to the throne in 1837, following the death of her uncle, William IV. She was crowned at Westminster on 28th June 1838.

The *West Riding Herald* reported on 20th October, 1837, although quoting a report from another newspaper:

MISS DESBOROUGH, – This lady opened the Queen's Theatre, London, on Monday evening. We find the following notice of the circumstance in the Sun of the following day:This theatre opened last night for the season, under the management of Miss Desborough, announced in the bills as the "Lessee of the Theatre Royal, Richmond," assisted by a dramatic corps, strong in numbers and good intentions. The fair lessee delivered an opening address, after which the National Anthem was sung by the strength of the company. The popular farce of *Bachelor's Buttons,* a new comic interlude called *The Miniature Painter,* and *Esmeralda, or the Deformed of Notre Dame,* followed in succession, and were favourably received by a well-filled house. It would be harsh-perhaps not altogether fair-to judge of the histrionic abilities of a company by a first night's performance, especially where several members of it find themselves for the first time in the presence of a London audience. Miss Desborough appeared quite at home on the stage, and in her varied performances displayed abilities, if not of a high, yet a respectable order.

The Queen's Theatre was the then current name of the theatre in Tottenham Street, off Tottenham Court Road, which later became known as The Prince of Wales's Theatre. At this stage its fortunes were at a particularly low ebb, as members of the press were anxious to inform her: 'The Queen's Theatre is again in the hands of a lady – a Miss Desborough – whose friends, if they have any sincere wishes for her present or future welfare, will make an empyrosis of this ruinous property, and avenge the hundreds it has destroyed."[31]

By December of that year Miss Desborough's foray into management hit the bumpers when she found herself unable to pay the rent to the theatre's owner, John Perry. He, in turn, seized what machinery, scenery and props there were, and even took their dresses, wigs, boots and other articles, which actually belonged to the cast members, while they were rehearsing in the theatre.[32]

Miss Desborough refused to vacate the theatre, and Mr Perry was unable to evict her, and he, apparently, had defaulted on his mortgage payments, hence the effort to strip the theatre of its assets. The holder of the mortgage had a deed of covenant prepared with powers of sale, and, in February of the following year, the theatre was indeed sold at auction for £2650.

What then happened to Miss Desborough I have been unable to glean, although a Miss Desborough appeared as a member of the company which performed for the Royal family at Windsor Castle, on 19th January 1854, produced and directed by Charles Kean. She also appeared in Charles Kean's company at the Royal Princess's Theatre in 1855. Also, whether or not this was the same one, there was an actress who appeared in Birmingham called Miss Desborough and who became very popular in the North East of England during the 1860s.

* * *

---

[31] Quoted in 'The History of the Prince of Wales's Theatre London, 1771-1903' by Richard L Lorenzen, pub. by The Society for Theatre Research, 2014

[32] As above. Quote of article in the Examiner, 24th December 1837

We next hear of Joseph's company in March, 1837 when they played at Horncastle; on 7th March they performed Colman's *Heir at Law*. The cast was as follows:

Mr Lockwood	Mr W. Chaplin	
Mr Hill	Mr Montague	
Mr Hayes	Mr J. Smedley	
Mr Smedley	Mr Coppin	Mr Jones
Mrs Lockwood	Miss A. Smedley	Miss Smedley

This was followed by 'A Character Dance' by Mr W. Chaplin, and 'Ladies' Tongues' sung by Mr Lockwood, with the final piece being *Widow's Victim*.

On 9th March they performed *Heart of Mid-Lothian* and *Bee Hive*. Still in Horncastle in April, they performed *The Green Man* with *Wanted A Valet* and *The Provoked Husband* with *Raymond and Agnes,* a melodrama.

Onwards to Beverley, where they performed, on the 'first race night' – April 12th, *The Provoked Husband,* with the following cast list:

Mr Smedley	Mr Lockwood	Mr Wright
Mr J. Smedley	Mr Hayes	Mr Jones
Mr G. Smedley	Mr Hill	
Miss A. Smedley	Mr W. Chaplin	
Miss Smedley`	Mr Coppin	

After this *Catching an Heiress* was presented.

In June, 1837, they returned to Bradford for a season, although as mentioned earlier in this chapter, this was a different, sturdier, wooden theatre in Hall Ings. Even in 1887, in his talk to the Bradford Historical and Archaeological Society, reported in The Era of 25th June,[33] William Scruton remarked: "Although Smedley had a good stock company he nevertheless went in for the 'star' system." However, Senior in his book *The Old Wakefield Theatre,* wrote "his domestic combination (and the rectitude of the Company's conduct)

---

[33] British Newspaper Archive, accessed 29th September 2016

seem to have been sufficient attraction without the assistance of 'stars', and I have not found any notable names…" They cannot both be correct. While it is true that Joseph occasionally presented a 'name' to appear at the top of the bill, he did not do this routinely. It seems that when he did so it was because he felt that the ticket sales required it, or else he detected that a particular actor was well-liked in that town. This was certainly true in this season at Bradford, where Joseph employed the talents of the actor G.V. Brooke to appear in a production of *Romeo and Juliet*, as announced in the playbill:

MR SMEDLEY

Has great pleasure in announcing to the public that he intends opening the theatre for a limited season on Saturday evening, June 17th, 1837 and that he has formed an engagement for THREE NIGHTS ONLY, viz. Saturday, Monday and Tuesday, with that celebrated Youthful Tragedian

MR G. V. BROOKE

Who has been making a most successful professional tour through all the provincial theatres in the United Kingdom, prior to the fulfilment of his engagements in London.

ROMEO AND JULIET
ROMEO…………MR G. V. BROOKE
Capulet…………Mr Lockwood
Mercutio…………Mr Smedley
Benvolio…………Mr Willey (from the Queen's Theatre, London)
Paris…………Mr Hill (from the Blackburn Theatre)
Tybalt…………Mr Hayes
Peter…………Mr J. Smedley
Apothecary…………Mr Coppin (from the Scarborough Theatre)
Balthazar…………Mr Reid
Friar Lawrence…………Mr Tannett
Juliet…………Miss A. Smedley
Lady Capulet…………Mrs Willey (from the Queen's Theatre, London)
Nurse…………Mrs Lockwood
Song, 'The Gypsy King' by Mr Willey
'Auld Robin Gray' by Mrs Willey
Dancing by Mr Chaplin from the Manchester Theatre
Comic Medley by Mr Hayes
Followed by the farce CAPTAIN IS NOT A-MISS

On 19th June, 1837, they performed *Othello*, again starring Brooke, with the farce *The Dead Shot*. After announcing Brooke's second night, the playbill for continued:

> The following notice of Mr G. V. Brooke, is from the Sheffield Iris, of May 30th. "We stated a fortnight ago that a numerously signed requisition had been presented to the manager of the Norwich Theatre, requesting him to re-engage Mr Brooke for one night to play 'Hamlet'. Mr B. having in his performance of the same character, previously given unbounded delight to a crowded audience, the manager at once complied with the wish of his patrons."

This continues with another quote, from the Norwich Chronicle, expressing similar sentiments

OTHELLO
The Moor of Venice
OTHELLO,MR G. V. BROOKE
Iago.......Mr Tannett   Cassio......Mr Chaplin   Brabantio.......Mr Lockwood
The Duke......Mr Hayes   Montano......Mr Willey
Ludovico......Mr Hill   Gratiano......Mr Coppin
Roderigo......Mr J. Smedley   Marco.......Mr Read
Desdemona......Miss Smedley   Emilia......Miss Chaplin

Gustavus Vaughan Brooke

Although forgotten now, not being classed among the top order of Tragedians, Brooke was nevertheless highly thought of. He was an Irishman, born in Dublin in 1818 and educated there. In 1833, aged 15, he stood in for an indisposed Edmund Kean at Dublin's Theatre Royal, and was immediately dubbed, unsurprisingly, 'Master Brooke, the Hibernian Roscius'. He toured many of the Irish and Scottish towns, and even played London's Victoria Theatre, but to little notice. He appeared with Joseph's company following a stint with the Kent Circuit and appearances at Sheffield. Although invited to appear with Macready at Drury Lane in 1841, he withdrew after an argument about his roles, and returned to act in the provinces where his reputation grew, culminating in his opening at the Olympic Theatre in 1848 as *Othello*, which was lauded. After his marriage to Marianne Bray in 1851, he sailed for

New York where he played with great success before a speculation in his own management brought financial disaster. He later tried his luck in Australia, initially with success, but after another spell of management, was again penniless. His first wife having died in 1860, he met and married an American actress Avonia Jones in 1863. On 28th December, 1865, she saw him off, with his younger sister, Fanny, from Gravesend, on the steamship *London*, bound again for Australia. On 10th January 1866, the ship foundered in heavy seas in the Bay of Biscay with the loss of 244 people. Afterwards the survivors, numbering 19, remarked on Brooke's heroic behaviour.[34]

* * *

On June 23rd, Joseph's playbill for the evening announced that –

Mr Smedley has the satisfaction of announcing the re-engagement of

MR G. V. BROOKE

for three nights more, viz Friday, Saturday and Monday next. It is useless now to comment on the extraordinary talent of this youthful actor, whose attractions have more than doubled the number of admiring audience each succeeding Night of his former engagement.

ON FRIDAY EVENING, JUNE 23RD 1837

Will be presented Shakespear's celebrated

Tragedy of Macbeth

King of Scotland

Macbeth............Mr G. V.Brooke

Macduff............Mr Tannett   Malcolm............Mr Chaplin

Rosse............Mr Hill   Lennox............Mr Coppin

Banquo............Mr Willey   Duncan............Mr Wright

Officer............Mr Reid   Bleeding Serjeant............Mr Hayes

Seyton............Mr Jones

Lady Macbeth............Miss A. Smedley

Gentlewoman............Miss Chaplin

---

[34] K. D. Reynolds, 'Brooke, Gustavus Vaughan (1818–1866)', *Oxford Dictionary of National Biography*, Oxford University Press, 2004 [http://www.oxforddnb.com/view/article/3542, accessed 25 Nov 2016]

Hecate............Mr Lockwood
Witches............Miss Smedley, Mrs Willey, Mrs Lockwood, &C
In the course of the play
ALL THE ORIGINAL CHORUSES
(composed by the celebrated Matthew Locke)
Miss Smedley, Mrs Willey, Mrs Lockwood, Messrs. Lockwood, Willey, Hayes, Hill, Smedley, &C
A Grand Banquet in which the Ghost of Banquo appears
THE WITCHES' DANCE
AN AWFUL INCANTATION OVER A MAGIC CAULDRON
THE APPARITION OF EIGHT KINGS
With a mysterious prophecy of a moving wood
The Storming of the Castle, with the Death of the Tyrant
Mr Lockwood will sing 'The Age of India Rubber'
Song, 'The Spell is Broken', by Mrs Willey
To conclude with the farce of
SPOILED CHILD
Little Pickle (the Spoiled Child)............Miss Smedley
Old Pickle............Mr Lockwood   John............Mr Hayes
Thomas............Mr Hill   Tag............Mr J. Smedley
Miss Pickle............Mrs Lockwood   Maria............Miss Chaplin
Susan............Miss A. Smedley   Margery............Mrs Willey
In the course of the farce
Miss Smedley will dance a hornpipe

On July 5th, "positively Mr G. V. Brooke's Last Night," they performed *Stranger* and *Heart of a Soldier, or, Ella Rosenberg*.[35]

On July 7th, for their 'last night of performing':

MR SMEDLEY finding that the excitement consequent on the approaching Election, together with other causes, is likely most materially to affect his Interest; the public is respectfully informed, that the Theatre will Close on FRIDAY NEXT, and Re-opened again, about Five WEEKS hence for usual Season.

---

[35] Bradford Playbills in West Yorkshire Archive, Bradford

Married Life,
Or, Fireside Sketches

After the cast list it gave the Opinions of the piece by the Press:

"The most amusing of all Comedies, Gravity itself could not defy its power over the risible faculties; and the moral it conveys is as excellent as the incidents are humourous"(sic).

– Leigh Hunt's *London Journal*

"Every married couple should see this piece, and learn a useful lesson while they laugh. It is full of nature, whim, eccentricity, and truth."

– *Sunday Times*

"A new piece was brought out in the Theatre on Tuesday night, and was repeated last night, with TREMENDOUS APPLAUSE. It is entitled "Married LIFE", and is from the pen of Mr Buckstone. Its merit lies in the ludicrousness of the situations, and the humour of the dialogue. The piece was very warmly received.

– *Edinburgh Evening Courant*

Underneath this they presented *High Notions*.

While in Brigg they performed, on August 15th, *Deformed, or, The Hunchback of Notre Dame*, and on 17th August, *The Wife, A Tale of Mantua*, before returning again to Bradford, where on the evening of August 26th, for one night only, they charged half the usual prices, i.e Boxes 1s6d, Pit 1s., and Gallery 6d. This was for *The Tragedy of George Barnwell* and *The Dunder Family*. Two nights later, they presented *Sweethearts and Wives* with *Too Late for Dinner*.

From here they went to Bradford, where, on 2nd September, they opened 'for a short season' presenting *Heir at Law*, including 'The Original Epilogue by the Characters,' finishing with *Love and Laugh or, All at Coventry*.

On 6th September they acted *Eugene Aram* with *Two Strings to your Bow*, and on 7th September, *Sam Weller – founded on Boz's*" *Posthumous Papers of The Pickwick Club*, with *Illustrious Stranger, or, Married and Buried*.

On 15th September they performed *Bottle Imp*, founded on a popular German legend. The cast then included Messrs Mosley, George, J. Smedley, Mungall, Lockwood, Letchford, Tannett, Waterfield, Smith, and Miss A. Smedley, Mrs Short, Miss Somers, Mrs Lockwood and Miss Smedley. This was followed by Dancing by Mr Mungall, and then *William Thompson* and *Married Rake*.

On Wednesday evening, September 20th they performed:

SWEETHEARTS AND WIVES
Written by Mr Poole, Author of Paul Pry, Simpson & Co.
After which a new Bagatelle
WINNING A HUSBAND
OR, SEVEN'S THE MAIN
To conclude with a new Burletta
PETTICOAT GOVERNMENT

Then on Friday, 22nd September, came a playbill announcing that evening's fayre of *My Poll and my Partner Joe,* and *Plot and Counterplot*, followed by this announcement:

MR SMEDLEY, at the suggestion of some of his best friends, is induced (as a temporary matter) to meet "the pressure without", and the decreased means within-at once to

REDUCE THE PRICE OF ADMISSION
VIZ. To the Boxes 2s6d—Pit 1s6d—Gallery 6d
Second Price to the Boxes 1s6d – Pit 1s.
No Second Price to the Gallery

In doing this he wishes it not to be misunderstood that the Prices are *permanently* lowered, but to shew(sic) his desire to adapt them to the peculiar depression of the times.

It is quite certain the Town of Bradford is entitled to amusements on the scale of talent and respectability equal to *any* in the County, but if so, they must be paid for at the same rate; Mr S. Therefore cannot pledge himself to the *continuance* of

Prices that will preclude him from forming future engagements with such talent as will not be placed on a par with Booths in a fair.

On Saturday Evening, Septem. 23rd 1837
Will be revived Massinger's Comedy of
A NEW WAY TO
PAY OLD DEBTS
As performed at the Theatre Royal, Drury Lane with great applause
BLUE BEARD
OR, FEMALE CURIOSITY

On 25th September, for 'The Benefit of Mr Smedley', they performed *The Wife, A Tale of Mantua* with *Catching an Heiress*.

Still at Bradford, on October 23rd 1837, a playbill informs us of a performance of an "entirely new domestic Drama, by the same author as *The Red Rover, the Flying Dutchman and the Soldier's Widow* [i.e. E. Fitzball], *Jonathan Bradford, or, The Murder at the Roadside Inn* with scenery by Mr J. Smedley and music by Mr Short."

On 25th October they performed *The Mountaineers, or, Love and Madness* with Joseph Snr playing the role of Octavian. Other cast members included Messrs Neville, Lockwood, Mosley, Rayner, J. Smedley and Miss Smedley. This was followed by a melodrama, *The Jew of Lubeck, or, The Heart of a Father*. *Therese, or, The Orphan of Geneva* was performed on 28th October, again with a cast again headed by Mr Smedley, with Messrs Jones, Mosley, Lockwood, Neville, Hill, Coppin, Rayner, and Mrs Short, Miss A Smedley, and Mrs Willey. Supporting the bill was an Interlude *Mr & Mrs Smith*, and a farce, *Sleeping Draught*.

The final performances of their Bradford season were announced in the *Bradford Observer* of 2nd November 1837:[36]

---

36 Bradford Observer, 2nd November 1837; British Newspaper Archive

On FRIDAY EVENING, Nov. 3rd
FOR THE BENEFIT OF THE MISS SMEDLEY'S
Will be revived, the Comedy of
Paul Pry,
Comic Song by Mr Lockwood;
And the Farce of
THE CORK LEG

* * *

ON SATURDAY EVENING, Nov. 4th,
THE HONEY MOON!
And
THE DUMB ORPHAN!!!

* * *

On MONDAY EVENING, Nov. 6th
Coleman's Comedy of
JOHN BULL, or the ENGLISHMAN'S FIRESIDE;
And the laughable Farce of
DEAF AS A POST!!!
Being the LASTNIGHT OF PERFORMING
Doors to be opened at half-past Six;
Performances to commence at Seven precisely.
Boxes, 2s 6d.; Pit, 1s 6d.; Gallery, 6d. Second Price
to commence at a quarter to nine o'clock.

Having concluded their season at Bradford, they moved the short distance south-east to Wakefield, where, on the playbill for the performance of 8th November, 1837, which was to be *Heir at Law* and *Love & Laugh, or, All at Coventry,* Joseph announced further new additions to the company:

The Life and Times of Joseph Smedley

In addition to the established favourites, the following new performers will make their appearance in the course of the week, viz:

Mr Litchford	from the Bristol Theatre
Mr Burton	from the Margate Theatre
Mr Callan	from the Norwich Theatre
Mr Jones	from the Cheltenham Theatre
Mr & Mrs Stamford	from the Nottingham Theatre
Mrs Short (late Miss Chaplin)	from the Liverpool Theatre
Together with Miss and Miss E. Grey	from the Margate Theatre and
Miss Johnson,	from the Birmingham Theatre
Leader of the Band	Mr Short
Mr Monkall (Dancer)	from the Theatre Royal, Drury Lane

On Saturday evening, December 16th, 1837, the following programme was announced:

Mr Gyngell
In the course of the evening
WILL GO THROUGH HIS EXTRAORDINARY EVOLUTIONS
ON THE SWINGING WIRE
The Performance will commence with SHAKESPEARE'S TRAGEDY
ROMEO AND JULIET

Romeo............Mr MOSLEY   Capulet............Mr MOSLEY
Mercutio............Mr SMEDLEY   Benvolio............Mr MUNGALL
Paris............Mr HILL
Tybalt............Mr WILTON   Peter............Mr J. SMEDLEY
Apothecary............Mr Coppin   Balthazar............Mr CULLENFORD
Friar Lawrence............Mr LITCHFORD
Masques   Messrs. NEVILLE, WILTON, GEORGE, RAYNER &C
Juliet............Miss A. Smedley   Lady Capulet............Miss Grey
Nurse............Mrs LOCKWOOD
MADAME DE IRVINE
Will Preside at the Pedal Harp
And Mr Gyngell
Will perform a Variety of Favorite Airs on the
MUSICAL GLASSES
'TWAS I

On January 5th, 1838, still at Wakefield, they performed *Bold Stroke for a Husband*, followed by dancing by Mr Mungall, a rendition of *Ladies Tongues* by Mr Lockwood and in conclusion repeated the comedy piece *'Twas I*.

At Gainsborough, on 29th January, they performed *Heir at Law* with *Miller and his Men* – "The principle Part of the Scenery will be entirely new, and painted by Mr TANNETT."

On 2nd February, 1838, "For the Benefit of Mr J. SMEDLEY," they offered *The Belle's Stratagem*, *Handsome Husband*, and *Hunting a Turtle*. The cast included Mr Tannett, J. Smedley, Miss A. Smedley (Annette), Messrs Lockwood, Coppin, Mosley, Smith, and Miss Smedley (Helen), but not Joseph Smedley Snr. Perhaps because he was making ready at their next venue at Downham where they opened on 17th February where

>MR SMEDLEY
>Respectfully informs his Patrons, Friends,
>and the public of Downham and it vicinity, that
>THE THEATRE
>Which has been entirely re-painted, decorated,
>and improved by Mr Tannett, Artist to the
>Company, will be opened for a limited Season
>ON SATURDAY, February 17th 1838
>with a numerous and effective Company. Added to which,
>ONE NEW PIECE at least, will be produced every night during his stay with new and appropriate Scenery, Dresses, Decorations, &C and that no Piece will be repeated, except by express desire. THE DRAMATIC REPRESENTATIONS will be SUPPORTED BYMessrs. Smedley, J. Smedley Lockwood, Litchford, Mosley, Tannett, Mungall, Coppin, George, Cullenford, and Smith. Messdames Smedley, Lockwood, and Short, Miss Smedley & Miss A. Smedley.
>THE ORCHESTRA –Mr Short, First Violin, Messrs. J. Smedley and Cullenford, Second Violins, Mr Coppin, Tenor;
>Mr Lockwood, Violincello, and an Auxiliary, Flute.
>THE RIVALS
>OR, A TRIP TO BATH
>THE DUNDER FAMILY

In April 1838 they returned to March in Cambridgeshire, where they presented *Wreck Ashore*, with *The Husband's Secret* and *Hunting a Turtle* (on 4th April), and on 6th April *Ivanhoe, or, The Jew of York* and *The Unfinished Gentleman*.

It was then on to Holbeach, where, on 16th May, Joseph informed everyone that the Theatre would be re-painted, and decorated, by Mr Tannett, Artist to the Company, and that the Theatre would be opened for three weeks only, commencing that night with *The Rivals* and *The Dunder Family*, and the following evening ('The Fair Night'), with *The Farmer's Story* and *'Twas I*.

While at Holbeach they also performed *The Wife, A Tale of Mantua* with *Love Laughs at Locksmiths*; *The Surrender of Calais* and *Deaf as a Post*; *Married Life, or, Fireside Sketches* with *Simpson & Co.*; *The Poor Gentleman* with *Gretna Green*, the latter in July.

On 14th July, now in Southwell, the Company performed *Country Squire, or, The Old English Gentleman*, with Messrs. Lockwood, Mosley, Letchford,

J. Smedley, G. Smedley, Mungall, Coppin, Smith and Miss Smedley, Mrs Short, Mrs Lockwood and Miss A. Smedley. (Joseph himself was missing from the cast.)

Mr Mungall then exhibited a living Tableau of Grecian Statues, followed by dancing by Miss Somers, and the farce of *The Haunted Inn*.

This was followed on the 16th by *Heir at Law*, with Joseph Smedley playing his usual role of Dr. Pangloss, L.L.D. & A.S.S.; with *Illustrious Stranger*. And on the 21st of July they presented *Virginius, or, The Liberation of Rome*, and 'The Overseer' by Mr Lockwood, dancing by Mr Mungall and Miss Somers, and ending with *William Thompson*. On the 26th of that month *The Rake's Progress* and *The Handsome Husband* (featuring Mr Tannett and Miss A. Smedley), with *Catching an Heiress*. Next, still at Southwell, they acted *Sam Weller*, which was a version of *The Pickwick Papers* and, unusually, featured Mrs Smedley as Mr Pickwick. Melinda had been increasingly absent from playbills since the mid-1820s, which is not to say she didn't have a role to play in the backstage organisation or supporting her husband's work, but her acting performances were becoming rarer. With this they presented a farce called *The Young Widow*, in which Miss Smedley (i.e. Helen) played three roles!

On 11th August they staged *The Lady of Lyons* with *A Day in Paris*; on 14th August *More Secrets than One, or, Man and Wife* wit*h 'Twas I.* On the 16th August, 1838, presumably to celebrate the newly crowned Queen Victoria, the company presented: *The Youthful Queen, or, Court Favorites*, with *A Pleasant Neighbour* and *Plot and Counterplot.*

They next went to Bradford, where there seems to have been some kind of uprising among the players, causing Joseph to make the following announcement in the *Bradford Observer* of 23rd August 1838, of which all but the first paragraph was repeated on a playbill:[37]

MR SMEDLEY
RESPECTFULLY announces to his Patrons, Friends,
and Supporters, that he proposes
OPENING THE THEATRE,
Which has been entirely re-painted by Mr Tannett, Artist to the Theatre,
ON THURSDAY, AUGUST 23rd, 1838,

With a Company which consists of most of the established favourites of the last season, and a numerous selection of new aspirants to become so; at the same time he promises, both for them and himself, that no effort shall be spared to merit a continuance of that estimation in which the Theatre was held during his former visit.

Mr S. having found a difficulty in retaining his old performers or in forming engagements with new ones of talent for a Theatre, where the prices put them on a level with a Booth (a thing which he never anticipated, is forced into the necessity of either advancing them to the scale of other provincial Theatres, or submit to have an inferior Company; the latter he is quite assured the Inhabitants of Bradford have no right to be satisfied with, a town which is second to none for

---

[37] Bradford Observer, 23rd August 1838; British Newspaper Archive; accessed 29th Sept 2016

its encouragement of all institutions by which society can be benefitted(sic), and that society may, nay <u>must</u> be benefitted by the amusements of a <u>well-conducted</u> Theatre, he dares to affirm without fear of contradiction. Convinced of this, he has engaged a very numerous and effective Company, not doubting that if their talent is found equal to others, they will be considered entitled to equal remuneration.

The prices in future will be the same as at Leeds, Doncaster, Wakefield, Huddersfield, &C viz Boxes, 3s, Pit 2s, Gall. 1s. Perf to commence at 7 precisely.

Second price to commence at a Quarter to Nine O'Clock.

Boxes 1s 6d, Pit 1s. Gall 6d.

The advertisement continued:

The first Representation will be the Comedy of
SPEED THE PLOUGH
Comic Singing. Dancing by Mr Mungall and
Miss Somers
TO CONCLUDE WITH
LUKE THE LABOURER, OR, THE LOST SON

* * *

On FRIDAY Evening, August 24th, 1838, an admired
Drama called
THE GYPSIE CHIEF
OR, THE FALLS OF CLYDE
Comic Singing.-A new Interlude of the FEMALE
FOX-HUNTER
DANCING BY MR MUNGALL – AND THE FARCE OF
MAKE YOUR WILLS

* * *

Richard E. Smedley

On MONDAY. The Twenty-Seventh of August,
KING RICHARD THE THIRD,
And the QUEER SUBJECTS

* * *

On WEDNESDAY (Fashionable Night), a new Comedy
Written by Sir E. L.Bulwer, Bart., M.P.
ENTITLED
THE LADY OF LYONS,
And the IRISH LION

* * *

On FRIDAY Evening, August 31st,
THE YORKSHIREMAN,
A PLEASANT NEIGHBOUR, and PLOT AND
COUNTERPLOT

* * *

Doors open at Half-past Six; Performance to commence
at Seven. Tickets to be had at the Printers' and the
Theatre, where Places for the Boxes may be taken.

In the event, Joseph changed the programme, and instead presented on

Friday, August 24th 1838:
THE YOUTHFUL QUEEN
OR, COURT FAVORITES
"God Save the Queen" by all the company.
A PLEASANT NEIGHBOUR
Dancing by Miss Somers
PLOT AND COUNTERPLOT

The part of 'The Youthful Queen' was taken by Miss A. Smedley (i.e. Annette). Clearly the falling-out was over pay, but many of his company had been with him for a long time, and he would have been upset at what he presumed was their disloyalty. However, it seems that in this case he acquiesced, and did so by raising his prices in line with other theatres in the immediate area, and found he could keep his regular players and still supplement his company further.

The *Leeds Times* of 25th August simply reported:[38]

> THEATRE, – Mr Smedley has again appeared among us and opened the temporary wood-built theatre in the Hall Ings, on Thursday night. The interior is very handsomely embellished and all the inside arrangements are very good. The company he has engaged is a superior one, and performed "Luke the Labourer" on Thursday night in capital style. We hope the inhabitants of Bradford will this time patronise Mr Smedley and his company as they deserve.

Also while in Bradford, on 12th September, they presented *Love Chase* with *The King's Command*.

Family Matters

As if to compound his problems, and to make matters much, much worse, it was about now, during the Bradford season, that Joseph received the following undated letter:

> Sir,
> When you receive this, I shall have made your daughter, Annette, my wife. I am well aware that such a proceeding will incur your displeasure – and I have no excuse to offer to palliate the offence (if it be an offence for a man to study his own happiness) from the first commencement of my affection for your daughter. I knew you had an utter abhorrence to any of your children marrying one in this profession, and I was obliged to adapt a line of conduct foreign to my nature. Had I asked your consent to our union I should have been refused, my poverty and my being an actor would have formed the objection, such refusal would have sent me

---

[38] Leeds Times, Saturday 25th August 1838; British Newspaper Archive, accessed 29th Sept. 2016

a wretched, nay, a heart-broken man through the world for my attachments are not those of the moment of such sentiment perhaps you can form no idea. The bright days of your youth have past and brought the cold calculating feelings of mature years – yet if you have any recollection of those days place yourself in my situation and you would have done as I have done and had I not been thoroughly satisfied within myself that I could take your daughter with the firm conviction of making her a good husband. If exerting these abilities, trifling as they are, with which I am blessed, to contribute to her comfort and happiness, I never would have married her "not what I have been but what I will be", shall best speak that I am sincere in what I write. My temper may be bad, but not innately so, it springs more from the trifling vexations of life than from my disposition. My past actions are such that I can look back to them without any reproach to my self. Many of them have been thoughtless, but not depraved – I do not write with a view to gain your pardon. I do not ask for it, for I have done nothing of which I am ashamed. I have taken your daughter from you with the determination of making her happy and not with any interested motives. There can be no blame attached to her for her love and duty to you was such that I had to exert all the interest I had gained in her heart to induce her to leave you. If by so doing she has lost the affection of a father, the husband she has gained will be that father to her.

I have provided a situation for her and myself in a respectable company which we join in the course of a fortnight. Till then we remain with my relations in Leeds. If our services are required till then you may command them – you may imagine that we have taken advantage of your difficulties to get married hoping that our services would induce you to forgive what we have done, but I assure you upon the word of a man we had no such motive. Circumstances and not inclination have compelled us to this step at the present moment – wishing you every success that can or may contribute to your happiness and assuring you of the affection of one, who, if he should ever have it in his power – and circumstances should require it, will show to you the same attachment as to his own father,

I remain
And shall be proud to add
Your affectionate son-in-law
B. Tannett

The shock and anguish that Joseph must have suffered upon receiving this letter is almost palpable. As young Tannett wrote, receiving such news did indeed "incur his displeasure." Not only had he always expressly forbidden his daughters to marry actors, but he had paired Annette and the Tannetts in the same bills when he split his company, and practically drove them toward each other. It is unlikely that he saw any irony in the situation, having himself eloped with Melinda to be married over thirty years earlier. He is likely to have been angry at Annette's wilfulness and defiance, particularly in consideration of the problems he recently encountered with other members of the company, which Tannett alluded to in his letter. Having left no diaries behind, we can only guess at Joseph's feelings, but the family's history, handed down from generation to generation, claims that Joseph never saw or spoke to her again. It is almost certain, however, that whatever strain their elopement put on Joseph's relationship with Tannett Senior, they continued to work together, and it is likely, but by no means certain, that Joseph received news of his daughter's activities through that medium.

In any case, six days after her eldest sister, Melinda Brunton Young, gave birth to her third child, a daughter whom they named Helen, Annette was married to Benjamin Tannett, Junior, on 23rd October, 1838, at St Peter's Church in Leeds, witnessed by a John Wright Wooly and Sarah Tannett. (Sarah was later to be married in the same church, in 1847.) B. Tannett's occupation was given as 'painter', while his father was named as 'Thomas Tannett, musician'; actually his grandfather. His address was given as 20 Bedford Place in Leeds. Annette's address was given as Holbeck, a suburb of Leeds, and she gave her father's occupation as 'musician' also. In both cases, their ages were given as 'full age'; Annette was now 29, but Benjamin was only 18 years and 7 months. This may be why, in almost every case, he gave his details as those of his father. The address he gave of Bedford Place is in the North East of Leeds. Holbeck was an industrialised area of Leeds with mills and other factories, which today is a red light area for controlled prostitution just south of Leeds city centre. Joseph was now 54 years of age.

* * *

Still, existing commitments must be kept, the show must go on, and the day following the marriage, with the company still at Bradford, and for the first time without Annette as a member of it, they performed as announced on the following playbill:

Richard E. Smedley

For the Benefit of Mr L S Thompson
TWO WILLS
OR, ALL RIGHT AT LAST
A New Song Improvements of Bradford
Or, A Peep at the Wool Trade
LADY OF PALERMO

Mr Undermine (an Executor and Steward, of course honest)	MR COPPIN
OLD NICHOLAS RUE (his factotum, commonly called Old Nick, and very like his namesake	MR L S THOMPSON
Mr April, (a real specimen of the John Bull genus)	MR LOCKWOOD
Rostrum (something like an auctioneer's Hammer, knocks down every thing that comes in its way)	MR MOSLEY
Mr Greville (married for love, but no objection to money)	MR TANNETT
Mr Egerton, (a soldier, not famed for his riches)	MR LETCHFORD
Plethora, (a Veterinary Surgeon in a galloping consumption)	MR J SMEDLEY
Coachman, (with the bad manners to ride before his master)	MR MUNGALL
Butler, (a good judge of the best wine in his Master's cellar)	MR GEORGE
Groom, (never known to cheat his master or his Horse)	MR WATERFIELD
Mrs Greville (full of honour and melancholy)	MRS SHORT
Sally Downright (can keep a secret)	MRS LOCKWOOD
Rose Sidney (no secrets to keep)	MISS SMEDLEY

A New Song, written for the Occasion, called The
Improvements of Bradford
Or, A Peep at the Wool Trade
BY MR L S THOMPSON
A New and Appropriate Scene,
Will be displayed on the Occasion
Painted by Mr J W Anderson
Dancing by Mr Mungall & Miss Somers

> Comic Singing by MR LOCKWOOD
> To Conclude with a celebrated Musical Farce
> The Lady of Palermo
> Or, The Haunted Apartment
> THE BRADFORD OLD BAND
> Have Kindly offered their Services on the Occasion

This marked the appearance of L. S. Thompson, a local favourite who had at one time managed the Wakefield and Huddersfield Theatres. He was a gifted character actor, especially in rustic parts,[39] who could speak the Yorkshire dialect, and who later made his name in London and then returned to his native parts a hero.

They finished the year in Wakefield, where they played *Lady of Lyons, or Love and Pride*, in which the company was joined by the talents of Mr Manly, who formerly ran the Nottingham and Derby Circuit. Other members of the company were Messrs J. Smedley, Lockwood, Coppin, Kingston, Horton, Mosley, George, Waterfield, Smith, Mrs Short, Miss Palmer, Mrs Lockwood, Miss Andrews and Miss Smedley. Mr Lockwood then sang 'Music Mad', followed by *A Highland Fling* by Miss Andrews; to be rounded off by *Tom Noddy's Secret*.

On the 14th December, Joseph and Mr Manly acted together in *The Poor Gentleman*, the playbill for which advised the public that the play for the following Monday was in preparation and was to be *Rory O'More*, for the benefit of Mr Smedley. On 21st December, they presented *A New Wonder! A Woman Never Vext*, with a Musical Romance entitled *Robert the Devil, or, The Statue Bride*, again featuring Messrs. Manly and Smedley. On 27th December they offered *The Provoked Husband* with *A Roland for an Oliver*.

At some time either while here at Wakefield, or possibly while still in Bradford, that Joseph introduced *Nicholas Nickleby* into their canon of work. Certainly they had played it at some stage prior to the playbill for Wakefield Theatre on 4th January, 1839 which advertised its last night there, where it was supported on the bill by *A Pleasant Neighbour* and *A Husband's Secret*. Mr and

---

[39] W Scruton; Pen and Pencil Pictures of Old Bradford

Mrs Smedley, Joseph Jnr, and Miss Smedley (Helen), appeared in this adaptation of Dickens' novel which was then being serialised in 19 monthly instalments. Only then was it published in its entirety in book form, in the latter months of 1839. Indeed the first theatrical adaptation was produced after only eight instalments, and therefore was presumably a dramatic representation of the first main theme of the book, set in Yorkshire. By December 1838 it was being played at theatres all over England, including the Theatre Royal, Newcastle, where it formed part of a benefit for the actress Mrs Ternan, "then seven months pregnant with her third daughter, Ellen,"[40] who herself became a central character in Dickens' own life. In fact, there were at least 25 stage productions of *Nicholas Nickleby* by the time the serialisation of the book was completed.[41]

It has been stated that much of Dickens' popularity sprang from the respect in which he was held by other writers and, not least, for his clearly delineated characters, and his situations, but also because he brought to his writing a campaigning zeal for bettering the conditions of ordinary people, and improving their lives. Although Dickens had a love of the theatre, there are conflicting views of how well he accepted the almost wholesale theft of what today we would call his 'intellectual property'. We mustn't forget that there was still no legal protection for an author's work until the Copyright Act of 1842. Some works suggest that Dickens accepted this practice, but other indications are that he was much discomfited by it, and angered by the "liberties which other writers were taking with his work."[42] So much so, that Dickens included in *Nicholas Nickleby* a diatribe spoken by Nicholas to a 'literary gentleman', "who had dramatised in his time two hundred and forty-seven novels, as fast as they had come out – some of them faster than they had come out." This so-called 'literary gentleman' was thought to be a caricature of William T. Moncrieff, who had brought out a fairly wayward version of *Nickleby*, (not listed by Nicoll) and to whom Dickens' character says:[43]

---

[40] Taken and Quoted from 'Charles Dickens: A Life' by Claire Tomalin, Viking Press, 2011

[41] University of Kent, Charles Dickens Theatre Collection, Information Services.

[42] do

[43] Do; quoted from Nicholas Nickleby

> If I were a writer of books, and you a thirsty dramatist, I would rather pay your tavern score for six months, large as it might be, than have a niche in the Temple of Fame with you for the humblest corner of my pedestal through six hundred generations.

However this caricature might also apply to Edward Stirling.

To make matters worse as far as plagiarism is concerned, the original serialisation of *Nicholas Nickleby* contained illustrations by Hablot Browne which were themselves copied during performances in the guise of Tableaux Vivants, a fairly common practice at the time.

It is not surprising that Joseph was drawn to this piece, not least because part of Dickens' own research for the book was undertaken in North Yorkshire, and that the character of Wackford Squeers was based on an amalgam of real people, occasioning quite a few attempted lawsuits from some of them.[44] Although that section of the storyline dealt with boys' schools and the ill-treatment of boys who were found and taken there, some of the characters were quite humorous and afforded tremendous dramatic scope, particularly in Squeers whose character displayed a dichotomy of grotesque humour with vileness and cruelty.[45]

What would be surprising, however, is if Joseph failed to recognise the irony of enacting on stage the roles of Vincent Crummles' acting company with its similarities to his own. Although undated, some wag wrote the following about Joseph's efforts with the play, which must have found some resonance with him since he kept it amongst his papers and it survives within the family archive:[46]

> *Oh hoh! On the stage*
> *Nickleby is the rage:*
> *Sent to Warde-but prigg'd by great Stirling,***

---

[44] From "Dickens" by Peter Ackroyd; pub Sinclair-Stevenson Ltd; 1990
[45] See Charles Dickens: A Life by Claire Tomalin; pub Viking, an imprint of Penguin; 2011
[46] Sumners Family Archive, by kind permission of Roy Sumners

Richard E. Smedley

Known as a Pirate,
Whose powers so high rate,
Hah! His thunder he'll at me be hurling.
The great Mr Downs***
Who visits three towns,
In Yorkshire said, " 'twas quite a Satire,
'Twould not do at all,
His friends great and small
So severely them to bespatter!"
Clever Joe Smedley,
Sent for the Medley,
The Wakefield folks to surprise so;
If into the shop,
The folks will but hop,
The Ghost, he quickly will raise, ho!
If Actors so ready,
And Managers so steady,
To handle your cash every night,
Shall make no amends,
For serving their ends,
It makes one swear ne'er more to write!
To the free Wakefield wights,
Who greet theatrical delights,
I fain would address a small verse
On this Pirate's* vile spirit,
What his behaviour does merit,
His praises I'll shortly rehearse.
   FOH
The supercilious tribe,
Richly merit my gibe,
Or I'd not wielded against them my feather;
But their most mean conceit,
Is so egregiously great,
They may go to the Devil together.

   Mr St—g**

**Mr Stirling refers to Edward Stirling, (1807–94), who wrote and presented the first adaptation of Nicholas Nickleby as a burletta. He was known as a 'theatrical pirate', and had written a stage adaptation of *Pickwick Papers* when only 12 instalments of the book had been published. When presented at the Adelphi Theatre, Nickleby, we are told, caused Dickens himself to groan when he went to see it.[47]

***Mr Downs probably refers to Mr Thomas James Downe, another provincial Actor-Manager, who had formerly run the Theatres Royal at York and Hull

While at Wakefield, as well as *Nicholas Nickleby*, they also presented, on 5th January 1839, *Heir at Law* with *Love, Law and Physic*, and on 7th January, *The Merchant of Venice* with *The Rival Valets*, being "by Desire and under the Patronage of the Worshipful Master, Officers, and Brethren of the Lodge of Unanimity of Free and Accepted Masons, and the last night of performing."

That performance of *Heir at Law* on 5th January was the last playbill to record the appearance of Mr Coppin with Mr Smedley's company, for he had succumbed to the demon drink, and consequently Joseph was forced to dispense with his services.

Coppin had first appeared on Smedley playbills in March 1837, and played mainly comedic roles. On a 1837 Wakefield playbill, Coppin is credited with having come from the Norwich Theatre, and, after leaving Joseph Smedley's employ, a G. Coppin joined the company at Leeds Theatre, (May 22nd 1839), *Rob Roy*, with Messrs Woolgar and Montague also, previously of the Smedley company, on the bill.

This leads me to the conclusion that he was most likely George Selth Coppin, (1819–1906), whose father, who came from Norwich, had given up medicine and become a theatrical manager.

Coppin's entry in the *Oxford DNB* states that as a child he had shown an ability on the violin and playing juvenile characters on stage, and that by 1837 he was a minor member of the Sheffield company. He developed his skills

---

[47] Charles Dickens A Life by Claire Tomalin. p 99

as a low comedian and was engaged at the Queen's Theatre, Manchester, which conveniently skates over the period he would have been employed by Smedley. Also in 1841 he went to Dublin where he met and eloped with an American actress to Australia. He became well known there and made a lot of money, most of which he lost in commercial enterprises. He returned to England in 1854 and toured; then returned to Australia with G.V. Brooke. He was responsible for presenting the Keans to Australia and taking them to America, he suffered several reversals of fortune. In 1858 he entered politics.

* * *

Joseph's Company then moved on to Gainsborough, where *Nicholas Nickleby* was played as one of three 'new pieces' on 14th January, the other two being *The Pleasant Neighbour* and *Comfortable Service*, as the benefit for Mr and Mrs Smedley; and on the 17th they presented *The Poor Gentleman* with *The Dancing Barber*. On 28th January, they enacted *Tom Cringle, or, The Black Wreckers*, with the drama, *Passion and Repentance, or, Love's Frailties*. On 30th January, for Joseph Jnr's benefit, they performed *The Rake's Progress*, *Middy Ashore*, and *The Irish Lion*.

It was also at about this time that Joseph made one of several, ultimately unsuccessful, efforts to find someone to take over the leases of his Yorkshire theatres, which he had so recently taken for himself. There is an undated notice announcing this in the family archive,[48] and offers to let "The Theatre at Wakefield, together with six others in the immediate neighbourhood, forming one of the most compact circuits in the kingdom." It goes on to state that if they remained unlet, Mr Smedley Junior would carry the business on. The six other theatres were Barnsley, Bradford, Huddersfield, Rotherham, Pontefract and probably Halifax.[49]

From this we have to assume that the running of so many theatres coupled with his longstanding dates, were proving either too strenuous or too expensive or both, and that he had made the decision to cut back his enterprise,

---

[48] Smedley Archive (Sumners deposit), Lincolnshire Archive:LLHS 38/5/6/2

[49] As above and quoted by CMP Taylor in "Right Royal" Wakefield Theatre, 1776-1994

and the recent reverses in fortune he had suffered may have led him to doubt the wisdom of continuing, despite the high regard in which he was held in those towns. There was little doubt that Joseph wanted to eventually leave the circuits he had built to his sons to run. Perhaps now, as he was getting older, he was thinking of this legacy, and whether or not his sons were capable of making a success of it. It may also be that the sons, Joseph Junior and George, might have expressed a preference to follow different avenues for themselves to those that their father had mapped out for them. Again, Joseph had only to look back to his own youthful past to find precedent for this.

At any rate, Joseph did manage to let the theatre at Wakefield, and other theatres in the circuit. He did his best, however, to warn the new lessees of the financial dangers that theatre management attracted.

It seems that Joseph had already managed to find some people to take over the Wakefield Theatre, and that this had already failed, as, in an indenture dated 22nd January, 1839, between Joseph, whose current residence was given as Gainsborough, and "Thomas Stennett of the County of Lincoln, yeoman, Sarah West of Boston in the County of Lincoln, widow, Susannah West of Boston in the County of Lincoln, John Rawson of the County of Lincoln, William Needham, George Kiallmark of Russell Place, Fitzroy Square in the County of Middlesex, and John Halls."[50]

According to the indenture, on paying the sum of five shillings, ("of lawful money of Great Britain") to each of the aforementioned, the ownership of the Wakefield Theatre, it's Cellars and attached buildings reverted to Joseph Smedley.

The document is signed and sealed by each of the parties. Present at the signing was Samuel Obbinson, chemist and druggist of New Sleaford. I cannot identify any others mentioned in the document except for George Kiallmark.

George Frederick Kiallmark (1804–87) was a pianist, born in Islington and educated at Margate. His father was George Kiallmark (1781–1835), a violinist and composer, and himself the son of John, an officer in the Swedish

---

[50] Indenture in West Yorkshire Archives at Wakefield, WYW1432/1

navy who married Margaret Meggitt, who, shortly after the birth of George Snr was deserted by her husband who then died, married her butler, named Pottle. She was an heiress from Wakefield in Yorkshire and was related to Sir Joseph Banks, the famous botanist who had accompanied James Cook on his voyage round the world on the *Endeavour*. It seems natural, therefore that George Frederick was close to his grandmother and this is the only connection to Wakefield that I can uncover. He had also helped his father in giving music lessons and opened an academy at his home at Percy Street, Tottenham Court Road, for the study of the piano. He was a fine exponent of Chopin's music and, on hearing him play, Mendelssohn is said to have commented "a fine sketch of what piano playing should be, and what he will one day make it."[51]

It is another bid to take over the circuit that Joseph refers to in the following letter, in reply to one received from Coppin. It gives their names as Hooley and Kirk, although there are no surviving playbills for that period and they're not mentioned by Senior or Kate Taylor. This letter, however, is worth including here as it indicates how disillusioned Joseph had become, and expresses his desire to retire from the stage:

Gainsborough, 5th Feb. 1839
Friend Coppin
    For I do consider you as such and indeed no one's enemy but your own. But the present letter is not to reproach but thank you. Now for the information – tis true I've let the Wakefield Circuit and the parties commence at Beverley on the 18th and I do fear will end (for want of sufficient funds to bear up against probable loss) ere they have been in two months. However they "sin with their eyes open" – there is not a thing, that I know of, that will operate against their success, but of which I've forewarned them and even after the deed was signed, and the deposit made – I offered to return the money and render the contract void – on the payment of a trifle for the expence they had put me to in going to Hull, Beverley and "Faintheart" and you know the proverb on they would go and must now take the consequences – if they should succeed, all well for I want them to do so, but if not, I am safe for they must pay me, as well as the tradesmen, weekly or they immediately forfeit the deposit £50 as well as the circuits.

---

[51] From entry in Oxford DNB by R.H.Legge and Anne Pimlott Baker. Accessed 01/03/2017

I therefore assure myself that without they have greater funds than I gave them credit for – it must again fall into my hands and very soon for which reason I am prepared to come to Huddersfield, and for which I've now a license, immediately after Passion week and Bradford, bad as it was and will try again, all attempts for any other person to get a license, whilst I have the funds "at court" I am now possessed of, will be futile and Thompson who did apply last year, knows it to his cost – it seems a matter of doubt to me, whether Hooley and Kirk, want to lose all they own by concertizing – but if not – play acting, I am sure, will soon swallow the remainder tis a strange infatuation! While they are so anxious to be in the pursuit – I would make any sacrifice to get out – men of sufficient capital will not embark in so hazardous an undertaking – and without a sufficiency as times are, they must fail, – consequently my prospect of getting permanently out – every day seems to get worse. I am glad to hear that you get on so well with the Conjurer – now Coppin, let me beg, let me entreat you as a sincere friend and Brother, that you will abstain from that, which has already brought you into distress and trouble and if persisted in must shorten your life – let me but hear that you have done so – and assure you the satisfaction, nay the pleasure will be great indeed to your sincere friend Brother and well-wisher

J. Smedley

All well and in status quo – except Green (my leader) formerly a drunkard, now very steady and a Mr Cooper heavy and Mrs Cooper (useful).

Joseph's warnings notwithstanding, the enterprise did fail, and the circuit reverted to Joseph's management.

In February 1839 they moved on to Gainsborough, where their programme included (on 4th Feb) *The Two Murderers*, with a cast including Messrs Horton, J. Smedley, Lockwood, Mosley, George and Waterfield. Underneath this, *Court Favour, or, Private and Confidential*, in which Miss Smedley (i.e. Helen) made an appearance; followed by a recitation by Mr Horton: 'Bucks have at ye all'; A Sailor's Hornpipe in Character by Miss Andrews, and concluding with *Petticoat Government*.

It was then on to Brigg, where the only surviving playbill informs us that they played their first night on the 19th, for "Half the Usual Prices", and that this was *The Tragedy of George Barnwell*. On 5th March, they played *Love Chase*, with the farce *Everybody's Husband*, and on 7th March, *Wonder!*

A Woman Keeps a Secret, featured both Joseph Snr and Jnr, with *The Doctor and His Man, or, Animal Magnetism*, which also featured an appearance by Mrs Smedley.

On 14th March 1839 they presented *John Bull* with *Merry Monarch*, and on the 16th, *Richard Parker, or The Mutiny at the Nore* with two farces, *Make Your Wills* and *The Liar*.

The tour continued to Barton, where, on 17th May they performed *Clari, The Maid of Milan*; a Burlesque tragic opera called *Bombastes Furioso*; and *Spectre Bridegroom*. On 20th May, *Robin Hood and Little John, or, Sherwood Forest*, a musical play featuring Joseph Jnr, was performed along with *Smoked Miser* and *Spoiled Child*.

On 27th May they performed the comedy *Where to Find a Friend*, and *Simpson & Co*. The playbill also announced that "after this evening the Company will remove to Beverley Races and re-open at Barton on Friday the 31st." They may have performed at the theatre in Beverley on this visit, for Joseph was its current licensee; however he may have reverted to a pop-up booth at the racecourse itself, as so many touring companies had been forced to do in the past, although this may not have suited Joseph at this point in his career. There are no surviving playbills of this visit to enlighten us. But true to his word, the 31st May saw Shakespeare's *Taming of the Shrew* back at Barton, performed with both Josephs appearing, with a farce, *The Female Fox-Hunter*, and the musical farce *Lady of Palermo, or, The Haunted Apartment*.

On June 11th, 1839 they were back in Huddersfield, this time with another guest artiste, this time Mons. Gouffe, the 'man-monkey'. This was really what we would today call a 'speciality act'. An actor (John Hornshaw) who dressed in an ape costume and, with excellent acrobatic ability, was able to appear in suitable productions mounted to show off these skills. He had made his name at the Surrey Theatre in London where he debuted in 1825 and where he appeared in a number of 'monkey plays'.[52] He had also appeared

---

[52] A Major London Minor; The Surrey Theatre 1805-1865 by William G Knight; STR 1997

at the old Prince of Wales' Theatre in 1829[53] However he retired and a 'new' Mons. Gouffe appeared in 1837, identified as Sam Todd,[54] who, as a pot-boy "amused the customers of the house by climbing and running round ceilings , shelves, and every available place in tap-rooms, and imitating in a most natural manner monkey tricks, utterances and habits." Apparently this act was extremely popular at the time.

The second night of Mons. Gouffe's engagement started with a presentation of *To Marry or not to Marry* with Mr Smedley, followed by *Jocko the Brazilian Ape*, with Gouffe and Joseph Jnr.

Another guest artiste was brought forth during the Huddersfield season, on June 21st, when Joseph presented:

MASTER OWEN
THE YOUNG ROSCIUS!
THE ORIGINAL OLIVER TWIST!
150 successful nights at the Surrey Theatre
MRS OWEN
(Late Miss Beaumont)
Of Theatre Royal Covent Garden
IN
DOUGLAS
Or, The Noble Shepherd
MERRY MONARCH

Yet another 'Young Roscius', this one old enough to be married! He had been chosen to play the title role of Oliver Twist in a pirated stage version of Dickens' novel which was still being serialised, in much the same way as *Nicholas Nickleby* had been. It also featured the appearance of another Roscius – the African one – who had played 'Mr Fang, the Sitting Magistrate of the Metropolitan Police Office' in an odd piece of casting for the times.

---

[53] See the History of The Prince of Wales's Theatre, 1771-1903, by Richard L. Lorenzen, pub STR 2014

[54] Identified by Edward Stirling in his 'Old Drury Lane', and quoted here from 'A Major London Minor'

Richard E. Smedley

An excellent account of the shenanigans surrounding that production is to be found in William G Knight's book on the Surrey Theatre, which explains how the ultimate loser in this sorry tale was the author himself-Dickens!

The following evening, 22nd June 1839 they performed *Barbarossa, Tyrant of Algiers*, again with Mr and Mrs Owen, and a musical farce, *No Song No Supper*, also with Mrs Owen.

Remaining in Huddersfield in July, they performed as follows:

5th July; *The Merchant of Venice, Tableaux Vivans* and *The Dancing Barber;*
10th July: *Married Life* and *The Invincibles!!*
8th July: *Rob Roy* with *Comfortable Service*
22nd July: *The Lady of Lyons* with *Simpson & Co* and
24th July: *The Love Chase* with *The Illustrious Stranger, or, Married & Buried.*

In Huddersfield on 5th August they presented *A New Wonder: A Woman Never Vexed*, and *The Wandering Boys* for the benefit of Joseph Snr. On 7th August *The Rake's Progress*, with *Wreck Ashore*; on the 17th *The Wife, or, A Tale of Mantua*, with the farce *High Notions*. On 23rd August they revived *Hunchback* with a *Tableaux Vivans* and *The Old Maid, or, Village Scandal*, and on 30th *Every One Has His Fault; Tableaux Vivans* and *Winning A Husband*.

Still at Huddersfield, on 13th September 1839, and for the Benefit of Mr L.S. Thompson Junior, "and on which occasion Mr Thompson Snr will appear in Two Fair Characters," was presented *The Gypsy Chief, or, The Falls of the Clyde*, with *Two Thompsons* (specially written for the father and son) and *Love Law and Physic*.

Back in Wakefield on 4th October, they presented *The Love Chase* with *The Illustrious* Stranger, and, on the following night, *The Moor's Revenge* and *The Liar*.

On 7th October, 1839 they performed *Macbeth* with *Two Strings to your Bow*; on the 9th, *Guy Mannering* with *The King's Command*; and on the 11th, *Taming a Shrew* with *The Rifle Brigade* and *Paul and Virginia*. The prices remained the same, i.e. Boxes 2s-6d; Pit 1s-6d; and Gallery 6d.

On 11th October, for the Benefit of Mr and Mrs Lockwood, the company performed *Henry the Fourth*, with *Simpson & Co*, and on the night of the 12th, *The Taming of the Shrew*, with *The Rifle Brigade* and *Paul and Virginia*. On 13th they played *Guy Mannering* and *The King's Command*.

On the 15th October, it was announced, that their main piece was to be *The Pilot* – "in which Mr THOMPSON Jnr from the Theatre Royal Liverpool (who is engaged for a limited number of nights) will make his first appearance in LONG TOM COFFIN." The evening concluded with *The Farmer's Boy* and "Bristles, by Mr Thompson Jnr".

On 18th October they performed *The Farmer's Story*, with *Tableaux Vivans* and *John of Paris*, while on the following night it was *The Revenge* and *A Day in Paris*.

On 21st October, the bill was topped by *Robert Macaire*, with *The Husband's Secret* and *The Female Fox-Hunter* completing the entertainment. The 23rd October had *Bertram* with *A Captain's Not A-Miss* on the programme, followed by October 25th: *The Wife*, followed by the farce *The British Legion;* then, on 26th, *Jane Shore* with *The Tragedy of George Barnwell*; and on the 28th, *Othello* with, as Iago, Mr Montague, who, we are assured, came "from the Manchester Theatre, his first appearance here these three years." This was supported by the farce *The Captain's Not A-Miss*. On 30th October it was Mr Smedley's Benefit, for which he chose to play *King Henry the Eighth*, with the farce of *The Doctor and his Man, or, Animal Magnetism*.

On 8th November, they again played *The Pilot*, with Mr Thompson reprising the role of Long Tom Coffin, followed by *Honest Thieves*; on the 9th they presented "the new play" of *Abelard and Heloise* with the farce *Love's Frailties*, a gifted piece of programming given the subject matter of the first piece!

On the 11th November (the fair night) they enacted *The School of Reform* and *Blue Beard*; on the 12th, *Tom Cringle, or, A Seaman's Log*, with *The Irish Widow*, and, for the 13th November, in a departure from the norm, it was announced, "For the Benefit of Mr Thompson Jnr, and last night of his engagement, A VARIETY OF ENTERTAINMENTS, As will be announced in the bills of the day." Alas, we do not know what these were, as the relevant daily playbills have not survived, but one can be sure that they were carefully chosen to show off the Mr Thompson's unique talents.

On 15th November, Joseph decided to return to Bulwer-Lytton's drama of *The Lady of Lyons*, which he played with *The Irish Lion*. The 16th of November was the Tragedy of *The Gamester*, and the *Warlock of the Glen*; the 18th, and for the Benefit of Messrs Gilfillan and Robinson (comparatively new members of the company) they chose *Rob Roy* and *The Artist's Wife*. The 20th November was the Benefit of another newcomer, Miss Walton, in *The Maid of Mariendorpt*, and *The Middy Ashore*, while on 22nd, and for the Benefit of Mr and Mrs Montague, they offered *Hamlet* and *Highways and Byways*. On 23rd it was *Venice Preserved* with *The Lady of the Rock*; 25th – By Desire for the Benefit of Mr J. Smedley – *How To Avoid the Road to Ruin* with *My Spouse and I*. For Mr Mosley's Benefit on 27th November, they repeated *Nicholas Nickleby*, which had just been published for the first time as a complete book on 28th October, i.e. the previous month, along with *Spectre Bridegroom* and *Therese*.

On 29th November, it was announced:[55]

> For the Benefit of Mr Woolgar, Sheridan Knowles'
> Historical Play of
> VIRGINIUS
> On this occasion, Mr WILSON has kindly consented to afford
> His valuable services, and will sing with Miss WOOLGAR, in
> TWO DUETTS (sic)
> In the course of the evening will be presented
> The Last Act of
> A NEW WAY TO PAY OLD DEBTS
> When Mr WOOLGAR will endeavour to perform Sir Giles
> Overreach, in imitation of the late Mr KEAN

---

[55] According to an advertisement in the Wakefield Journal and West Riding Herald; Wakefield Local Studies Library

On 24th January, 1840, while still at Wakefield, Joseph made the following announcement in the newspaper:[56]

> Mr Smedley has the justification of announcing to
> His Friends and the Public that he has succeeded in
> Forming an engagement with the celebrated vocalist
> MR BRAHAM
> Of the Theatres Royal Drury Lane and Covent Garden
> FOR THREE NIGHTS ONLY
> Viz. On MONDAY the 27th, TUESDAY the 28th, and
> WEDNESDAY the 29th instant, when Mr B will appear in a
> Favourite Character each night; viz MONDAY
> HENRY BERTRAM
> IN
> GUY MANNERING
> TUESDAY HAWTHORN
> IN
> LOVE IN A VILLAGE
> And Wednesday, for the Benefit of MR BRAHAM, a Play
> And Farce that will be announced in the Bills of the Day
> And the last night of performing.

* * *

Another advertisement appeared in the same paper on 31st January, 1840, which is somewhat mysterious:

> THEATRE, WAKEFIELD
> (For one night only)
> Mr Mosley has the honor to inform his Friends
> And the Play-going Public in general that he Purposes
> OPENING THE THEATRE FOR ONE NIGHT ONLY
> In the course of next week, on which occasion
> He is enabled to announce the first and only

---

[56] The Wakefield Journal and West Riding Herald of 17th January and 24th January, 1840

Appearance of
MISS REEVE,
Of the Theatre Royal, Hull, Leeds, Lincoln &C
MR ROGERS
Of the Theatres Royal, Glasgow, Belfast, and
formerly of Wakefield, is also engaged on this occasion,
and will appear in two of his favourite Characters
The Evening's Entertainments will commence with
THE COUNTRY SQUIRE
OR
THE OLD ENGLISH GENTLEMAN
Squire Broadlands   Mr Rogers
Fanny Markham   Miss Reeve
A Song by Mr Rogers
To conclude with the domestic Drama of the
MILLER'S MAID
Giles   Mr Rogers
Phoebe   Miss Reeve

Here, there is no mention of Joseph, or indeed whether Mosley is acting on Joseph's behalf or his own. It certainly looks as though Mosley has leased the theatre from Joseph for the day on his own account; perhaps the first fledgling steps of his own management.

I estimate that it was about now that Joseph tried again to find someone to take over the leases of the Yorkshire circuit from him:

TO THEATRICALS
TO BE LET

THE THEATRE at Wakefield, together with six others in the Immediate Neighbourhood, forming one of the most Compact Circuits in the Kingdom, and with them will be let The USE of all the Scenery, Machinery and Properties, as well as the Wardrobe, Books and Music such as few can boast of. The Company Has been under the present management for thirty-six years, and offers a rare opportunity of embarking in a large concern with a comparative small capital.
    For particulars apply to Mr SMEDLEY, Wakefield

NB The Company will be carried on after the First of January next, by Mr SMEDLEY Jun., if an eligible Tenant does not offer in the mean time.[57]

In February of 1840, the company visited Worksop in Nottinghamshire where Mr Braham was to begin a further two-night engagement.

John Braham

Here it is perhaps worth including a note about John Braham. Relatively unknown and forgotten today, Braham was an operatic tenor, and, in his time, popular and famous. In February 1840, while at Worksop, Joseph presented him as another guest-artiste in what was a departure for Joseph's company. Probably born in 1777,[58] he was brought up (after his father's death) and taught to sing by his uncle Michael Leoni (Myer Lyon), also a tenor. He made his first stage appearance in 1787 at Covent Garden, with his new stage name (a corruption of his family name, Abraham) and made several more appearances at London theatres over the next eighteen months. In 1797, his voice having settled in adulthood to a tenor, he sang in Bath where he studied under Venanzio Rauzzini and met Nancy Storace, a soprano of international repute. Her brother, Stephen, a composer, engaged him to sing in his forthcoming opera *Mahmoud* which premiered at Drury Lane on 30th April 1796, after the death of the composer. His success in the role established him at the top of his profession, although still only 19 years of age. He was said to be considered ugly, short (he was 5 feet 3 inches tall), and of swarthy complexion.

He and Nancy Storace had a relationship spanning the next 20 years. In 1797 she drew up her will in which she bequeathed Braham £2000. They then embarked on a continental tour, lasting until 1801, where, after eight months in Paris where they sang for Napoleon and Josephine, they went to Florence where they performed, and again at La Scala, Milan.

---

[57] Undated printed advertisement in the Smedley Archive; Lincolnshire Archive, LLHS 38/5/6/2

[58] Extracted from his entry in the Oxford DNB by George Biddlecombe

Richard E. Smedley

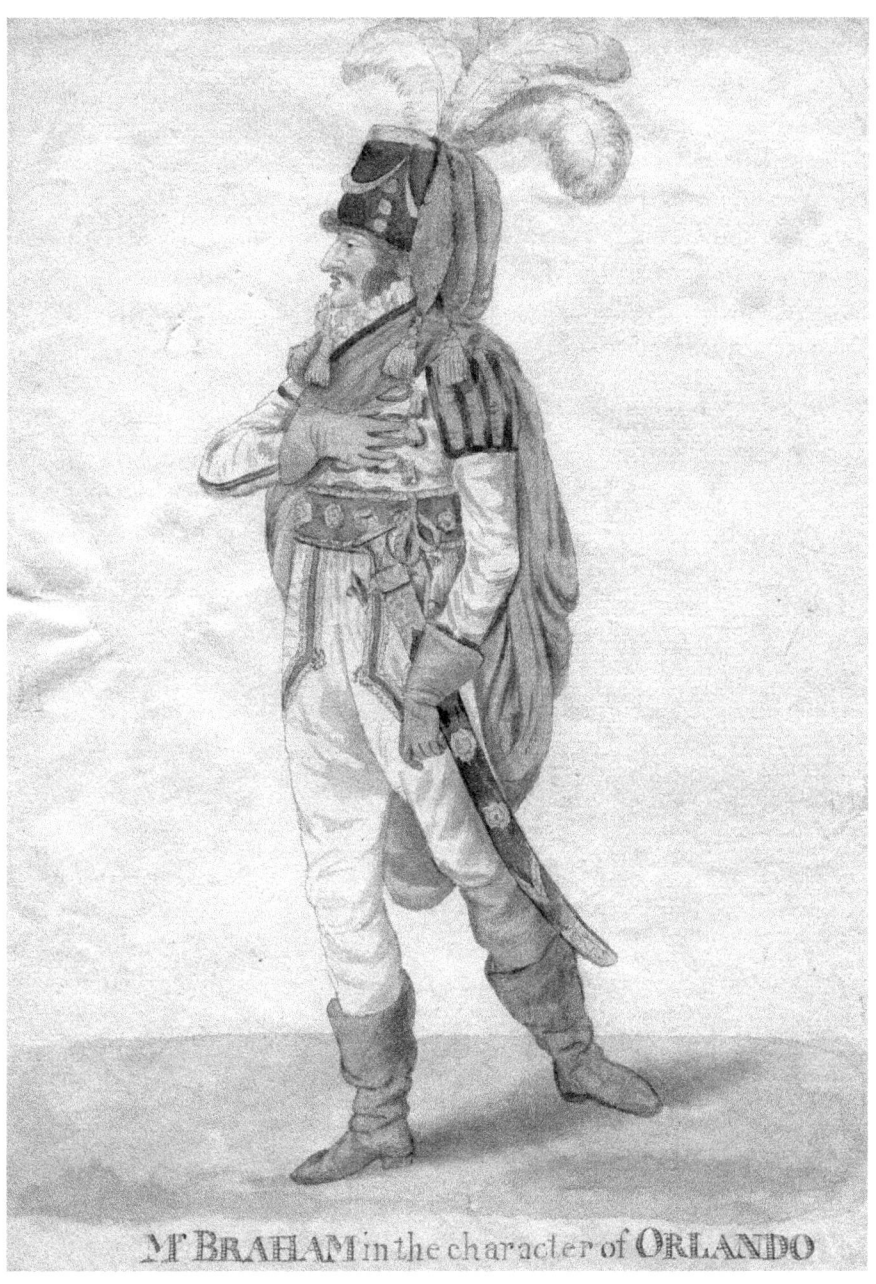

Print of portrait of John Braham as Orlando – one of a series produced by Robert Dighton

Once back in London he was in constant demand, and his reputation grew further. On 3ʳᵈ May, 1802, Storace gave birth to their son, William Spencer Harris Braham. Able to command huge sums to perform, Braham's vocal range was huge, from low A to high F, and including high C in full voice. In line with the convention of the time, he sang high notes in falsetto, but so great was his control that the change was successfully disguised. He mingled with the highest society; George IV was a fan, as was Charles Lamb. He was not renowned as an actor, however, but this was accepted as he was first and foremost a singer.

Nancy Storace's husband, from whom she had been separated for years, passed away in 1806, and, although free to marry, they didn't, and their relationship foundered in 1815, when Braham had an affair with a Mrs Wright, and descended into a bitter and ferocious exchange of insults as to who owned what.

Not long after, and having left Mrs Wright, he met and married Frances (Fanny) Elizabeth Bolton (1799–1846) in Manchester; she was then aged 17, the daughter of a dancing-master, very tall, blonde, and considered very beautiful. She was also stage-struck and ambitious to rise in society. Although seemingly unsuited, they made a devoted couple and between 1819 and 1829 they had six surviving children.

A memoir about him, published in 1825, notes that

> to attempt a summary of Mr Braham's talent is almost absurd. His severest critics once accused him of exuberance of ornament-that fault he has long since corrected. From the simplicity of *There was a jolly Miller,* to the difficulty of *Amid a thousand racking woes,* he has no competitor. He is equally above censure and praise...as a composer, he has more taste than originality... He is reserved, indeed haughty, in the theatre; but he is neither tyrannical nor imperious; in private life, he is agreeable, and tolerably unassuming; for a man who has been so deluged by praise, he has the least apparent vanity of any one we know."

Braham's successful career continued. In 1826 he created the role of Huon in Weber's *Oberon*, and after Weber's death he was appointed to the committee responsible for the funeral arrangements.

By 1830 Braham had amassed a fortune of £90,000, and he signed a 21 year lease for a large property at Brompton. In 1834 he was said to have "surpassed himself" when he appeared in the Handel commemoration at Westminster Abbey, and, during the York festival in September 1835 he lunched with the future Queen Victoria and her mother, the Duchess of Kent. Earlier in that year, on 18th May, he became co-manager, with Frederick Yates, of the Colosseum, Regent's Park, in which he invested £30,000, and two days later he purchased the site for a new theatre, the St. James's, at a cost of £26,000. These ventures proved to be financially disastrous, and forced him to re-think his wish to retire. In 1838 and 1839 he sang the title roles in *Don Giovanni*, by Mozart, and *Guillaume Tell* by Rossini. By now in his sixties, his voice had become a baritone. According to his entry in the *Oxford DNB*,[59] his last stage appearance was in February 1839 and he next appeared at the Birmingham festival in September 1840, singing Mendelssohn's 'Lobgesang'. Between these performances, however, Braham obviously arranged some performances in the provinces, presumably to try and recoup some of his recent losses, and this is when he performed at Worksop. On 1st October 1840 he embarked with his wife and son Charles to start a tour of America, from which they did not return until January 1843.

He did also write some music, although it did not appeal, except for 'The Death of Nelson', which was well-known in its day to every patriotic Briton. His entry in the *Oxford Companion to Music* summed up his career succinctly: "He made a fortune as a musician and lost it as a theatre manager."

Braham opened at Worksop on 7th February, 1840, playing one of his better-known roles as Henry Bertram in *Guy Mannering*, supported by the farce *Maid and Wife,* and the following evening, his last, he performed the opera *Love in a Village* and *The Waterman.*

On Monday, 17th February, Joseph and his company were honoured to receive His Grace the Duke of Newcastle and party to the Worksop Theatre where, to honour the wedding of the Queen to Prince Albert, the Duke bought out the house, i.e. the audience were invited to attend at the Duke's

---

[59] Oxford Dictionary of National Biography. Braham's entry written by George Biddlecombe, accessed on-line 18/10/2016

expense. In his diary for 10th February, 1840, the Duke wrote:[60] "This day our Queen Victoria is united to Prince Albert of Saxe Coburg. We all drank their health wishing that the unison may be amply productive of good and happiness to the wedded pair and of benefit and prosperity to the Country." In her book, C.M.P. Taylor[61] states that this visit took place in the March of that year, confusing the occasion with another visit by the Duke. The *Lincolnshire Chronicle* of 21st February, 1840, reported it thus:

> THEATRE, WORKSOP. This place of amusement, under the management of Mr Smedley, has been unusually attractive. It has been patronised and honoured with the presence of the Duke of Newcastle, Lord Wm. Clinton, Ladies H. And G. Clinton, Sir Thos. and Lady White, &c. & c. The Duke of Newcastle, in honour of the Queen's marriage, caused the theatre to be opened gratis on Monday last, and, we need not add, it was filled to overflow; hundreds were obliged to go away disappointed. The national anthem was sung by the company, the audience joining heartily in the chorus. His Grace was loudly cheered on his entrance as well as at his departure.

The *Sheffield Iris* of 25th February was more effusive:

> THE WORKSOP THEATRE. On Monday week, Sheridan Knowles's play of "The Love Chace"(sic) was performed at this theatre, and through the liberality of his Grace the Duke of Newcastle the theatre was thrown open to the public, in honour of the Queen's marriage. Long before the regular hour of admission the theatre was besieged by hundreds of both sexes, and some difficulty was experienced in keeping possession of the doors. About seven o'clock his Grace and family arrived, and were loudly cheered on their entrance. Shortly afterwards, Sir Thomas and Lady White and family were in attendance. Great credit is due to Mr Smedley and company for the respectable manner in which both the play and farce were performed. Indeed it was a general remark that a better company of comedians had never been seen in any country theatre. They certainly deserve success. The Duke was loudly cheered on leaving the theatre.

---

[60] Newcastle Collection; University of Nottingham, MSS and Special Collections Dept

[61] Right Royal; The Wakefield Theatre, 1776-1994

Richard E. Smedley

The Duke's diary for the 18th February[62] gives the following account:

I bespoke a Play at Worksop last night and I thought it might produce a good affect if I opened the house in honor of the Queen's marriage – I was not mistaken – the measure has given the greatest satisfaction and I am told has been wonderfully beneficial as a popular act. We were all much amused – I never before was in the theatre which for scenery and decorations on the stage was floor to ceiling well conducted. The company too was unusually good for a country theatre.

The Duke of Newcastle

He was Henry Pelham, the 4th Duke of Newcastle, owner of Clumber Park in North Nottinghamshire, and had been, since 1809, Lord Lieutenant, and as such the Queen's representative, of that county. He was a major landowner and employer in the area, but cut a controversial figure, and was uncompromising in his views, opposing the views of Protestant dissenters, Catholic emancipation and Parliamentary Reform.

In 1831 his mansion, Nottingham Castle, was burnt down by a mob, forcing him to fortify his Clumber Park residence and his house in Portman Square, London. He views on the Reform Act, which was at Committee stage, were hostile, and in 1839, after refusing to retract an offensive letter to the Lord Chancellor, he was sacked as Lord Lieutenant. He acquired Worksop Manor and its lands, and brought in Gladstone as M.P. for Newark.[63]

Despite inheriting land and properties, he had married, in 1807, a wealthy heiress, Georgiana Mundy.[64] They went on to have 14 children together, eight sons and six daughters, one of whom, Anna Marie, died when only 14

---

[62] Newcastle Collection; University of Nottingham MSS and Special Collections Dept.
[63] Taken from Pelham's entry in Dictionary of National Biography, George C. Boase, 1887; and repeated in History Home website, accessed 13/01/2017
[64] Adapted from article in Spotlight on Tuxford Magazine; Nov/Dec 2016, and quoted by kind permission of the author, Dawn Johnson

years of age. Only four months after this, in 1822, Georgiana died in childbirth to twins, neither of whom survived.

So great was the Duke's grief that he decided to build a church and mausoleum in memory of his wife in the village of Milton, to be designed by England's top architect Robert Smirke (1783–1845), who, incidentally, had been hired by J.P. Kemble to rebuild the Theatre Royal Covent Garden in 1808–09. The Mausoleum was to contain a marble monument to Georgiana and the twins designed by Sir Richard Westmacott, a well-known Royal Academician. The church was completed in 1833 and became the parish church.[65]

Smirke and Westmacott must have known each other's work as they were both members of the Royal Academy and foremost in their areas of expertise at this time. Indeed Westmacott had testified before the House of Commons in favour of the purchase of the Elgin Marbles; Smirke designed their temporary accommodation (1815–16) at the British Museum, then at Montague House, Bloomsbury.

During this period, his was the premier Dukedom of the country, and, as owner of Worksop Manor, had a role to play in the Sovereign's Coronation, by supplying a glove to cover the Sovereign's right hand during the ceremony.

On 2nd March, still at Worksop, Smedley's company presented "a new play for the first time here," *The Lady of Lyons, or, Love and Pride*, after which Miss Woolgar danced the Highland Fling, and the evening's finale was the farce *Lock and Key*.

On 6th March, they played *The Green Man* and ended with the operatic comedy *Love-Will Find Out the Way*, again with an interlude of dancing by Miss Woolgar. This performance was again attended by the 4th Duke of Newcastle accompanied by Sir Thomas White, Bart. and Lady White.

---

[65] Taken from entries for Smirke and Westmacott in Oxford DNB, by Richard Riddell and Marie Busco, accessed 13/01/2017

The Duke's diary entry for that day says[66]:

> In the evening we all went to the theatre at Worksop, it being the Manager's benefit – we were much amused, the company is an excellent one and the farce "Love will find out the way" very droll & entertaining – the parts were exceedingly well [sustained?? – unclear-RS].

It is perhaps appropriate here to discuss William and his daughter, Sarah Jane Woolgar, who, as best I can judge, joined Joseph's company while at Huddersfield the previous July, prior to which they had been in the Nottingham Company, and with whom they had performed at Halifax in the Benefit for Mr Manly, the Acting Manager[67]. Mr Woolgar was a tailor as well as actor, who is described by the *Dictionary of National Biography* as an "indifferent tragedian."[68] His daughter was born at Gosport, Hampshire, and she was raised and trained by her father who also guided, and to an extent managed, her career. She would therefore have been 15 years of age when she joined Joseph's company, although she had made her first appearance at Plymouth in May, 1836, as Leolyn in The Wood Demon. She then studied music at Birmingham, where she went on to sing, for five nights, the role of Adalgisa in Bellini's *Norma* in support of Mr and Mrs Wood. In 1842 she appeared in *Guy Mannering* at Edinburgh, and was Ophelia at Manchester later that year. In 1843 she made her London debut at the Adelphi Theatre in a burletta, *Antony and Cleopatra*, and she was to be associated with that theatre for many years. In 1855 she married Alfred Mellon, the leader of the Adelphi orchestra, and thereafter acted under her married name. Born in 1820, and raised in Birmingham, Mellon could not have been the same Mellon who acted for Joseph in 1831, and it is unlikely that the two were related.

There were, in fact, several theatrical Mellons during this time, and although in those days there were fewer degrees of separation than today, I have not been able to establish any connection between them. As far as I can tell, he

---

[66] Newcastle Collection, Manuscript and Special Collections Department, University of Nottingham

[67] Playbill in West Yorkshire Archive at Bradford

[68] According to entry in the Oxford DNB, written by W.J.Lawrence and Rev. J Gilliland, accessed 09/01/2017

was not related in any way to the Miss Harriot Mellon, who grew up the daughter of strolling players, became a popular actress herself and eventually married Thomas Coutts, the banker, and later, the Duke of St Albans; nor to the Mr and Mrs H. Mellon who headlined the bills at the Leeds Theatre in the early 1840s and later. It was this Mrs H Mellon presumably who forfeited her membership of the General Theatrical Fund for making a false declaration about her age.

* * *

The company's next port of call was Southwell, where, on 25th March, 1840, and for the Benefit of Mr and Mrs Wilton, they performed *Rob Roy, or, Auld Lang Syne* and *Hunter of the Alps, or, The Forest of Savoy*.[69] The casts were as follows:

ROB ROY

Sir Frederic Vernon............Mr DUVAL   Rob Roy............Mr WOOLGAR
Francis Osbaldiston............Mr WILTON
Rashley Osbaldiston............Mr MONTAGUE
Dougal............Mr J. Smedley
Captain Thornton............Mr PERKINS   McStuart............Mr George
Major Galbraith............Mr CLIFFORD
Corporal Cramp............Mr ROBINSON
Andrew............Mr WATERFIELD
Robert and Hamish, By Young Gentlemen
Bailie Nicol Jarvie............Mr SMEDLEY
Owen............Mr CLIFFORD
Diana Vernon............Miss WOOLGAR
Hostess............Mrs MONTAGUE   Mattie............Mrs BECKWITH
Martha............Mrs Wilton   Helen Macgregor............Mrs CLIFFORD

HUNTER OF THE ALPS

Felix............Mr PERKINS
Jeronymo............Mr CLIFFORD   Baptista............Mr DUVAL
Marco............Mr George   Pietro............Mr DUVAL
Stephano............Mr ROBINSON

---

[69] Playbill

Rosalvi............Mr MONTAGUE		Julio............Miss Wilton	
Florio............Miss MONTAGUE			
Genevieve............Miss WOOLGAR		Helena............Mrs CLIFFORD	
Georgette............Mrs BECKWITH		Annette............Mrs WILTON	
Claudine............Mrs MONTAGUE			

Little is known about Mr and Mrs Wilton, and, their daughter, presumably, billed as Miss Wilton, who were fairly recent additions to the company.

According to Senior,[70] Miss Wilton first appeared as Curio in *Twelfth Night*, on 5th December, 1839. Apparently there had been a child actress at Wakefield of the same name, and who later recited epilogues and "other dreadful things" and was the daughter of Mr and Mrs Wilton who appeared from time to time listed amongst Joseph's company. However, in 1842 she is described as being five years old, and it is therefore unlikely that she could have played Curio three years earlier. It is quite possible, though, that her age may have been exaggerated downwards in order to increase her appeal. She was, however, certainly not related to the Miss Marie Wilton, who later became Mrs Bancroft, and subsequently Lady Bancroft.

Still at Southwell, on 11th April, *A New Way to Pay Old Debts* was played with Mr Woolgar as Sir Giles Overreach again, and supported by a musical entertainment called *Rosin, or, The Harvest Home*; Joseph Snr appeared in neither piece.

On 31st May 1840, Joseph and Melinda's eldest daughter, Melinda Brunton Young, gave birth to another daughter, this time to be named Marianne

Later, in June 1840, at March, Joseph and his company played the comedy *The Rajah's Daughter, or, Englishmen in India* with a *Tableaux Vivans*, arranged by Joseph Smedley Jnr, dancing by Miss Woolgar, and ending with a farce, *The British Legion*.

In July 1840, Joseph's company visited Downham Market. Throughout his career touring the country's theatres, the company usually travelled via the

---

[70] The Old Wakefield Theatre, William Senior, First pub. 1894

road system in carts and other horse-drawn vehicles. However, occasionally, they utilised the canal systems, and this was perhaps more convenient when playing in East Anglia, where the fens and broads afforded a greater choice of transport. This is illustrated by a letter addressed to Joseph while at Downham Market, from a firm in King's Lynn and dated 18th July 1840:[71]

> Sir,
> I have had a letter from Mr Furley and he will take your goods and passengers upon the following terms viz passengers in the best cabin at 10/6 each and will be allowed 2 boxes each not exceeding 1 cwt which of course would reduce your luggage considerably – fore cabin 6/- each but in that case the luggage would go as cargo and be paid for as I stated to you at 1/- per cwt.
> I would feel obliged if you would give me a week's notice.
> I am yours most obediently
> H H Cook

Although we no longer have playbills to refer to, we know that Joseph's company continued to tour to their usual venues, and we do know that on 30th October, 1840, they were at Gainsborough, for it was here, on that date, and following disappointing receipts and playing to "empty benches," that Joseph announced that he was quitting the stage.[72] Senior's book informs us[73] that by now, Joseph's company included Mr Young "of the Theatre Royal Drury Lane" and that on the 30th October, Young appeared as 'Gloster', which would suggest that they performed *King Lear*. He goes on to tell us that during November and December he played Damon in *Damon and Pythius*, Brutus in *The Fall of Tarquin*, Hamlet (for his benefit), Octavian in *The Mountaineers*, Alexander in *Alexander the Great*, Master Walter in *The Hunchback*, Bertram in *Guy Mannering*, Jacques in *As You Like It*, the Chevalier St. Franc in *The Point of Honour*, and Doricourt in *The Belle's Stratagem*.

On 22nd December, *Heir at Law*, with Mr Rayner playing Homespun, Mr Bedford as Dick Dowlas, and Joseph Smedley in his usual role of Doctor

---

[71] Letter in family archive, reproduced by kind permission of Mr Roy Sumners
[72] CMP Taylor, Right Royal; The Wakefield Theatre, 1776-1994
[73] The Old Wakefield Theatre, William Senior, first pub. 1894

Pangloss, LL.D and A.S.S.; on 23rd December *The School of Reform*, with Mr Bedford as Ferment and Mr Rayner as Tyke. Senior also tells us that Messrs. Bedford and Rayner were "leading comedians in their day, and the latter had succeeded Emery in the representation of broad Yorkshire parts."

On 24th December, Rayner appeared as Giles in *The Miller's Maid*, Chip in *A Chip of the Old Block*, and Fixture in *A Roland for an Oliver*. On 26th Rayner played Harry Wakefield in *The Two Drovers*, and Paddock in *My Spouse and I*.

On 30th December, G.V. Brooke appeared as Othello; and on 1st January 1841, and the following nights, *Ravenswood*, Rolla in *Pizarro*, Selim in *Barbarossa*, Romeo, and O'Callaghan in *His Last Legs*; and on the 9th, for his benefit, as Claude Melnotte in *The Lady of Lyons*, and Lieutenant Kingston in *Naval Engagements*.

On 13th January, Joseph's career as an active theatre manager at Wakefield ended. Although we are told[74] by Kate Taylor, that Joseph actually ended his acting career at the end of the Huddersfield season on 7th March, 1841, where he claimed he was "giving up the pursuit", but this was actually the announcement of his eldest son Joseph, Jnr, who was also to leave the stage.

Joseph Snr was now aged 57 years to the month. He had been touring constantly for nearly 40 years. He had been comparatively successful, and yet he had suffered the reverses that every manager faced. He had fought back against the stigma which the Church attached to his profession, and did his best to rebut the incriminations bestowed upon it. He had worked hard to provide entertainment to largely provincial audiences with a talented company of good conduct. As a family man he also knew the meaning of joy and of heartbreak. As the poet Tennyson described Ulysses, first published the following year, Joseph was perhaps "weakened by time and fate", but he was still "strong in will."

---

[74] In *Right Royal* by C.M.P. Taylor

12

In Retirement

By 1841, Joseph had domiciled his family in Sleaford in Lincolnshire, where he had built, and still owned, a theatre. He had toured to Sleaford early in his theatrical career and had friends there. It was a growing town with a population of 3181, and had been lighted with gas since October 1839, by a company of proprietors holding £20 shares.

In the theatre's company in the early days was a R. Obbinson, and it was probably his son, Samuel Obbinson, with whom Joseph (a year younger) enjoyed a long friendship. However, it seems that their relationship was deeper than that. There are letters from Obbinson in the Smedley family archive which are friendly and amusing, such as when Obbinson wrote a plea to Joseph, written entirely in rhyme, to borrow a book to take his mind off illness. There are also letters which refer to business, in which Obbinson sympathised with Joseph when he was depressed by low ticket sales, but also refers to his own stewardship of Joseph's money.

From these letters it appears that it was Obbinson who acted as an agent for Joseph, collecting rents for the theatres when Joseph wasn't using them and for the hiring out of rooms. According to Simon Pawley[1], the theatre was "only opened for a few weeks in any one year, being leased out for storage for the rest of the time by its local manager, Samuel Obbinson (a Sleaford Chemist)." He was certainly a reputable and solidly respectable businessman, listed in *Whites Directory* for 1842 as Postmaster and also listed under 'druggists'. Indeed in an Indenture of 1839 returning the Wakefield Theatre back to Joseph's management, Obbinson, a witness to the transaction, is described there as a chemist and druggist of New Sleaford.

---

[1] Simon Pawley, author of The Book of Sleaford published in a limited edition by Baron Birch for Quotes Ltd, 1996

In the Post Office Directory for 1849 he is listed as chemist, druggist, post office and sub-distributor of stamps. The Post Office premises were in the Market Square, just round the corner from Thornhill Lane and Thornhills the Printers.

One may speculate as to what Obbinson knew as to Thornhill's intention of retiring, and whether that is how Joseph came to know of it, but the following announcement was made on 19th January, 1841:[2]

> R. THORNHILL, Printer, Bookbinder, and Stationer, gratefully impressed with a sense of the kindness of his friends for a period of nearly half a century, begs to announce that he has declined business in favour of Mr SMEDLEY, whom he can with confidence commend, and for whom he respectfully solicits a continuance of that support which has been for so many years conferred upon him.

Immediately underneath this was the following:

> J. SMEDLEY, in succeeding to the Shop of Mr. Thornhill, begs leave to assure *his* friends, as well as those of his predecessor, that no effort will be spared to deserve a continuance of their favours in this his *new place of business*. In a few weeks he proposes considerably *to enlarge* and otherwise improve his Shop; after which, it will be re-opened with an entirely new Stock, purposely selected by himself from the first houses in London. In the meanwhile, the whole of the present stock of Books, Stationery, &c. will be sold off at very reduced prices, in many cases less than half their original cost, particularly in the article of Paper Hangings, which will be offered at a price not much exceeding the expense of white-washing the walls.
>
> Periodicals and other Works, together with every article connected with the business, regularly obtained from London weekly.
>
> N.B. Dealer in Genuine Patent Medicines.
>
> *Sleaford.* Jan. 19th, 1841

---

[2] Reported in Stamford Mercury, 22nd January 1841; British Newspaper Archives

This was followed by a letter from the Postmaster at Bingham near Nottingham dated January 23rd, 1841[3]:

> Dear Brother,
>   I am exceedingly happy to have the opportunity of wishing you every success and prosperity in your new business which I find by your advertisements in the Stamford of having succeeded Thornhill in his concern. I hope it will answer your expectations. I am sure it will not (if it does not) be owing to any neglect or assiduity on your part and therefore I am not fearful respecting it. I sincerely congratulate you on your having at last procured a comfortable retreat from your unsettled state in this troublesome world and have a good and warm fireside of your own which I hope you will enjoy with long life and good health. Mrs Strong and Mary joins their sincere good wishes to Mrs Smedley and yourself and requests me to say that we all shall be happy to see you at Bingham whenever you can make it convenient. I write half starved in the Post Office you must excuse my scrawl.
>   I am dear Smedley
>   Yours fraternally,
>   John Strong.

If one includes the business of Mr Thornhill which Joseph purchased, there were four such businesses in Sleaford at that time; one run by a man called Creasey and another by a Mr Heald. Joseph, it seems, set out immediately to ensure that his was the better equipped and the most efficient. Hence his placing of the following advertisement:

J. SMEDLEY
PRINTER, BOOKSELLER, STATIONER,
BOOKBINDER,
COPPER-PLATE PRINTER
DEALER IN PATENT MEDICINE
AND PAPER HANGINGS
At all times desirous of deserving the support which
his friends and a liberal public

---

[3] From an original letter in the family collection and with kind permission of Mr. Roy Sumners.

Richard E. Smedley

have awarded him, again begs to thank each and all for the past,
and inform them that for the future, he shall not only be
enabled to execute all orders he may be favoured with in the
PRINTING DEPARTMENT
with punctuality and despatch, but with an entire
NEW TYPE,
Just received from the first Houses in London;
He has likewise just received and fitted up
A NEW COPPER-PLATE PRESS,
With which he can execute all orders

In addition to this he continued to operate the circulating library started by his predecessor, whose bookplate read thus:[4]

THIS BOOK
Belongs to
THORNHILL'S
Circulating Library
SLEAFORD

* * *

When thou art hired by a friend,
Right welcome shall he be
To read it over, *not to lend,*
But to return to me.
Not that imparted knowledge doth
Diminish Learning's store;
But Books, I find, if often lent,
Return to me no more.
Now quickly read, and seldom pause;
Observe the Book keep clean;
And when return'd to me, let not
A damag'd leaf be seen.

---

[4] From original document in collection of Mr Roy Sumners, copied by kind permission; also copy available in Lincolnshire Archives

However it appears that Joseph wished to adopt a more stringent scheme and introduced the following scale of terms:[5]

Terms of Subscription

Yearly 10s-0d
Half-Yearly 5s-6d
Quaterly 3s-0d

Rules

I   Subscriptions to be paid at the time of subscribing, and a deposit left if required
II Non-Subscribers to pay for each volume when taken out, and strangers to deposit the value of the book.
III Non-Subscribers to pay 2*d.* per volume for new works and octavos, and 1*d.* for others
IV New publications to be kept two days per volume, nor any above *one week*.
V   Subscribers and Non-Subscribers keeping books past the time allowed, shall pay a 1*d.* for each additional day.
VI Readers *not to lend any book or books* belonging to the Library, *on pain of paying for the same.*
VII If any book be written in, torn or otherwise damaged, *or lost,* whilst in the reader's possession, that book, or if belonging to a set, that set of books *to be paid for* at the publisher's price.
VIII Any Subscriber retaining books beyond the period of Subscription, becomes responsible for a renewal of the same.

In time these charges were increased, firstly to 12s per year and then to 17s per year, with further rules to cover the cost of borrowing new publications and periodicals.[6]

Joseph, having spent most of his working life in theatrical endeavour, now used his business acumen in promoting his printing concern, and in doing so used the same principles of fairness and honesty that he had practised all his life. He was helped by having already been known in his former guise by

---

[5] do
[6] Do

people of the town, and, possibly by his Masonic contacts, and he quickly became established in the business community. Still, for now, the owner of the theatre at Sleaford, he was able to gain the business of any lessees of the theatre for the printing of their daily playbills.

It may also have given him the opportunity to reunite with his old friend George Oliver who was by this time the Vicar of Scopwick, a village approximately half way between Lincoln and Sleaford, where he had various parish responsibilities. In addition to these he had his Masonic duties as Deputy Provincial Grand Master to carry out, as well as those of the post of Vicar of Wolverhampton, an office to which he had been appointed by the Dean of Windsor, also Dean of Wolverhampton, who was, at the time, the Hon. and Very Reverend Dr H.L. Hobart, whose home, coincidentally, was near Scopwick.[7] It is almost certain that Joseph and George Oliver were still in contact, even though the extant copies of their correspondence cease in 1834.

On 23rd September, 1841, Melinda Brunton Young, Joseph's eldest daughter again gave birth, this time to a son whose name was Arthur. Sadly, the child passed away on 10th June 1843 aged just under a year and nine months.

While Joseph was initiating himself into the world of commerce, he was still in control of the leases of a number of theatres. In that year, however, he sold the theatre in Sleaford to a Mr J. Hyde.

As the following letter shows, Joseph was still the titular head of a circuit of theatres. The writer of the letter is seeking to book a theatre for his show.

The letter is dated 1st May, 1842, and was sent from Halifax:[8]

> My Dear Sir,
>   On the way home from the north my brother & self think of performing one night each in the towns of your old circuit and therefore write to you, to enquire <u>what towns</u> you still have the <u>theatres</u> and what will be the <u>lowest</u> you will <u>charge me</u> for them, at each night.

---

[7] See Priest and Freemason by R.S.E. Sandbach (1988)
[8] In collection of Mr Roy Sumners, with his kind permission

It is now the very worst season of the year and I can <u>assure you</u> we have enough to do to make it answer – my father has left off travelling <u>some time</u> and is now in business in <u>Reading.</u>

Please to send me an answer by return of post – and also inform me whether I shall send <u>you</u> the cash or pay your agent.

Be sure and give me a <u>list of the towns</u> as I will <u>forget</u> them, I think <u>Wakefield</u> will be the <u>first</u> and on my last tour I paid Mr Hurst £2 for it <u>for a night</u>- but only had 30/- in the house – I should not therefore venture more than 20/- for it <u>at most.</u> The next I think is Beverley and then Grimsby.

I am sure I need not tell you that things are not as they used to be in the <u>theatrical world</u>-you must be aware of the fact-and therefore I am certain you will do all you can for an old friend.

Please write by return if you can-as I am waiting to fix either for the <u>theatre</u> or the <u>room</u> at <u>Wakefield</u>-before Mr Hurst prints the bills.

Hoping you and yours are well,

I am yours

W.R. Grossmith**

P.S. Please divert to me at post office Halifax

**W.R Grossmith (William Robert), was a juvenile actor, and another entitled the "Young Roscius". He was born in 1818, and by now would be twenty-four years of age. He also toured with his younger brother, Benjamin, or 'Master B' as he was billed. They had appeared on a bill in Grimsby, under Smedley's management, on 14th August, 1833 when 'Master B' was only six years old. They were advertised as playing 23 characters between them. W.R.G. became the father of George Grossmith, the famous Savoyard and, who, with his brother Weedon, co-authored *The Diary of a Nobody*. (RS)

It was true that Joseph was still the owner of the Wakefield theatre, and still had the leases of the other theatres in the circuit in his name. However, the theatre had been let to a succession of people with varying success. Edward Hopper was the first; he had taken over the leases of York, Hull and Leeds theatres, i.e. the remnants of the old Tate Wilkinson circuit, from Thomas Downe.

He opened the theatre in May 1841 for two weeks, when he presented Mr Cathcart ("from Drury Lane"), and a Mr Davidson ("comic singer from Theatre Royal, English Opera, London").[9]

Cathcart was undoubtedly James Leander Cathcart, born in Ireland in about 1800, and was indeed a tragedian who worked at Drury Lane Theatre. He was the father of James Faucit Cathcart who became a stalwart of Charles Kean's company, and who, by chance also came to Wakefield during this period, right after, in September 1841, Hooper brought W.J. Hammond back to Wakefield, where he was very popular in his famous role of Sam Weller. In May 1842 William Farren, one of the greatest names in nineteenth century theatre, played there. Hooper also returned Mr and Mrs Wood, the opera singers, to the theatre where they were well known as they lived locally, and Madame Celeste, the dancer and mime artiste.

Clearly, Hooper was pursuing a policy of presenting famous names to fill the theatre, but this was insufficient to make a sustained policy, particularly as he employed few actors to provide a stock company for the visits of such worthies, and too few to manage without them. Certainly, Hooper decided it was time to move on, which he did, to Bath.

The theatre was closed for most of 1843, but reopened for a three-month season under the management of John Mosley (late of Joseph Smedley's company) and Charles Edmund Rice. Mosley had become quite popular in Wakefield and other areas he had visited with Joseph, and his reputation stood him in good stead. According to William Scruton,[10] Mosley and Rice first met each other at Oundle in Northamptonshire where Mr Mosley was presenting theatrical performances in a barn. The partnership with Rice spent a few seasons performing in similarly rustic and poorly-equipped venues before trying to improve their lot in Wakefield. This they did successfully, playing to good houses there and at Huddersfield, their next call. In the autumn of 1844 they arrived at Bradford's Duke Street Theatre, where they opened, on 12th August, with *The Hunchback* followed by the farce of *The Illustrious Stranger, or, Married and Buried*. The cast was considered to

---

[9] CMP Taylor, Right Royal
[10] Pen and pencil Pictures of Old Bradford

be superior and was augmented during its first two seasons by the addition of Lysander Thompson, a local favourite as we have seen, and Mr and Miss Woolgar as well as Miss Julia St. George.

In 1833 The Dramatic Literary Property Act had been passed into law to protect playwrights from the unauthorised performance of their works, and to punish by means of fines any transgressors. However this was not considered sufficient to protect *dramatic* copyright or to ensure payment of fees for the stage representation of the works. Some of the playwrights in London formed the Dramatic Authors Society which established a scale of fees for the performance of specific dramatic genres, and appointed the publisher John Miller to act as its agent.[11] In 1842 the Copyright Act was passed which revised and consolidated this legislation and affirmed the rights of authors. Perhaps taking a lesson from his former boss and mentor, or acting in his own right to establish his own reputation for probity, Mosley now included on all his printed matter: "Authorized to perform the Pieces of the Dramatic Authors Society."

More to the point, however, was that another new act had been passed by Parliament which had a greater and longer-reaching effect: the Theatre Regulation Act, better known as the Theatres Act 1843.

Mosley and Rice's visit to Wakefield was the first season there under the terms of the new Act which effectively did away with the old patent system and the restrictions under which the stock and touring companies of performers such as Joseph Smedley's had laboured since the previous Act of 1788. It restricted the powers of the Lord Chamberlain, and gave additional powers to local authorities to license theatres, and in doing so encouraged other popular entertainments which ultimately led to the formation of music halls attached to public houses, and, in a convoluted way saved theatre in Wakefield in the coming years. Because of this Act's effect on the patent theatres, Mosley and Rice, presumably misunderstanding its importance, renamed the Wakefield Theatre, anointing it 'Theatre Royal'.

---

[11] Women and Playwriting in the Nineteenth Century, ed. Tracy C Davis, Ellen Donkin, Cambridge University Press, 1999; see Appendix II

Richard E. Smedley

Just what Joseph Jnr's occupation was now, I cannot say, although he was possibly maintaining the leased theatres for his father. From now on, though, it is shrouded in doubt if not mystery, possibly obscured by the passage of time; but there are one or two anomalies that I have been unable to resolve, and which will have to remain in concealment.

By comparison, George's life is an open book. The youngest surviving son of Joseph and Melinda, he was 21 years old in 1841, and the following year he married a Miss Sarah Brewitt at the Church of St. Martin in Lincoln.

Sarah's trade was in the retail of china and glass, and she and George opened a shop together in Sleaford's Market Place.

Helen and Georgiana, as far as we know, continued to help Joseph in his work, although it is likely that this was when Helen had the time to write the books which her great niece referred to in her family memoir.

On 30th September, Joseph announced:[12]

> Sleaford Society for Promoting
> Christian Knowledge
> Quarterly meeting will be held at the
> house of the Librarian, Mr Smedley,
> bookseller, on 4th Oct. 1842

Also, in what was evidently a promotion for his business, Joseph announced (in print, of course):[13]

> Sleaford, 26th October 1842
> The Subscribers are respectfully informed that the drawing
> For the Papier Machee
> WRITING CASE
> INKSTAND
> AND

---

[12] Stamford Mercury, 30/09/1842

[13] Original in Lincolnshire Archive,

OTHER FANCY ARTICLES
Will take place at the house of
MR SMEDLEY, BOOKSELLER,
On Friday next,
At six o'Clock in the evening

On 26th August 1843 Joseph's eldest daughter Melinda Brunton Young gave birth to a daughter who was named Annette Josephine.

In October 1843, Joseph received a letter from a nephew, Abraham, then residing at Thorpe Understone near Richmond in North Yorkshire, containing some family news, not all of it good:

Dear Uncle,

Tis long since we received a letter from you but has been very ungrateful in not writing in return. The reason is I have been very much troubled in my mind as I have had the misfortune of losing two of my dear children. My only daughter Jane died the 20th April/40 and my son Bengm. died the 20th ~April/42.

The remainder of my family is all in good health at present, thank God, except my father who is very poorly, has had two paralysing strokes and has taken nearly his speech from him. He can neither read nor write, dress or undress himself. My mother is tolerable considering her age. My eldest son John has not married and is living with them as they are not capable of doing anything for themselves. But thank God they are very comfortable. My father has desired me to write to you many times, but through trouble and anxiety have neglected till now, has wrote to London two or three times but got no answer. My father is very uneasy to know if Uncle John be living or not if you know...

My youngest son Chris is at home with me.

I have two farms at present, but times being so bad has given one of them in. My Brother and Sister both send their kind love to you and Family. Should you have the goodness to write it would greatly oblige,

Your ever loving nephew,
Abraham Smedley

P.S. If Uncle John have removed please to give me the direction to him or cousins if you can as I do not know their names.

Joseph continued to grow his business, seeking to offer services that the other booksellers did not. For instance, the following advertisement which Joseph printed and issued around 1844 or 45:

SLEAFORD
SUBSCRIPTION MUSIC LIBRARY
J. SMEDLEY
Respectfully informs his Friends and the
Public that he has established
A MUSIC LIBRARY,
Or Club, on the same plan as a
BOOK CLUB
Viz. That each Subscriber of
ONE GUINEA, PER ANNUM
(IN ADVANCE)
Shall select and be entitled to Music of the value of ONE POUND, as well as the use of every other Subscriber's Selection to the same amount, (for the period of a month each) thus, if the Subscribers consisted of no more than Twelve, that number would be entitled To the use of
ELEVEN POUNDS WORTH OF MUSIC
every year, beside being the owner of ONE POUND'S
worth for every GUINEA thus paid.
The Music to be returned at least once per month, for the Librarian to forward a fresh supply to each Subscriber respectively

Also, in January 1844, we find Joseph named as the printer for a performance at the Sleaford Theatre for the last appearance of Monsieur Gouffe, the celebrated man-monkey, under the management of Mosley and Rice and with, as Gaspard, Mr Tannett.

Joseph Jnr's turn to marry also came in 1844, when he married a girl from Worksop, a Miss Frances (Fanny) Skelton. It appears that they lived initially at Goxhill, a small village close to the Humber estuary in North Lincolnshire, about five miles from Barton on Humber, where his father had started his career. In December of the following year, at Goxhill, Lincolnshire, Frances gave birth to their son whom they called... Joseph!

Unfortunately, this event was no doubt overshadowed by the news that Helen, perhaps the daughter closest to Joseph Snr, and certainly his greatest supporter during their nomadic theatrical career, had been diagnosed as suffering from *phthisis pulmonalis*, a type of wasting disease, usually pulmonary tuberculosis, or a type of consumption.

It is far from clear what Joseph Jnr was doing for a living, but family folklore contends that he became a publican around this time at Kirton, not far from Brigg, where, it is rumoured, he was initiated into the Old Ancholme Lodge of Freemasons. This lodge was formed in 1847, although I have been unable to find Joseph Boleyn Smedley on its list of members. It is also rumoured that at some stage Joseph Jnr worked as a coal merchant in Kirton too. Joseph Jnr seems to have developed a love of the Lincolnshire dialect, which, although fast disappearing, was still used by many in the fenlands, and wrote poems in dialect form some of which were published.

Meanwhile George and his wife continued to run their shop in the Market Place in Sleaford.

Throughout his career, it seems, whenever Joseph's life seemed to be stable and happy, something would come along to cause sadness or unrest. He could not have been prepared for the double sorrow that was to befall him and his wife, when, in April 1846 they received word that their daughter Annette had died as a result of childbirth in Clonmell, Ireland, and there she was buried. She was aged 37 years.

Despite their differences, and her refusal to obey her father's wishes, this must have been a terrible blow. Annette had been a very popular member of Joseph's acting company, and the most talented actress. The infant, named Helen, survived and later went on to marry and became Mrs Helen Nield.[14]

The following month, on 29th May, Helen Winner Cooke Smedley passed away at Sleaford, aged 39, of the disease with which she had been diagnosed two years earlier.

---

[14] Family history from conversation with Mr Roy Sumners

Richard E. Smedley

Helen was buried in the churchyard of St. Deny's Parish Church next to the Market Place in a corner less than a stone's throw from her father's business. The grave marker was also used to memorialise Joseph and Melinda's other children who died prematurely:

Grave marker and Memorial in St. Denys' Churchyard, Sleaford.

TO THE MEMORY OF
HELEN
Affectionate and beloved daughter of
JOSEPH AND MELINDA SMEDLEY
who died May 29th 1846 aged 39
ALSO
ANNETTE
Who died and was buried at Clonmell
Ireland April 18th 1846 aged 37
HENRY
New Malton Dec. 1st, 1823 aged 12
JANE
At Market Rasen
July 22nd 1821 aged 7
ABRAHAM
Caistor August 5th 1821 aged 3
JANE WINNER
Grimsby March 6th 1808 aged 2
All children of the above
On earth apart. In heaven to meet

There was, however, brighter news in June 1847 when Melinda Brunton again bore a daughter, this one named Georgiana; and two years later, in June 1849 another daughter, Edith Jane.

During this period, it is worth noting, public health became a matter for concern. Principal health issues were outbreaks of cholera, influenza, typhus and typhoid. Mortality rates were not recorded between 1842 and 1846 during which period the number of epidemics declined. The cause of many of them was due to, and encouraged in their spread by, weather conditions and poverty. During the 1820s and 30s almost one infant in three failed to reach the age of five.[15]

The poorer classes were underfed and undernourished and therefore had little resistance to contagion. Overcrowding was another factor which aided the

---

[15] The Victorian Web on-line resource

spread of disease, with mortality figures twice as high in crowded areas of London than middle-class areas.

Statistics such as these were used by reformers to try to persuade central government to act. Reports by the Poor Law Commission in 1838 looked at causes of, and means of preventing, the spread of disease in poor areas in London such as Bethnal Green and Whitechapel.

However another campaigner, Edwin Chadwick (1800–90), was more concerned about the national picture. From his work, and a Royal Commission in 1845 on the Health of Towns and Popular Places, they found that where drains were made of stone, seepage from sewers was considerable, hygiene was poor and water was often drawn from infected and polluted sources. The Public Health Act of 1848 allowed local boards to see that new homes had proper drainage and their local water supplies were clean and dependable.[16]

There was huge resistance to the theory of pollution as a source of infection which contributed to the steady prevalence of typhoid and cholera, but the cleaning up of towns and cities did bring about a reduction in deaths from typhus which today is known to be transmitted by lice.

The town of Sleaford was far from immune to these concerns. As elsewhere, the advent of the Industrial Revolution highlighted the failings of the previous regional arrangement of local politics. Countryside towns were managed by parish councils and local justices. Company towns were controlled by small groups of people, rate-payers, but often corrupt. However with the arrival of factories and steam engines before the provision of efficient water and sewage systems horrendous conditions ensued in congested and highly populated towns. The Municipal Corporations Act of 1835 gave corporate towns an administrative body which could pass progressive legislation. Other areas, such as Sleaford, didn't have such a body of local government, and even ordinary people were starting to press for some relief from the poor working conditions.

Edwin Chadwick's and others' work in enquiring into the health of towns and their findings thus established resulted in the Public Health Act in 1848,

---

[16] Mid-Victorian Sleaford, Charles Ellis (ed)

as we have seen, and this enabled the formation of Local Boards of Health providing that ten per-cent of people requested one, or if the death rate in the area exceeded 23 per 1,000 people per annum. If that was the case, the Central Board could impose a Local Board on the district. These boards could then appoint a Medical Officer of Health who in turn had the power to pave streets, introduce sewage schemes and inaugurating a clean water supply.[17]

In 1850 a man called William Ranger, a superintending inspector, published a report on the parish of New Sleaford as a result of sufficient rate-payers petitioning to allow the Public Health Act to apply to Sleaford. Even if they hadn't, the incidence of death was so high as to have a Local Board imposed on them.

A number of local inhabitants of Sleaford helped Mr Ranger to write his report, and these people were considered men of substance and public spirit. These included three doctors, two churchwardens, and three solicitors. Special mention also was made of the contribution of Thomas Pinder, the Southgate ironmonger, and Joseph Smedley the printer, who by this time had moved his business to larger premises on Northgate, on the site of what today is Lloyds Bank.[18]

The report detailed the cost of ill-health, as well as conditions in various sections of the town, including major instances of overcrowding. In addition the sewage scheme was hopelessly inadequate. The Northgate sewer, 285 yards long, ran into a cesspool at the corner of Northgate and Eastgate, from where the Eastgate sewer flowed into two more cesspools, and, from one of these an open drain ran southward. The Westgate sewer, 383 yards long, ran into the Northgate sewer, and in Southgate where there was no fall, the sewer had to be flushed periodically by letting in river water.

The cost of resolving these issues was, regrettably, considered too great at a Vestry Meeting in June 1850, as was the cost of providing pure drinking water, and these issues continued to cause suffering and hardship into the latter part of the century.

---

[17] do

[18] do

Richard E. Smedley

Although still used as a theatre, and let to visiting companies and individuals, the theatre in Sleaford was by now in decline, as was the area in which it stood on Westgate, with prostitutes and drinking houses abounding, and it soon became the red light district of the town, with the worst slums said to centre around Playhouse Yard itself. The theatre closed its doors in 1855. The building was purchased by Thomas Parry (of Kirk & Parry, architects and builders) on 25th August 1856 on behalf of a committee of the non-conformist church who wanted to build a school for young children near the town's centre. Kirk and Parry were employed to carry out the necessary alterations. They paid £380 for it, compared with the £478 cost to Joseph Smedley of building it in 1825.[19]

In William Ranger's report of 1850 on the health of the town, he had pointed out the overcrowded state of the churchyard. This was not just a local matter but was a common occurrence everywhere, and prompted the government of the day to pressurise local authorities to act. In 1853 the Burial Act was passed which prohibited burial within two hundred yards of a dwelling without consent from the owner.[20] In Sleaford there were no further churchyard burials after 1855, whilst in that year land was purchased for use as a cemetery, together with sufficient land to provide for an access road.

We do not know to what extent Joseph missed the world of theatre, if at all. He certainly kept busy, and in his leisure time he sat and read or wrote short stories for himself with such titles as 'My Cousin's Portfolio', 'The Artist's Picture' and 'Our Christmas Visitor'. He also attempted a play, and some verse.[21] He was still growing his business, having moved premises to Northgate. He was now listed as 'printer, bookseller, bookbinder, dealer in patent medicines and honorary secretary to the Art Union, emigration agent for Australia and the Cape of Good Hope, Northgate'. Among his papers is a playbill for Dumfries, dated 16th January 1850 for a production of *King Charles ll, or, the Merry Monarch*, and advertising a Benefit and last appearance for Madame Castaglioni on 18th January in *The Lady of Lyons* and concluding with the comedy *Rory O'More*. One wonders why Joseph kept this

---

[19] Mid Victorian Sleaford, 1851-1871
[20] Mid Victorian Sleaford 1851-1871; Ed.Charles Ellis
[21] All these items in the Lincolnshire Archive: LLHS 38/5/8/3; LLHS 38/5/9/8;

until one's eyes alight on the performer of a comic song whose name on the bill in small print, was Mr Frimbley, a previous member of Joseph's acting company, who was evidently keen to stay in touch with his former boss.

Joseph was still effectively in charge of the Wakefield Theatre, and with the visit of Mosley and Rice had in a way presided over a continuation of his old company, particularly as they also continued a similar programme of visiting artistes and novelty acts such as Monsieur Gouffe. After their three-month season at Wakefield finished, there were a number of events including a visit by W.J. Hammond, the singer and comedian who was always popular in the town having been a former lessee of the theatre; a miners' conference, lectures, and a season of plays presented by a stock company headed by a Mr Clifford, but which did poor business.[22]

When Mosley and Rice returned to Wakefield for their second and final season there, the theatre had been completely redecorated, though at whose cost is unknown. They had now added Halifax to their circuit, and the company now numbered thirty. Their season spanned the Christmas period, and Mr Rice had an enthusiastic liking for pantomime, until now an entertainment without seasonal connotation, but usually derived from the *Commedia dell'Arte*. For its first Christmas pantomime, and probably among the first of its type in the country, he chose to present, following *She Stoops to Conquer*, and the pantomime of *Harlequin and the Magic Pancake, or, The Fairy of the Well*.

Notwithstanding the success of this venture, they found it difficult to compete with other entertainments in the town, particularly the new Corn Exchange, which had opened further up Westgate in 1838 and became more popular and fashionable, to the extent that when John Braham next returned to Wakefield it was to the Corn Exchange.

From here Mosley and Rice continued to Bradford, and it was here, in 1847, that Rice ended his association with John Mosley.[23]

---

[22] *Right Royal* by CMP Taylor

[23] do

Their tenure at Wakefield was followed by a series of dubious and some downright unscrupulous managers, one of whom was a Mr Sylvester. His company included a Mr and Mrs Maddocks, and a Mr and Mrs Tannett (!) and a Miss Temple. The Maddocks's were to take the parts of Macbeth and Lady Macbeth but withdrew citing some misunderstanding, about unpaid salaries, before Mr Sylvester absconded with the company wages.[24] Who these members of the Tannett family were I cannot ascertain, although they, and certainly Mrs Tannett alone, were later to appear on Bradford playbills under John Mosley in March, April and May 1859 and October 1860. There was a succession of managers, almost all of whom failed.

After this somewhat squalid period in the history of the Wakefield theatre, an upturn in fortunes was indicated when the lease was taken by Henry Farren, for he belonged to a dynastic theatrical family, and someone I feel sure Joseph would have enjoyed talking with, and discussing theatrical news, gossip and trends.

Henry was the grandson of actor William Farren (1754–95), and son of William Farren (1786–1861) who was a very popular actor, particularly of comedic roles, specialising in old men and Irishmen. He had begun his career in around 1806 at Plymouth, working under his brother Percy's management, then on the Worcester and Shrewsbury Circuit. While acting in Dublin he married a young lady named Mary (surname unknown) and, in 1818, left Dublin to appear at Covent Garden where he had a triumphant debut.

In 1821, or thereabouts, he parted with his wife and, after making financial arrangements for her future maintenance, he began living with the actress Mrs Faucit (Harriet Elizabeth Savill), managing and guiding her career and giving a home to her two daughters as well as the two sons they had together, William and Henry, both of whom became actors. After they were both widowed, Farren and Mrs Faucit married in 1853.[25]

---

[24] do

[25] Entry in Oxford DNB by Carol J. Carlisle, accessed 19th April 2017

As the scion of this great family, Henry now leased the theatre at Wakefield from Joseph. Henry was born in 1827 in London and made some appearances in the provinces, notably at Birmingham and Manchester in 1846 and at Nottingham, Liverpool, Norwich in 1847, during which year he married Ellen Smithson, the daughter of a solicitor's clerk. Together they eventually had three daughters, Ellen (called Nellie), Harriet Letitia and Florence, all of whom became actresses. Nellie Farren later became quite famous in musical comedy at the Gaiety Theatre. Thus the famous Victorian actress Helen Faucit was Henry's half-sister

In November 1847 he made his London debut at the Haymarket Theatre, acting the part of Charles Surface to his father's Sir Peter Teazle in *The School for Scandal*.

Henry Farren's opening night at Wakefield was on 7th February 1848. The theatre had been cleaned and advertised as "rendered fit for the patronage of the nobility, gentry and inhabitants of Wakefield."[26] He had garnered his acting company (ten men and five women) from other towns, and a "stage and acting manager" called Mr Bisson.[27] Farren had promised, too, some established stars, and engaged Mr and Mrs Dillon (then managers of the theatres at Sheffield and Wolverhampton), and John Vandenhoff and his daughter.

The programme consisted of a mixture of tried and tested plays; a mixture of Shakespeare, Sheridan and Knowles, with Bulwer Lytton's *Lady of Lyons* included too.

Henry also initiated a list of rules for members of his company in whatever theatre of which he was manager, which gave a list of transgressions and fines which would not be out of place today. One of these was for "being imperfect on stage" and "reading a part at last rehearsal." These two rules, coupled with the engagement of a "stage and acting manager", show to what extent the acting of drama had changed, with emphasis on the text and rehearsed performances, spelling the end of improvisation to a large degree, although such change comes about slowly. This list, published

---

[26] Source unknown; quoted by CMP Taylor in 'Right Royal'.
[27] CMP Taylor: Right Royal.

Richard E. Smedley

RULES
AND
REGULATIONS
TO BE OBSERVED
IN ALL THEATRES,
Under the direction of Mr. HENRY FARREN.

All the Ladies and Gentlemen will be obliged to sign to the following Rules.

                                                             £. s. d.

1.—The Manager trusts he need not observe that all cases of Inebriety, during business, will subject the party to a Fine of (or instant Dismissal at the option of the Manager,) ... 1 1 0

2.—For Refusing any Part assigned by the Manager—such being their line of business— (or instant Dismissal, at the option of the Manager,) ... 10 0

3.—For being Imperfect on the Stage at night, sufficient time having been given for study, ... 2 6

4.—For keeping the Stage Waiting at night, ... 1 0

5.—For Refusing to Obey the Orders of the Stage-Manager, ... 2 0

6.—For Reading a Part at a Last Rehearsal, sufficient time having been given for Study ... 1 0

7.—For Detaining the Prompt Book or Music beyond the time appointed, ... 1 0

8.—For being Absent from the First Scene at Rehearsal, ... 1 0

9.—For every subsequent Scene, ... 0 6

10.—For using Improper Language on the Stage, Talking during a Scene, or wilfully making an exit, at a different part of the stage to that appointed, ... 1 0

11.—Any Lady or Gentleman taking a Book or Paper from the Prompter's table or shelf without permission, will forfeit ... 0 6

All Persons in the Establishment to be on in all Chorusses, Processions, the National Anthem, Pantomimes, Extravaganzas and Dances.

All Benefits to be fixed by the Manager.

No Bespeaks will be allowed on the occasion of a Benefit, unless previously arranged with the Manager.

All Engagements will Terminate with a Fortnight's Notice on either side, unless a previous agreement is made to the contrary by Mr. H. FARREN *himself.*

NICHOLS & SONS, PRINTERS, 17, NORTHGATE, WAKEFIELD.

Henry Farren's Rules of the Theatre

in Wakefield, is shown in full here, a copy of it survives among Joseph Smedley's papers,[28] suggesting closer ties with the theatre and/or the lessee than might otherwise be supposed.

Henry's first season ended on 15th April, and he returned for a second season to run from 27th November 1848 until 19th January 1849, with a new company. This included Barry Sullivan, Juliet Powers (Farren's wife), and a singer and low comedian, Wood Benson.[29] After Christmas Farren staged a pantomime, *Card Castle, or, Harlequin Tom Tiddle* as an after-piece, and, in January he brought the eminent tragedian Gustavus Vaughan Brooke back to Wakefield. On 5th January, Brooke's last night, Brooke played Othello, E.M Duret played Desdemona, with Farren as Cassio and F.B. Egan as Iago.[30]

Despite such a strong cast and varied programme the business was not as good as one might expect, and, even with the price of boxes being reduced to as little as two shillings, the houses remained unfilled, causing the local paper to ask if there was "any taste for legitimate drama in Wakefield?"

This financial state of affairs caused considerable concern to Henry Farren, and when suppliers who had not been paid got together, efforts were made to make Farren bankrupt. The following is a report from The Era of Sunday, September 23rd, 1849:

INSOLVENT DEBTORS' COURT

IN THE MATTER OF HENRY FARREN. – This insolvent, comedian, applied on Wednesday to be discharged. Mr Dowse opposed for two creditors, named Nicholwaite and Winter; and Mr Cooke supported the application. Mr Nicolwaite stated that he was a printer at Wakefield. Prior to November last the insolvent was indebted to him £38 for printing and advertisements connected with the Wakefield Theatre, of which the insolvent was manager. On that debt he had been paid a composition of five shilling in the pound. Subsequently the insolvent contracted another debt with him for printing for the same theatre,

---

[28] Lincolnshire Archive, LLHS 38/5/6/11
[29] CMP Taylor; Right Royal
[30] do

and promised to pay him the balance of the former debt after the payment of the composition. He had received £26, including £9 10s. paid on account of the composition. The insolvent left Wakefield in January last, and when he ascertained that he was connected with the Olympic Theatre he applied for payment of his debt. Mr Winter was a creditor for £8 at Wakefield. He had signed a receipt for the composition, stating that it was paid in full, but Mr Farren had told him he would pay him the balance. The Chief Commissioner thought there could be no case on the part of a creditor who had consented to take a composition and then obtained a security for the balance. Mr Dowse said he had a point of vexatious defence, and also wished to make some inquiries of the insolvent. It appeared that an action was brought at the suit of Mr Nicolwaite for £44 9s., including the balance of the old debt, to which the insolvent pleaded, and a verdict was given for only £36 14s. The costs had been taxed at £63 11s. The sum paid was allowed. Subsequently an offer of £10 and £1 a week was made, but it was not carried into affect. His Honour said that the point of a vexatious defence could not be established. The insolvent was then examined. He now owed about £100. His father, Mr W. Farren, had paid his former creditors five shillings in the pound to upwards of £600 when he petitioned this court. In June last year he was manager of the Gravesend Theatre, and in about two months lost nearly £150. He afterwards took Yarmouth, Cambridge, Wakefield, and other theatres. In June he had a ticket night at the Haymarket Theatre, but it was no benefit to him. He was engaged at the Olympic Theatre, and his father was about to sign an agreement for that theatre, when it was burnt down. His father was lessee of the Strand Theatre, and it was only under his direction. The "properties" were not his own, but his father's. As well as the theatrical dresses he used, and also the furniture in his house. He was a married man, with two children. It appeared that the insolvent had a book at Wigan of his taking of the Wakefield Theatre, on which an application was made that it might be produced, but it was refused. The learned Commissioner, in discharging the insolvent, recommended him not again to appear in the court. "Do try", added His Honour, "and keep out of the insolvent's box". The insolvent remarked that, had the opposing creditor been a little indulgent, he should not have made his present appearance before the court. He was ordered to be discharged.

Alas, this was not to be the end of Henry's problems, for later, in 1852, he took over the management of the Brighton Theatre Royal where he formed an excellent partnership on stage with Louisa Howard as his leading lady. Unfortunately, this, too ended in financial failure, and on 4th March 1854 he fled from the theatre to avoid arrest for debt. He went to London, leaving his wife in Brighton, and after a brief acting job at Sadler's Wells, he decamped for New York, again leaving his wife behind. There he again acted with Louisa Howard, joined a company in New Orleans where he married, bigamously, Kate Reignolds (1836–1911). He died of diabetes while in St. Louis in 1860. He was aged just 32.[31]

In the meanwhile, George and Sarah had a daughter whom they unsurprisingly named Helen, and, in June 1851, a son whom they named George. Also, in January 1852 Joseph and Frances had a daughter who was named Sarah Holmes Smedley, again christened at Goxhill in Lincolnshire. However, at the time of the 1851 census, Joseph Jun. is listed as a brewer and maltster living at Kirton, and Frances (given as Fanny) as a visitor at Normanby by Spittall, presumably family, and listed as a brewer's wife.[32] This is perfectly normal given that one is listed in a census wherever one happens to be at the time. The birth of their daughter and the 1851 census are the final records of Joseph and Frances being together: the marriage does not appear to have lasted beyond this time. Samuel Obbinson was still listed in the 1851 census as Druggist and Postmaster, residing on the west side of Market Place with his wife, Sarah (11 years younger than Samuel), and his two sons, Robert, then aged 27, and Samuel, 24, and a daughter, Mary Ann, aged five. Sadly, Joseph's friend Samuel died in the following year, 1852.[33]

The theatre at Wakefield continued to stagger on through an incredibly long list of lessees, many of whom were led by inexperienced managers of poor calibre, such as a Mr Croom ("of the Theatres Royal Brighton, Southampton, etc."). An amateur group put on a charity performance in 1854 for the families of soldiers fighting in the Crimea. This too was a financial failure. Indeed very little success was experienced at the Wakefield Theatre during this period, particularly as the named artistes in better-class productions were playing at the Corn Exchange.

---

[31] Oxford DNB, Henry Farren entry by Carol J. Carlyle, accessed 19th April 2017

[32] "England Births and Christenings, 1538-1975" database, *FamilySearch* (https//familysearch.org/ark:61903/1:NTHJ-Q83: 30 December 2014) Fanny Smedley: Ancestry.com 1851 England Census (database on-line)

[33] "England and Wales Census, 1851" database with images *FamilySearch*

In the early weeks of 1855 the theatre was taken by a Benjamin Young, with a W. Simpson as Stage Manager, and opened with the tragedian Charles Pitt. However, less than two weeks later they had both abandoned the company, leaving nothing but debts behind them. Two members of the company tried to continue, but they had to end the season prematurely. The viability and future of the theatre at Wakefield was now in doubt, and Joseph was, by early 1857, advertising it as "to be sold or let, by the night, week, month or year," and offered "separately if required, a cellar under it, and a stable, gig house, and yard in which is a pump and two privies". The previous year Joseph had mortgaged the building for £800, and his desperation to find a buyer or a lessee of some standing was apparently becoming a financial necessity.[34]

Joseph's advertisement asked interested parties to contact a Mr Whitaker of the Gas Office in Wakefield.[35] John Whitaker had become the agent for the Gas Company in 1846 and became its secretary in 1862, and was clearly now acting as Joseph Smedley's local representative as well. Later, during the 1860s this task was passed on to another employee of the Gas Company, William Milsom.[36] In the 1841 census he was described as Engineer at Wakefield Gas Works, living in Gas House Yard, Warrengate. In 1862 he applied for a stage licence for the theatre in his own name to discourage the erection of theatre booths in the area around the market.[37]

Another major change had been put into effect in 1844 when a scheme was hatched to operate a direct railway line from London to York, to be operated by the Great Northern Railway. The line was to be routed through Peterborough and Grantham from which a spur line would loop through Boston and Lincoln. This was not the first such plan to be mooted, the first having been promoted in 1827, with another one in 1836 which proposed a line from Nottingham to Boston via Sleaford, but this came to nothing.

---

[34] CMP Taylor; Right Royal
[35] Wakefield Journal and Examiner, 27.2.1857
[36] CMP Taylor; Right Royal
[37] Wakefield Journal and Examiner 14.2.1862, quoted by CMP Taylor in Right Royal

The scheme was hotly contested, not least by those with vested interests in the canal network, and who thought at first that the railways were a good way of transporting Ancaster stone to the Sleaford Canal only to realise that the railways were set to replace canals in the transport of goods as well as people. In the event, the loop line from Boston to Lincoln opened in 1848, and Grantham was linked to Nottingham by rail in 1850.

In 1852 the Boston, Sleaford and Midland Counties Railway, initiated a plan to link Boston with Grantham and to build new docks at Boston. This plan obtained much support, not least by the people and business interests of Sleaford. When the plan came before a parliamentary committee, it was argued that Sleaford was at a disadvantage by not having a railway when Boston, Grantham and Lincoln had railway services. The Bill was passed in August 1853, and construction began. On 13th June 1857 the first passenger service ran from Barkston Junction to Sleaford, with an intermediate station at Ancaster.[38] The launch of this railway was a reason for celebration, and tickets for the dinner were to be handed out to all men over the age of 18 upon application in person to the Committee in the Old White Hart Yard on Thursday, 11th June between 7 and 8 p.m.[39] We know that Joseph Smedley attended, and his invitation to do so remains amongst his papers. The entire day was planned thus:

Programme for the Opening of the Sleaford Railway
On Saturday 13th June 1857

1. The church bells will commence ringing at 7.30a.m. and will ring at intervals during the day.
2. At 8 o'clock a band will play round the town.
3. At 10 o'clock the shops and places of business will be closed. The public will assemble in the Market Place and, accompanied by the band, will escort the directors, contractors and officials in procession to the station.
4. At 10.30 the train for Grantham will leave the station, returning with the London directors and a second band from Grantham, arriving at Sleaford at 1.00 p.m.

---

[38] From mid Victorian Sleaford 1851-1871 ed. Charles Ellis
[39] Do.

5. A procession will then be formed of the directors, contractors, officials, visitors and others, accompanied by both bands, and proceed through the btown. This procession will be preceded by the children of the various schools, bedesmen etc.
6. On returning to the station the working men of New and Old Sleaford, Holdingham and Quarrington will proceed to dine in the tents erected for them on the cricket field, and the directors, contractors and their visitors will proceed to their dinner.
7. The tents erected for the working men are to be vacated by 5 o'clock to allow of provision being made for the general tea drinking.
8. Tea and cake will be provided for the women at 5 o'clock,
9. The masters and mistresses of the different schools will assemble their pupils on the cricket field at 7 o'clock when each scholar will receive a silver threepence and a bun. Youths under eighteen will be eligible for this class.
10. The proceedings of the day will close with a display of fireworks at 9.30 p.m.

In 1855, one of Joseph's competitors, Mr James Creasey, passed away. Indeed in the entry in the Post Office directory for that year, his business is listed as being run by "the executors of the late Mr Creasey." Not being one to let grass grow under his feet, Joseph advertised to try and gain Mr Creasey's custom for himself, in an effort which today might be considered rather crass and unfeeling:[40]

> The Family of the late MR CREASEY Bookseller, Stationer, &c have disposed of their interest in the Shop and Business; but as the favours of customers and patronage of Friends are not necessarily transferred with the Stock-in-Trade, J. Smedley feels himself at Liberty respectfully to solicit a share of that support which the deservedly high character of Mr Creasey had long obtained for that establishment, assuring those who may honour him by their encouragement that his utmost endeavours shall be used to deserve it.
>
> North Street, Sleaford, May 5th, 1855

---

[40] Copy of advertisement in Smedley Archive; part of the Sumners Collection in Lincolnshire Archives LLHS 38/5/6/8

In the 1861 census, Joseph Smedley was still listed as Printer and Bookseller, and employing one man and two apprentices. At about this time, the glass and china shop of George and his wife Sarah had closed, and George was now working as a gas fitter for the Sleaford Gas Company. Also listed under the 1861 census, Joseph Jnr was then living as a lodger with the Aulton family at Carlton Road in Sneinton, a suburb of Nottingham, just east of the city centre, and listed his occupation as a 'wine broker'.

* * *

On 1st March, 1863 Joseph Smedley, Actor, Manager, Theatre owner, and Printer, died in the presence of his son George at George's East Street home, of typhus. He was aged 79 years. Although not a bad age for those times, it was nevertheless the result of the poor sanitation and public health issues of the day, as previously described, and, ironically, of a cause which he had helped to try and eradicate.

He was buried in the 'new' cemetery, on 3rd March, in what today is a corner caused by the meeting of two hedges. The grave is in an almost direct line with the cemetery entrance. This part of the cemetery today is no longer tended, being left as a nature reserve with particular regard to the habitat of butterflies.

13
Coda

In his will, Joseph left all of his property and personal estate, valued for probate purposes at under £1500, to his wife Melinda and his daughter Georgiana '*for and during the term of their joint natural lives*' and, after the decease of Melinda, to Georgiana and her heirs. Georgiana carried on the printing business and library.

Joseph's wider legacy, should perhaps be adjudged, however disillusioned he became, by his theatrical career.

At a time when legitimate drama was the province of the patent houses, which in the latter part of the eighteenth century had swelled to include provincial houses in Bath, Bristol, Norwich, Ipswich, York and Edinburgh, companies of actors still roamed the country from shire to shire, seeking support where they could find it; playing in barns and booths, and, where they existed, purpose-built playhouses. They were still treated as being no better than criminals; thieves, drunks and scoundrels with low morals. Joseph Smedley chose to enter this profession at the juncture, albeit an arbitrary one, of the eighteenth century with the nineteenth. He joined an established company based at Lincoln and which played its circuit of theatres, where he learned his craft, and no doubt also observed some of the bad conduct of other company members, and experienced for himself some of the disparagement his business attracted.

Joseph came from good Yorkshire stock, religious and educated, he was, for the time in which he lived, considered well-read. His fledgling career in law may well have given him an understanding of contracts and torts. He must have drunk thirstily from the keg of theatrical ambition to have had the desire to strike out under his own banner, along with his new wife.

From the outset, he was determined to ensure the reputation of his company was without blemish. He attempted to provide the best possible standard of theatrical production to the widest rural audiences, and to use the nature of the entertainment, often containing themes of morality, to further enhance his reputation.

As we have seen, there was a huge sea-change in attitudes to certain types of amusement and entertainment during Joseph's lifetime. This provoked attacks on theatrical entertainments which caused Joseph to defend his living. Another result of the 'new Culture' was the rapid rise of Freemasonry and other societies, which he used for brotherly support and also to give testimony to his professional and moral integrity.

He was a family man. His family meant a great deal to him. He ensured that they each received a good standard of education for the time, but that they also, by virtue of their stage experience, understood much of the outside world, and by their training were equipped to make their own way in that world.

From material left behind, we know that Joseph kept up with the trends of the time, particularly in regard to new plays, as he read, and saved, cuttings from reviews of new productions in the patent houses, as well as articles about the well-known actors of the day. He certainly travelled around to see the work of other companies, and eyed the competition keenly. He made it his business to know what other companies were doing and which actors were proficient in various roles.

Joseph did not base himself at any one particular theatre and reach out from there. He chose to operate in more rural and less-populated areas often underneath an existing circuit. This gave him more territorial scope and was much less limiting. It enabled his company to play in theatres or other venues more usually visited by such circuits as those based in Lincoln, Nottingham and Derby, Norwich, York and Hull to name a few. Although visiting such towns, villages and hamlets perhaps once every two years, and then mostly on market days or hiring days, it increased the frequency by which such a group attended these areas.

Joseph had learned the business of theatre management well. He was careful in his choice of programme, and seldom took additional financial risks outside those inherent to the business (he was robbed of the takings more than once), and it was always a gamble as to how many seats would be sold. He was therefore loath to hire 'named' actors, preferring to use his own well-coached and rehearsed company of established members and members of his family. Certainly the programme of plays and entertainments which he presented over a period of 35 years was as varied and interesting as any other provincial manager, as was the quality of production. He was considered to be 'successful' even though at times he was disappointed by small houses and empty seats. Such were the vagaries of theatre management that one could be on top of the world one day and down in the pits of despair the next, and yet Joseph does not seem to have experienced these extremes often.

We have seen how the Robertson family's fortunes fluctuated and how they diced with bankruptcy, and how their affairs were not helped by employing famous actors from London, something only occasionally attempted by Joseph. Although they had theatres in cities to maintain as well as those on the circuit, with the attending overheads, Joseph had enough faith and self-confidence to actually build new theatres as well (as did the Robertson family), and to invest in others by purchasing shares. The list of theatres of which he was manager was extensive, and as he leased the majority of them, had to maintain them too. This must have caused considerable expense in addition to the capital he invested in the ownership of some. Yet despite declining audiences in the latter part of the 1830s, he still managed to keep his head above the water-line. In part this may have been due to income he received from the hire of rooms at his theatres when he was not using them, and the siting of a billiard room beneath the stages of some of them.

It is my belief that Joseph Smedley deliberately built up his circuit of theatres over a period of many years, supplemented by a smaller, more compact one in south Yorkshire, for his sons to operate after he retired. Perhaps he had the intention of creating a dynastic theatre chain akin to that of the Robertsons. We don't know. However I feel sure that when the time came, a decision was made about their future which caused a schism in the family, and might even account for what amounted to Joseph Jnr's exile, and George's change in career path. Unfortunately, there is a lack of documentary evidence to support this theory.

In the aforementioned memoir about the family written by Joseph Snr's granddaughter Annette Josephine Young (daughter of Melinda Brunton Young) for her own grandchildren, she says of Joseph Sr : "he was a man of fine intellect, clever, well read, honourable in principle but stern and one who would never brook to servility." These traits we have witnessed in his dealings with actors (particularly during the Desborough fiasco), and in his financial and commercial dealings. It is a small step to consider what his reaction might be to his plans for the future being thwarted.

The same memoir says the following of Joseph Jnr:

> He spent his last days in a small cottage, leading the life of a recluse, much dependant on his younger sister Georgiana for support who also undertook a mortgage in his favour in consequence of which at his death all the nieces including myself and sisters were losers to the amount of about £2000 – besides interest for years which would have come to them.

It is tempting to wonder how Joseph would have reacted to the changes that affected the world of theatre after he chose to retire. I may be doing him a disservice, but I think it likely, given his character, that Joseph did not take kindly to change. The changes in licensing, the onset of fees payable for performing plays, enforced by legislation, he might well have seen as interference in his business. However I believe that he was enlightened enough to understand what was wrong with the status quo and to see such changes as a necessary correction to the illegality and piracy which heretofore robbed playwrights of their living and regulated the ways in which licenses were collected. To an honest, honourable and upright member of the theatrical community, I feel sure that he would have supported such innovation, particularly if it helped to improve the reputation of the members of the said community.

There is no doubt that Joseph built a solid reputation for probity, fairness and sobriety, not just for himself but for members of his company. He stated repeatedly in his own printed playbills that he sought to raise theatre to an art form, and, without any London experience, he presaged the sentiments and practice of Henry Irving who achieved exactly this 40 years later.

It is impossible to know whether or not Joseph saw the business and theatrical possibilities that were ushered in by the advent of steam railways. Did he welcome a new and comparatively quick and clean mode of transport that would help to revolutionise travel between venues for touring companies in the future? Did he foresee an age when the biggest stars of the London stage would be able to travel to a provincial theatre to perform in the afternoon and return to London on the same day, in a 'flying' visit? Did he rue the opportunities that this could have afforded him and his income? Or had he become too disillusioned and tired to contemplate it? We'll never know.

Joseph's old friend, George Oliver passed away in 1867 and was buried in the churchyard of St Swithin's church near the centre of Lincoln. His grave is no longer there, as the graveyard was cleared some years ago to accommodate a redevelopment of the area, and its graves were removed for re-interment elsewhere. However the local History and Archaelogical Society kept details of the inscriptions of the headstones which ranged in date from 1822 to 1957:[1]

> *In memory of the Rev George Oliver DD who died 3rd March 1867 in the 85th year of his age.*
>
> *In Memory of MARY ANN wife of the Rev George OliverDD who died 13th October who died 13 October 1856 in the 80th year of her age.*

Joseph himself continued to take an interest in Freemasonry, or perhaps sought the company of like-minded individuals, and, in 1857 when he was 74 years old, he joined St Botolph's Lodge in Sleaford.

After Joseph's death, as we have seen, Georgiana continued to run the printing and library business which had been left to her and her mother. On 26th February 1870, however, Melinda Bullen Smedley died. She was buried in a separate matching grave next to that of her husband, with the plots surrounded by a metal link chain.

---

[1] Records kept by Lincoln Central Library

The Life and Times of Joseph Smedley

George and his family moved shortly after Joseph's death, to Buxton in Derbyshire where he gained employment as the manager of the new Buxton Gas Works. Here he was highly thought of, and became a Consultant Gas Engineer to the Urban District Council of Buxton and when he eventually retired in 1900 (aged 89!) they kept him on retainer until his death in 1909.

Joseph continued in a variety of jobs until retiring to a cottage by himself. In the 1891 census he was living at Tothill in Lincolnshire, and listed as "living on his own means," next to a Mabel Skelton, aged 88 and her son, Mark Skelton, then aged 65. It may be more than a coincidence that they shared Fanny's maiden name. However, Joseph passed away in Sleaford in July 1895, outliving his eldest sister, Melinda Brunton Young, who had died at her home in Gayton-le-Marsh in Lincolnshire, on 20th February 1883.

Picture of the overgrown graves of Joseph and Melinda Smedley in Sleaford Cemetery.

Melinda Brunton Young had played an important role in the lives of her parents and of her siblings, despite her early marriage to Joseph Tindal Young. She remained close to her mother and her younger brothers and sisters enjoyed staying with her at Gayton during their holidays. She also provided welcome shelter for Joseph and his acting company when they were travelling in the area of Alford. She and her husband had eight children, two of whom died in infancy. All of them were born at Gayton-le-Marsh.

Melinda's husband, John Tindal Young died at the Collegiate School, Gospelgate, Louth on 10th July 1893 aged 91. The great bell of St. James tolled out for him in the midst of festivities for the Duke of York's (the future King George V) wedding with Princess Mary of Teck. He was buried with his wife at Gayton-le-Marsh.

Appendix 1
The Plays
(AND OTHER ENTERTAINMENTS)

In each case, an entry attributed to Nicoll refers to information listed in 'A History of English Drama, 1660-1900' by Allardyce Nicoll and published by the Cambridge University Press in five volumes (second edition, published 1955)

Abelard and Heloise	D. John Baldwin Buckstone. First perf. Surrey Theatre, 1837 (Nicoll)
A Bold Stroke for a Husband	C. Mrs Susannah Centlivre. First perf. 1717/18 at new theatre in Lincoln's Inn Fields, (Nicoll), and frequently revived thereafter, notably by Charles Mathews at the Haymarket Theatre in 1859
A Chip of the Old Block	
A Dead Shot	Ba. John Baldwin Buckstone. First perf. Adelphi Theatre, 1827 (Nicoll)
Adelgitha	T. Matthew Gregory "Monk" Lewis. Sub-titled 'The Fruits of a Single Error' First Perf. D.L. 1807 (Nicoll)
Adrian and Orrila	D. William Dimond. (sub titled 'or, A Mother's Vengeance') First perf. C.G. 1806 (Nicoll) with cast inc. Cooke, Munden, C. Kemble. Liston, Davenport and Miss Brunton. (RS)

Richard E. Smedley

A Fish out of Water

Alexander

A New Way to Pay　　　(C) by Philip Massinger, 1633. This may
Old Debts　　　　　　　however refer J.P.Kemble's adaptation of 1810
　　　　　　　　　　　　(Nicoll)

A Queer Subject

Artist's Wife (The)

A Seaman's Log

A Woman never Vext　　C. Or, The Widow of Cornhill, by James
　　　　　　　　　　　　Robinson Planche. First perf. C.G. 1824

A Rowland for an　　　F. by Thomas Morton. First perf. C.G. 1819
Oliver　　　　　　　　 (Nicoll)

Bachelors' Buttons　　　F. By Edward Stirling, first perf Strand Theatre,
　　　　　　　　　　　　1837. (Nicoll)

Barbarossa　　　　　　 T.

Battle of Hexham　　　 Titled A Comedy. George Colman the Younger
(The) M.D.　　　　　　First Perf. Little Theatre in the Haymarket, 1789
　　　　　　　　　　　　(Nicoll)

Bee Hive (The)　　　　 O.F. by John Gideon Millingen sub-titled "or,
　　　　　　　　　　　　Lots of Fun". First perf. Lyc. 1811 (Nicoll)

Belle's Strategem (The)　C by Hannah Cowley. First perf C.G. 1780
　　　　　　　　　　　　(Oxford Comp. To Theatre)

Benevolent Tar (The)

Black-Eyed Susan	M.D. with a nautical theme, sub-titled "or, All in the Downs" by Douglas Jerrold, first perf. Surrey Theatre, 1829 (Nicoll)
Bleeding Nun	
Blind Boy (The)	M.D. James Kenney. First perf. C.G. 1807 (Nicoll)
Blue Beard	M.D. George Colman the Younger. Sub-titled 'Female Curiosity'. First perf. D.L. 1798. (Nicoll). A Burletta of the same name, by Charles Dance, was produced at the Lyceum in 1842 (Nicoll)
Bon Ton	F. David Garrick. Sub-titled High Life Above Stairs. First perf. D.L. 1775 (Nicoll)
Bottle Imp (The)	
Brigand (The)	
British Legion (The)	Ba. Thomas Haynes Baily; first perf. St. James Theatre, 1838 (Nicoll)
Captain is not A-miss	F. (OF in Nicoll); Thomas Egerton Wilks. First perf. Eng. Opera House, 1836 (Nicoll)
Castle Spectre (The)	M.D. Matthew Gregory "Monk" Lewis. First perf. D.L. 1797 (Nicoll)
Catching an Heiress	F. Charles Selby. First perf. Queens Theatre 1835 (Nicoll)

Richard E. Smedley

Chapter of Accidents	C. F. Scrimshaw, a writer from York and perf there in 1861, but I cannot find any other record of it.(The York Theatre, Sybil Rosenfeld)
Children in the Wood	O. by T. Morton (Rosenfeld: The York Theatre)
Christian Gambols	
Cinderella	
Clari	O. Attrib. To both J H Payne and J R Planche, variously sub-titled as The Maid of Milan; or, the Milanese Peasant Girl, or, in Jos. Smedley's production, The Broken-Hearted Father. First perf. C.G. 1823 (Nicoll)
Country Squire (The)	C. sub-titled "or, The Old English Gentleman
Cork Leg (The)	Apparently written by Mr Locking of Joseph Smedley's company; not to be confused with a burletta, Cork Legs, or, What a Coincidence!- first perf. New City Theatre, 1833 by unknown author.(Nicoll), but previously had played the Strand (Nicoll)
Court Favour	
Cure for Heartache	C. Thomas Morton. First perf. C.G. 1797 (Nicoll)

Damon and Pythias	T. By John Banim. First perf. C.G. 1821. Altered and revised by R.L. Sheil and perf. C.G. 1821. (Nicoll). However, a farce of the same tile was written by J.B.Buckstone and perf. at the Adelphi Theatre in 1831 and may be the more likely. Joseph Smedley used this as a sub-title to 'The Two Mr Smiths'
Darkness Visible	F. Theodore Edward Hook.First perf. Little Theatre in the Haymarket, 1811 (Nicoll)
Deaf as a Post	F. By John Poole. First perf. Little Theatre in the Haymarket, 1823. (Nicoll)
Deformed	"or, The Hunchback of Notre Dame".
Dunder Family	F.
Die for Love	
Doctor and his Man (The)	or, Animal Magnetism
Don Juan	Probably P by Carlo Delpini, sub-titled 'The Libertine Destroy'd'. Described in Nicoll as A Tragic Pantomimical Entertainment. 1790
Douglas	T. John Home. First perf. Edinburgh, 1756; London, C.G. 1757 (Nicoll)
Dream at Sea (The)	D. J.B.Buckstone. First perf. Adelphi Theatre, 1835 (Nicoll)
Earl of Essex(The)	T. Henry Jones. First perf. C.G. 1753. (Nicoll)
Education	C. By T. Morton (Rosenfeld: The York Theatre)

Ella Rosenberg	M.D. James Kenney. First perf. D.L. 1807 (Nicoll) While at Bradford, JS used this as a sub-title to "Heart of a Stranger".
Empty House (The)	F. By Miss Helen Smedley. First perf. Grimsby, 1833 (Playbill)
Every Body's Husband	F. Richard Ryan. First perf. Queen's Theatre, 1831 (Nicoll)
Everyone has his Fault	C. Sub-titled "or, The Old Bachelor's Wedding. Mrs Elizabeth Inchbald. First perf. C.G. 1793 (Nicoll)
Eugene Aram	M.D. by W T Moncrieff, sub-titled "or, St. Robert's Cave. First perf. Surrey Theatre, 1832 (Nicoll)
Exile of Siberia (The)	
Fall of Tarquin (The)	
False Friend (The)	C. Sir Charles Vanbrugh. First perf. D.L. (no date) First pub. 1701/2 (Nicoll)
Farmer's Wife (The)	T.J. Dibdin (Rosenfeld: The York Theatre) Apparently unlisted in Nicoll
Farmer's Story (The)	M.D. by William Bayle Bernard. First perf. E.O.H 1836 (Nicoll)
Female Fox-Hunter (The)	
Fortunes Frolic	

Foundling of the Forest	M.D. William Dimond. First perf. Little Theatre in the Haymarket 1809 (Nicoll)
Free Knights	opD by F. Reynolds; First perf. C.G. 1810; sub-titled or, the Edict of Charlemagne
Gamester(The)	C. Mrs Susannah Centlivre. First perf. 1704 (Nicoll)
Gay Deceivers	O.F. George Colman the Younger. Sub-titled 'More Laugh than Love' First perf. Little Theatre in the Haymarket, 1804 (Nicoll)
Gazette Extraordinary (The)	C. Joseph George Holman. First perf. C.G. 1811 (Nicoll)
George Barnwell (The	T. George Lillo. Orig. 'The London Merchant, or The Tragedy of) History of George Barnwell'. First perf. 1731. Re-worked Anonymously, 1811, perf. New Theatre, Tottenham Court Road. (Nicoll).
Gipsy Chief	
Grace Darling	
Green Man (The)	C. Richard Jones. First perf.1811 at the Little Theatre in the Haymarket. (Nicoll)
Gretna Green	F. By C Stuart
Grievings A Folly	C. Richard Leigh. First perf. 1809 (Nicoll)
Guy Mannering	M.D. by Daniel Terry. Sub-titled 'or, The Gipsy's Prophesy'. First perf. C.G. 1816, adapted from Scott's Waverly Novels.

Richard E. Smedley

Hamlet	adapted from Shakespeare's play
Handsome Husband (A)	Ba. Mrs J R (Elizabeth) Planche. First perf. Olympic Theatre, 1836. (Nicoll)
Happiest Day of My Life	Ba. J.B. Buckstone. First perf. The Little Theatre in the Haymarket, 1829 (Nicoll)
Happy Man (The)	F.
Haunted Inn (The)	F. (M.D. in Nicoll) by Richard Brinsley Peake. First perf. D.L. 1828 (Nicoll)
Heart of Mid Lothian (The)	M.D. T J Dibdin. Based on the book by Walter Scott (1818). First perf. Royal Circus Theatre (later Surrey), 1819 (Nicoll). However this version performed by Smedley's company is attributed to Daniel Terry, and listed by Nicoll as first perf. C.G. 1819
Heir at Law	C. George Colman the Younger. First perf. Little Theatre in the Haymarket, 1797 (Nicoll)
High Notions	O.F. sub-titled "or, A Trip to Exmouth" by John Parry. First perf. D.L. 1819 (Nicoll)
Highways and Byways	
His Last Legs	
Hit or Miss	O.F. Isaac Pocock. First perf. London (Lyc M) 1810 (Nicoll)
Honey Moon (The)	C. John Tobin. First perf. D.L. 1805 (Nicoll)

How to Avoid the Road To Ruin	
Hunchback (The)	D. by J Sheridan Knowles. First perf. C.G. 1832 (Nicoll)
Hunter of the Alps(The)	M.D. William Dimond. First perf. Little Theatre in the Haymarket, 1804 (Nicoll)
Hunting the Trolle	
Hunting a Turtle	F. Charles Selby. First perf. Queen's Theatre, 1835 (Nicoll)
Husband's Secret (The)	
Hypocrite (The)	C. Isaac Bickerstaff (taken from Moliere and Cibber) D.L. 1768 (Nicoll)
Illustrious Stranger	F. Sub-titled "or, Married and Buried"
Inkle and Yarico	CO G. Coleman the Younger (Rosenfeld, The York Theatre)
Invincibles (The)	OF by Thomas Morton; sub-titled "or, The Female Soldiers"
Ion	T. Sir Thomas Noon Talfourd. First perf. C.G. 1836 (Nicoll)
Irishman in London	F. William Macready. (sub-titled 'The Happy African') First perf. C.G. 1792 (Nicoll)
Irish Tutor	F. by Lord Glengall (Richard Butler) sub-titled or, The New Lights. First perf. Cheltenham, 1822; London, 1822. (Nicoll)

Richard E. Smedley

Irish Widow (The)	
Iron Chest	M.D. A Play with a Preface and a Postscript. George Colman the Younger. First perf. DL 1796 (Nicoll)
Irish Lion (The)	F. By J.B.Buckstone, first perf. Little Theatre in the Haymarket, 1838 (Nicoll)
Irish Widow (The)	
Is He Jealous?	
Ivanhoe	M.D. sub-titled "or, The Jew's Daughter" by Thomas John Dibdin, based on Scott's novel. First perf. Surrey Theatre, 1820 (Nicoll) But could be any one of many adaptations.
Jack Sheppard	Moncrieff wrote a musical drama of this title first perf. 1825, based on the real-life thief and gaol-breaker upon whom the character of Macheath was based in John Gay's Beggar's Opera. However, following the publication of William Harrison Ainsworth's novel, pub. 1839, at least eight plays of that name sprang up, one of them by Buckstone (Adelphi). The Censor, worried about public morals, banned such plays appearing in London for 40 years. The author of Joseph's version of the play is therefore unknown.
Jane Shore	T. Nicholas Rowe. First perf. D.L. 1713/4 (Nicoll)
Jew and the Doctor(The)	F. By Thomas Dibdin first perf. C.G 1798

Jocko	Ba. Or, The Ape of Brazil, by Charles Dibdin, Jnr. first perf. Sadlers Wells 1825 (Nicoll)
Jocko	M.D. or, The Brazilian Monkey. First perf. C.G. 1825 (Nicoll)
John Bull	C. George Colman the Younger. (sub-titled 'or, The Gentleman's Fireside'). First perf. C.G. 1803. (Nicoll)
John Buzzby	C. James Kenney. Sub-titled "or, A Day's Pleasure". First perf. The Little Theatre in the Haymarket, 1822. (Nicoll)
John of Paris	
Killing No Murder	O.F. Theodore Edward Hook, First perf. little Theatre in the Haymarket, 1809 (Nicoll)
King's Command (The)	
Kiss (The)	C. Stephen Clarke. Sub-titled "or, The Lawyer Outwitted". First perf. Lyceum Theatre, 1811 (Nicoll) (adapted from Beaumont and Fletcher's *Spanish Curate*) (Rosenfeld' The York Theatre)
Ladies Club (The)	C.
Lady and the Devil (The)	O.F. W. Dimond. First perf. D.L. 1820 (Nicoll)
Lady of Lyons (The)	D. By Bulwer-Lytton. Sub-titled 'or, Love and Pride'. First perf. C.G. 1838
Lady of the Rock	

Laugh When You Can	C. Frederick Reynolds. First perf. C.G. 1798 (Nicoll)
Law of Java (The)	
Liar (The)	C. By Samual Foote (The Lyar) First perf. C.G. 1762. (Nicoll)
Lock and Key	O.F. Prince Hoare. First perf. C.G. 1796 (Nicoll)
Love	D. By Sheridan Knowles. First perf. C.G. 1839 (Nicoll)
Love Chase (The)	C. By Sheridan Knowles. First perf. Little Theatre in the Haymarket, 1837
Love and Laugh	F. sub-titled "or, All at Coventry"
Love and Laurel	
Love in a Village	C.O. Isaac Bickerstaffe. First perf. C.G. 1762 (Nicoll)
Love Laughs at Locksmiths	F. G. Colman, the Younger. First Perf. Little Theatre in the Haymarket, 1803 (Nicoll)
Love's Frailties	F.
Luke the Labourer	MD by J B Buckstone; sub-titled "or, The Lost Son"
M.P.	C.O. Thomas Moore. Sub-titled "or, The Blue Stocking. First perf. Lyc M. 1811
Mr & Mrs Smith	

Macbeth

Maid and Magpie (The)

| Maid of Mariendorpt (The) | D. By Sheridan Knowles. First perf. Little Theatre in the Haymarket, 1838 (Nicoll) |

Maid of Orleans

Maids as they Are

| Man and Wife | F. George Colman the Elder; first perf. C.G 1769 (Nicoll) |

Married Life

Married Lovers (The)

| Married and Single | C. By John Poole. Sub-titled "or, Belles and Bailiffs". First perf. Little Theatre in the Haymarket, 1824 (Nicoll) |

| Matrimony | O.F. James Kenney. First perf. D.L. 1804 |

| Mayor of Garratt | C. Samuel Foote. First perf. Little Theatre in the Haymarket 1763 (Nicoll) |

| Merchant of Venice (The) | adapted from the play by Shakespeare |

Merry Mourners

| Midas | Burl. Kane O'Hara. First perf. Crow-Street, Dublin 1762; C.G.1764 (Nicoll) |

Richard E. Smedley

Miller and his Men (The)	M.D. J.S. Faucit. (Rosenfeld; The York Theatre) Apparently unlisted by Nicoll.
Miller's Maid	M.D. John Saville Faucit. First perf. The Lyceum, 1821. founded on Bloomfield's poem of the same name
Milliner's Revolt	Written by Miss Smedley
Mountaineers (The)	
Mutiny at the Nore (The)	M.D. sub-titled "or, British Sailors in 1797", by Douglas William Jerrold, first perf. The Pavilion Theatre, Whitechapel, June,1830. (Nicoll). Other sources quote the Royal Coburg Theatre, in August, 1930
My Spouse and I	
Naval Engagements	F.
Neighbours and their Wives	
Nicholas Nickleby	Ba. By Edward Stirling, adapted from the first instalments of Charles Dickens' book. First perf. Adelphi Theatre Nov. 1838. (Nicoll)
No!	
No Song No Supper	O.F. Prince Hoare. First perf. D.L. 1790 (Pirated version, Dublin 1792) (Nicoll)
Of Age-Tomorrow	F.
Old and Young	

Old Maid	C. Arthur Murphy. First perf D.L. 1761 (Nicoll).
Orphan of Geneva	M.D. Originally entitled Therese, or The Orphan of Geneva. By John Howard Payne, adapted from the French. First perf. D.L. 1821 (Nicoll)
Othello	
Paul and Virginia	O.F. James Cobb. First perf. C.G. 1800 (Nicoll)
Peasant Boy (The)	M.D. or Dramatic Opera by William Dimond. First perf. Lyceum Theatre 1811 (Nicoll)
Perfection	F. Sub-titled "or, The Lady of Munster"
Petticoat Government	Int. Charles Dance, first perf. Drury Lane, 1832 (Nicoll)
Pilot (The)	Ba. Sub-titled "or, A Tale of the Sea" by Edward Fitzball. First perf. Adelphi Theatre 1825
Pizarro	T. Richard Brinsley Sheridan, adapted from the German of Kotzebue. First perf. D.L. 1799. Many other adaptations and alternate translations existed and performed. (Nicoll)
Plot and Counterplot	F. Charles Kemble.sub-titled "or, The Portrait of Michael Cervantes. First nperf. Little Theatre in the Haymarket, 1808 (Nicoll)
Point of Honour	D. Charles Kemble. Sub-titled "or, The Fortunate Deserter".First perf. Little Theatre in the Haymarket, 1800. (An adaptation from Mercier, *Le Deserteur*) (Nicoll)

Richard E. Smedley

Poison Tree	Credited on a 1836 Smedley playbill from Market Rasen to George Colman the Younger, but not listed by Nicoll
Poor Gentleman	C. George Colman, the Younger. First perf. C.G. 1801, and published by Mrs Inchbald (Nicoll)
Popping the Question	F. John Baldwin Buckstone. First perf. D.L. 1830 (Nicoll)
Prize	O.F. A Musical Farce Prince Hoare, First perf. Little Haymarket, 1793 (Nicoll)
Provoked Husband	C. Started by John Vanbrugh as 'Journey to London' and finished after his death by Colley Cibber. First perf. D.L. 1727/8 (Nicoll) A Literary History of England, Ed. Baugh, 1948)
Raising the Wind	F. James Kenney. First perf.C.G 1803 Sometimes called 'How to Raise the Wind' (Nicoll)
Rajah's Daughter (The)	M.D. Alternative title to "The Cataract of the Ganges", by William Thomas Moncrieff, first perf. D.L. 1823 (Nicoll)
Rake's Progress (The)	by W L Rede
Raymond & Agnes	
Rendezvous	sub-titled "or, Which is the Lady".
Rent Day (The)	D.by D W Jerrold. First perf. D.L. 1832 (Nicoll)
Richard III	D. William Shakespeare (adaptation of)

Riches	D. Sir James Bland Burges. Sub-titled "or, The Wife and Brother". First perf. Lyceum by the D.L. company, 1810 (Nicoll)
Rifle Brigade (The)	
Rivals (The)	C. Richard Brinsley Sheridan. First perf. C.G. 1775 (Nicoll)
Rival Valets (The)	F. Joseph Ebsworth. First perf. Little Theatre in the Haymarket, 1825 (Nicoll)
Ro House	
Road to Ruin	C. Thomas Holcroft. First perf. C.G. 1792 (Nicoll)
Robert Macaire	probably adapted from a subversive melodrama repeatedly banned in France from 1823 until the 1880s. Original play by Antier, Lacoste & Chapponier which satirised social hierarchy, wealth, etc.
Robinson Crusoe	
Rob Roy	probably one of many adaptations of the book by Walter Scott
Romeo and Juliet	
Romp (The)	F.by T.A. Lloyd(Rosenfeld; The York Theatre) Nicoll calls it O.F. with music by C. Dibdin, altered from 'Love in the City' C.G. 1778

Rosina	C.O. by Frances Brooke, sub-titled 'Love in a Cottage', music W. Shield. First perf. C.G 1782 (Nicoll)
Royal Oak (The)	M.D. W.W. Dimond. First Perf. Little Theatre in the Haymarket 1811 (Nicoll/ Rosenfeld; The York Theatre)
Sam Weller	Ba. William Thomas Moncrieff, based on Dickens' sketches. First perf. Strand Theatre, 1837 (Nicoll)
School for Scandal (The)	C. Richard Brinsley Sheridan. First perf. D.L. 1777
School of Reform (The)	C. Thomas Morton. Sub-titled 'How to Rule a Husband' First perf. C.G. 1805 (Nicoll)
Secrets Worth Knowing	C. By T. Morton (Rosenfeld: The York Theatre)
Sharp and Flat	O.F. Dennis Lawler (music by J. Hook) First perf. Lyceum Theatre, 1813 (Nicoll)
She Stoops to Conquer	C. Oliver Goldsmith. Sub-titled "or, The Mistakes of a Night". First perf. C.G. 1773 (Nicoll)
Simpson and Company	C. John Poole. First perf. D.L. 1823
Slave (The)	M.D. by Thomas Morton. First perf. C.G. 1816. (Nicoll)
Sleeping Draught	

Sleepwalk	sub-titled "or, Love and Landowner". Probably The Sleepwalker (C) by Elizabeth, Baroness Craven, Born Elizabeth Brunton) later Margravine of Anspach, translated from the French and published privately in 1778 (Nicoll).
Soldiers Daughter (The)	C. Andrew Cherry. First perf. D.L. 1804 (Nicoll)
Spectre Bridegroom (The)	F. By W. T Moncrieff, sub-titled "or a Ghost in Spite of Himself". First perf. D.L. 1821 (Nicoll)
Speed the Plough	C. Thomas Morton. First perf. C.G. 1800 (Nicoll)
Spoiled Child (The)	F. Isaac Bickerstaff. First perf. D.L. 1790 (Nicoll) – also ascribed to Mrs Jordan and Ford
Stranger (The)	D. George Papendick (sub titled 'or Misanthropy and Repentance') translated from the German of Augustus von Kotzebue (1798) (Nicoll) May have been an alternative translation by A Schink.
Sultan	T. Francis Gentleman. Sub-titled 'or Love and Fame'. A New Tragedy perf'd Bath, York and Scarborough c. 1754, Little Haymarket, 1769. (Nicoll). OR: O.F. Isaac Bickerstaffe (sub-titled 'or, A Peep into the Seraglio') First perf. as a Farce D.L. 1775 (Nicoll)
Surrender of Calais (The)	M.D. by George Colman the Younger. First perf. Little Theatre in the Haymarket, 1791 (and Dublin – pirated-1792) (Nicoll)

Sweethearts and Wives	CO by James Kenney, first perf. Little Theatre in the Haymarket, 1823. (Nicoll) Joseph Smedley mistakenly attributed this to "Mr Poole, author of Paul Pry and Simpson & Co." on both Brigg and Bradford playbills, however Nicoll doesn't give any such attribution.
Tekeli	M.D. Theodore Edward Hook. Sub-titled 'or, The Siege of Montgatz'. First perf. D.L. 1806 (Nicoll)
The Moor's Revenge	D. Restoration piece, usually the sub-title to "Abdelazer" by Mrs Aphra Behn, based on "Lust's Dominion" by Marlowe. First perf. Dorset Garden Theatre, 1676 (Nicoll)
Therese	M.D. sub-titled "or, The Orphan of Geneva" by John Kerr, first perf. The New Royal West London Theatre, 1821 (Nicoll and Lorenzen's History of the Prince of Wales's Theatre).
The Thespian Barber	C. Dr George Oliver Sub-titled:'or, Rhyme without Reason. (Playbill)
The Two Drovers	D. Based on a story by Walter Scott, first pub. 1827 and included in his 'Chronicles of the Canongate'. Play's author unknown, but perf. at the Caledonian, Edinburgh, 1828 A Musical Drama of the same name by Henry Goff first perf at Edinburgh in 1841 (Nicoll).
The Two Mr Smiths	See 'Damon and Pythius'
The Two Pages of Frederick the Great	F. John Poole. First perf. C.G 1821

Three Fingered Jack	P. Usually titled "Obi, or, Three-fingered Jack by John Fawcett. First perf. Little Theatre in the Haymarket, 1800. (Nicoll)
To Marry or Not to Marry	C. By Mrs Elizabeth Inchbald. First perf. C.G. 1805 (Nicoll)
Tom Cringle	D. Sub-titled "or, The Man With the Iron Hand, by Edward Fitzball, first perf. Surrey Theatre, 1834. (Nicoll).
Tom Noddy's Secret	F. Thomas Haynes Bayly. First perf. Little Theatre in the Haymarket, 1838. (Nicoll)
Tom Thumb	Ba.
Two Murderers (The)	
The Way to Avoid the Road to Ruin!	C. Thomas Holcroft. First perf. C.G. 1792 (Nicoll)
Weird Woman (The)	or, Foundling Boy
Werner	
The Wife: A Tale of Mantua Winning a Husband	D. Sheridan Knowles. First perf. C.G. 1833 (Nicoll)
The Wonder: A Woman Keeps a Secret	C. Mrs Susannah Centlivre. First Perf. April 1714 (D.L.) (Nicoll)
Timour the Tartar	M.D. Matthew Gregory "Monk" Lewis First perf. C.G. 1811 (Nicoll)

To Marry or Not to Marry	C. Mrs Elizabeth Inchbald. First perf. C.G. 1805. (Nicoll)
Tom Thumb	May have been a different adaptation of the Fielding story, but more likely to be: Burl. Kane O'Hara. First perf. C.G. 1780 (1ˢᵗ pub. 1805) (Nicoll)
Too Late for Dinner	F by Richard Jones, first perf. C.G. 1820 –variously sub-titled as "or, Ins and Outs" and "A Little Too Late". (Nicoll)
Tough at Times	
Trial by Jury	F. Theodore Edward Hook. First perf. Little Theatre in the Haymarket, 1811 (Nicoll)
Turn Gate	
Turning the Tables	F.
Turn-Out	O.F. James Kenney. Orig. Called "Turn Him Out". First perf. Lyceum, 1812 (Nicoll)
Twenty Years Ago	M.D. Isaac Pocock. First perf. 1810 (Nicoll)
Two Strings to your Bow	F. Robert Jephson. First perf. C.G. 1791 (Nicoll)
Uncle John	C. by J.B. Buckstone. First perf. Little Theatre in the Haymarket, 1833 (Nicoll)
Unfinished Gentleman (The)	F.
Valentine and Orson	

Virginius	T. Sub-titled "or, The Liberation of Rome", by Sheridan Knowles, first perf. Glasgow, 1820; C.G. 1820. (Nicoll)
Water Witch (The)	
Ways & Means	C. Sub-titled, or, A Trip to Dover by George Colman, the Younger; first perf. Little Theatre in the Haymarket, 1788 (Nicoll)
Village Lawyer	F. Translated from French *L'Avocat Pathelin by David Augustin de Brueys* reputedly by George Colman, the Elder. But not listed by Nicoll. Performed by and sometimes attributed to, Macready. First perf. T.R.Haymarket 1787 (various sources)
Valentine and Orson	
Ways & Means	C. Sub-titled, or, A Trip to Dover by George Colman, the Younger; first perf. Little Theatre in the Haymarket, 1788 (Nicoll)
Wags of Windsor	According to Nicoll, this was included as part of a postscript to Henry Lee's operatic piece called Caleb Quotem, although omitted from the edition published by Colman in 1809. Nicoll also attributed the piece to: George Colman, the Younger. According to Nicoll, called "The Review, or, The ways of Windsor" First perf. The Little Theatre in the Haymarket, 1800 (Nicoll) Performed by Macready as The Review, or The Wags of Windsor at Leeds Theatre, 1823.-(RS)
Wandering Boys	M. D. John Kerr. First perf. Sadlers Wells, 1830 (Nicoll)

Wanted – A Valet	Adapted from a story of the same name by Miss Helen Smedley
Waterman (The)	B.O. Charles Dibdin sub-titled 'or The First of August' First perf. Little Theatre in the Haymarket,1774 (Nicoll)
Ways & Means	C. George Colman, the Younger. Sub-titled "or, A Trip to Dover". First perf. The Little Theatre in the Haymarket, 1788
Way to Get Married (The)	C. Thomas Morton. First perf. C.G. 1796 (Nicoll)
Weathercock (The)	O.F.A Musical Entertainment by Theodosius Forrest. First perf. C.G 1775 (Nicoll); but more probably: F. John Till. Allingham. First perf. D.L. 1805 (Nicoll) especially as it has an ideal leading comedic role in Tristram Fickle.
Wedding-Day (The)	By Henry Fielding. First perf (London D.L. and Norwich) 1743. (Rosenfeld: Strolling Players 1660-1765); (Nicoll) However, this version, according to a playbill of 1836 at Market Rasen is by Mrs Inchbald, and so listed by Nicoll; first perf. D.L. 1794
We Fly by Night	
West Indian (The)	C. Richard Cumberland, First perf. D.L. 1771 (Nicoll)
Wheel of Fortune (The)	C. Richard Cumberland. First perf. D.L. 1795 (Nicoll)

Who Wins	O.F. John Till. Allingham. Sub-titled 'The Widow's Choice. First perf. C.G. 1808. (Nicoll)
Widow's Victim	F.
Wild Oats	C. John O'Keeffe. Sub-titled "or, The Strolling Gentleman" First perf. C.G.1791 (Nicoll)
Wives as they Were and Maids as they Are	C. Elizabeth Inchbald. First perf. C.G. 1791 (Nicoll)
Wood Daemon (The)	M.D. Matthew Gregory "Monk" Lewis. Sub-titled "The Clock has Struck" First perf. 1807 (D.L.)
Wreck Ashore (The)	Ba. Sub-titled or, A Bridegroom from the Sea, by J.B. Buckstone. First perf. 1830 (Nicoll)
X, Y, Z.	Or, How to get a Wife
Young Hussar (The)	C.O. William Dimond. (sub-titled 'Love and Mercy'. First perf. D.L. 1807 (Nicoll)
Young Widow (The)	
Youth, Love, & Folly	C.O. By W W Dimond. Sub-titled in Jos Smedley's production "or, the Female Jockey". First perf. D.L. 1805 (Nicoll)

Appendix II
The Theatres

Working by playbills and newspaper, it is not always easy to state with certainty the dates when Smedley started to manage which theatres. Those that I know he was leasing, and touring to, in 1828 are listed below. Those theatres that he was managing in 1833 are listed below that. These are taken from *An Alphabetical List of Theatres in the United Kingdom, with the Names of Managers* which was compiled in 1833, by John Miller, who had been appointed Agent by the Dramatic Authors' Society (and listed here by kind permission of the Cadbury Research Library at the University of Birmingham). They were also quoted by Allardyce Nicoll in his *A History of English Drama*, but corrected in light of recently obtained information.

Section 1: Theatres known to manage in 1828:

Grimsby
Market Deeping
Malton
Barton on Humber
Howden
March
Sleaford
Southwell
Alford
Holbeach
Folkingham
Bourn
Caistor
Burlington Quay (now called Bridlington)
Hedon

Market Rasen
He also toured to
Bingham (outside Nottingham)
Melton Mowbray
Driffield
Belper
Ripley
Alfreton
Wirksworth
Castle Donington
Aston (Matlock)
Oakham

Theatres known to manage in 1833 according to Nicoll)

Barnsley
Barton
Beverley
Bishop's Castle (Shropshire)
Brigg
Burlington Quay (Bridlington)
Gainsborough (listed as Huggins and Clarke, but already taken by Smedley)
Grimsby
Horncastle
Howden
Malton
Mansfield
March
Market Deeping
Melton Mowbray
Pontefract
Sleaford
Southwell

Theatres which Smedley went on to manage after 1833:

Wakefield
Bradford
Beverley
Huddersfield
Selby
Spilsby
Worksop

Theatres managed by the Robertson family in 1833

Boston
Grantham
Huntingdon
Lincoln
Newark
Oundle
Peterborough
Spalding
Whittlesea
Wisbeach

To which were later added those theatres run by T W Manley (sic) in 1833:

Derby
Halifax
Nottingham
Retford

Bibliography

Ackroyd, Peter	Dickens (1990)
Bates, Anderson	A History of Freemasonry in Grimsby (1892)
Bates, Anderson	A Gossip about Old Grimsby (1893)
Baugh, Albert C.(ed)	A Literary History of England (1948)
Briggs, Asa	A Social History of England (1984)
Brown, Jonathan	The English Market Town (A Social and Economic History 1750-1914 (1986)
Burley, T.L.G.	Playhouses and Players of East Anglia (1928)
Carleton, Don	The Prince's of Park Row, 1983, for the University Historical Association.
Carol Jones Carlyle	Helen Faucit; Fire and Ice on the Victorian Stage
Chapman, F.J.A	History of Freemasonry in Grimsby 1802-1938
Coleman, Terry	The Old Vic (2014)
Crossland & Turner	Great Grimsby – A History of the World Renowned Fishing Port
Davies, M (Rev)	A History of Grimsby (1942)
Davis, Tracy C & Donkin, Ellen	Women & Playwriting in the Nineteenth Century, Cambridge University Press, 1999

Dickens, Charles	Nicholas Nickleby
Donaldson, Walter	Recollections of an Actor (1865)
Egan, Pierce	The Life of an Actor (1904); orig. Edn. 1825
Ellis, C (ed)	Mid Victorian Sleaford 1851-1871 (1981)
Eshleman, Dorothy (ed)	The Committee Books of the Theatre Royal, Norwich (1970)
Gillett, Edward	A History of Grimsby
Grice, Elizabeth	Rogues and Vagabonds, or the Actors' Road to Respectability (1977)
Hartnoll, Phyllis (ed)	The Oxford Companion to the Theatre (1951; 2nd ed. 1957)
Hartnoll, Phyllis	The Theatre: A Concise History (1968)
Hill, Francis (Sir)	Georgian Lincoln (1966)
Horn, Pamela	Pleasures and Pastimes in Victorian Britain (1999)
Hoyles, Martin	Ira Aldridge (2008)
Kelly, Ian	Mr Foote's Other Leg (2012)
Kelly, Linda	The Kemble Era (1980)
Kendal, Margaret	Dame Madge Kendal by Herself (1933)
Klepac, Richard L.	Mr Mathews At Home (1979)
Knight, William G.A	Major London 'Minor', (1997)
Lincoln, Bob	The Rise of Grimsby
Lorenzen, Richard L.	The History of The Prince of Wales's Theatre, 1771-1903 (2014)
Mullin, Donald	Victorian Actors and Actresses in Review (1983)
Nicoll, Allardyce	The Development of the Theatre (1927)
Nicoll, Allardyce	A History of English Drama 1660-1900. 5 vols. (1969)

Oliver, George	Ye Bird of Gryme (1866)
Parker, B.J.	The Theatre of Gainsborough: 1772-1850
Pawley, Simon	The Book of Sleaford; Pub. in a limited edition by Baron Birch
Perkin, Joan	The Merry Duchess (2002)
Pollack, Frederick (ed)	Macready's Reminiscences (1875)
Richards and Thompson (ed)	Nineteenth Century British Theatre (1971)
Rosenfeld, Sybil	Strolling Players and Drama in the Provinces 1660-1765 (1939)
Rosenfeld, Sybil	The York Theatre (2001)
Rowell, George	The Victorian Theatre, A Survey 1956)
Russell, Rex C.	From Cock-Fighting to Chapel Building (2004)
Russell, W. Clark	Representative Actors (1883)
Russell, W. Clark	The Book of Authors (undated) and the above published by Frederick Warne & Co. now an imprint of Penguin Random Hse
Sandbach, R.S.E.	Priest and Freemason, The Life of George Oliver (1988)
Scruton, William	Pen and Pencil Pictures of Old Bradford (re-pub. 1968)
Senior, William	The Old Wakefield Theatre (1894)
Sherson, Erroll	London's Lost Theatres of the XIX Century (1925)
Shaw, George (Rev)	Old Grimsby (1897)
Shilton, Richard P.	History of Southwell
Sissons, Eddie & 'The Delvers'	That's Entertainment II; A History of the Theatre in Gainsborough and other diversions, 1772-1910

Sturman & Purton	Poems by Two Brothers: George Clayton Tennyson and Charles Tennyson d'Eynecourt (1993)
Taylor, C.M.P.	Right Royal, Wakefield Theatre 1776-1994
Tennyson, Hallam (Lord)	Tennyson A Memoir (1897) 2 Vols.
Tomalin, Claire	The Invisible Woman (1990)
Tomalin, Claire	Charles Dickens A Life (2011)
Vernon, Rolf	Newark before Victoria; 1807-1837
Wheatcroft, Andrew	The Tennyson Album, 1980
Wilkinson, Tate	The Wandering Patentee (1795) Facsimile edn. 1973
Winston, James	The Theatric Tourist (1805); Facsimile Edn. STR, 2008
Wright, Neil R.	Treading the Boards; Actors and Theatres in Georgian Lincolnshire (2016)

Other Publications, Pamphlets & Unpublished Material

Lincolnshire Family Historian Vol. 6 No.1	Society for Lincolnshire History and Archaeology

Lippincott's Dictionary of Biography, 1910

Spotlight on Tuxford, Issue No. 3

Memoir of Mr C. Kemble, Pub 1825

Memoir of Mr Braham, Pub. 1825

The Thespian Dictionary, 1802

On-Line Resources

Archaeology Service-Heritage Lincolnshire "Advancing Lincolnshire Past"

Desktop evaluation for Conging Street, Horncastle, Lincolnshire by B. Riddle, P. Riddle and P. Goodrum

The Theatres Trust web-site: Nineteenth Century Theatre

Romantic and Revolutionary Theatre, 1789-1860; ed. Donald Roy (Theatre in Europe: a documentary history, pub. Cambridge University Press.

Hansard: State of the Drama, 31st May 1832, Commons Sitting, accessed 18/08/2016

Primary Sources on Copyright (1450-1900): R. Deazley (2008) 'Commentary *Dramatic Literary Property Act 1833*

The Penny Illustrated Newspaper

British Fiction, 1800-1829: Subscription Lists, accessed 23/07/2015

Strolling Players and Provincial Drama after Shakespeare, Early Journal content on JSTOR, Accessed 27/07/2015

University of Kent Information Services – Charles Dickens Theatre Collection, accessed 07/01/2017

The Henry Goodman Collection of Theatre Playbills (Collection 2286) UCLA Special Collections, Charles E. Young Research Library, UCLA

The Victorian Web; Health & Hygiene in the nineteenth century Cornell University Library;

"Catalogue of the valuable collection of playbills, portraits, photographs, engravings, etc., etc., formed by the late James H. Brown....comprising about 180,000 American and English play-bills". Pub. C.F. Libbie & Co., auctioneers, Boston, Mass.

Acknowledgements

Many people have helped me in researching and writing this book, and in varying ways. I must firstly acknowledge the help of Mr Roy Sumners, a direct descendant of Joseph Smedley, and with whom I have enjoyed many interesting conversations. He and his wife Pat have always been most welcoming and eager to share tales from their family history and their archive of material relating to Joseph Smedley. I value his knowledge, insight and friendship very highly.

I would particularly like to acknowledge here the research carried out by Guy Yeoman Hemingway (1899–1986), who was a civil engineer, and whose home was in a nearby village to where I now live, which he shared with his sister Ida, who died in 1981. Hemingway worked on various engineering projects throughout the Middle East. He had many hobbies, and he retired in 1965 and spent his time in pursuing them. These included all forms of transport, including railways, canals, ports and bridges; the family histories of various local worthies, the coaching system and inns, and the early theatre in the region. I have drawn heavily on his unpublished research on the Robertson family and their theatrical circuits, and would like to thank Dr Mike Rogers of the Lincolnshire Archive for permission to do so. I have found all of Guy's research to be absolutely accurate, and where I have relied on his citations I have used his initials against them. He also found time to research the theatres at Gainsborough, Retford and Sheffield. These typed papers are bound and placed in various libraries in the Newark and Lincoln area.

I have also used research carried out by Arthur Avison, a local historian in the Grimsby area, whose unpublished work is in the Grimsby local studies department of the Library.

I also wish to acknowledge the help of the late C.M.P. Taylor.

I would like to acknowledge and thank the staff of the Lincolnshire Archives for their expertise and their assistance and unfailing courtesy. They have been an enormous help, as has the staff of the following: Lincoln Central Library, Susan Snell and her colleagues at Freemason's Hall Library and Museum in London; The Forum and Public Record Office at Norwich; Maria Andrew at the Theatre Royal, Norwich; The West Yorkshire Archive at Wakefield Library and Museum , in particular Matthew Thomas for his knowledge of the Pontefract theatre; and their counterpart at Bradford; Helen Fox and staff at Worksop Library; Gainsborough Library; the staff of the Old Hall at Gainsborough for their enthusiasm and desire to help; Northallerton Public Record Office; Tim Warner of Nottinghamshire Libraries based at Newark, and Simon Balderson of the Local Studies section of Grimsby public library, both of whom have been unfailingly helpful, and knowledgeable in the history of their respective areas and the source materials under their care. Thanks too to the staff of the Bassetlaw Museum at Retford.

I am grateful, too, to the staff of the Manuscripts and Special Collections Department of Nottingham University, and to the Special Collections Department at the Cadbury Research Library at the University of Birmingham.

Thanks must also go to Beryl Venables of the Milton Mausoleum, Peter Chapman of the Grimsby Telegraph, Mrs Doreen Whittingham of Grimsby,and Mr George Shields of the Sleaford Theatre. Thanks also to Dr Paul V.W. Schlicke, Hon. Senior Lecturer at the University of Aberdeen and world authority on the works of Charles Dickens for his permission to quote from his article on N.C. Nantz which was later published in The Theatre Annual.

Thanks also to Claire Tomalin for permission to quote from her book *The Invisible Woman* (pub. Penguin Random House); Marion O'Connor of the Society for Theatre Research for her advice and assistance, particularly with regard to permissions for use of quotes from STR publications; Iain Mackintosh, theatre historian and expert on Georgian Theatre for his sage advice and permission to quote from his notes accompanying the exhibition on Georgian Theatre, (Hayward Gallery, 1975); The Heritage Trust of

Lincolnshire for their permission to draw on the changes to rural culture detailed in 'From Cock Fighting to Chapel Building'; Neil R Wright for his permission to quote from his excellent book on theatre in Lincolnshire, 'Treading the Boards'.

Thanks too to Cambridge University Press for permission under license to quote from several of their publications.

I wish too to thank Mr Will Jennings and Mr Gareth Walters, for their technical wizardry, computer know-how and patience.

I found the writing and research to be a solitary endeavour but would like to thank those who supported and encouraged me at all stages, in particular Mr John Causebrook of Anthony Field Associates for his interest in the project.

If I have neglected to thank anyone, please forgive me; it is entirely my fault. Please let me know and I will correct it in any subsequent print.

www.ingramcontent.com/pod-product-compliance
Lightning Source LLC
Chambersburg PA
CBHW031818110426
42743CB00057B/649